city baby chicago

By Karin Horgan Sullivan

universe publishing

First published in the United States of America in 2004
by UNIVERSE PUBLISHING
A Division of Rizzoli International Publications, Inc.
300 Park Avenue South
New York, NY 10010
www.rizzoliusa.com

2003 2004 2005 2006 2007 / 10 9 8 7 6 5 4 3 2 1

Printed in the United States of America

ISBN: 0-7893-1077-5

Library of Congress Catalog Control Number: 2004113251

contents

Dedication

To Matt and Clare, the two loves of my life.

Acknowledgments

Writing a book of this scope wouldn't be possible without a lot of help. Many, many thanks:

To Sharon Bloyd-Peshkin, for the many years of friendship and the recommendation that relaunched my career.

To the many city parents who shared their insider tips and resources.

To Corinne Peterson of Sweet Pea's Studio, an absolute fount of information for pregnant women and new parents.

To my editor, Holly Rothman, whose combination of professionalism and humor made every communication a pleasure.

To my extremely thorough and tenacious fact-checker, Elizabeth Johnson.

To Amy Fenton, Stephanie Kirchner, Jill Pacyna, Rossana Torres, and Anne Wakely. I could not possibly have written this book without the loving care you took of Clare in your homes and at school.

To the Posse: Andrea, Anna, Claire, Deb, Emily, Julie, Michele, and Tina (and honorary member Paul). It may be possible to survive motherhood without friends like you, but I certainly wouldn't be getting any style points for it.

To my parents, Steve and Peggy Horgan, who showed me by example, first, how to be a great parent, and now, how to be a great grandparent.

To my wonderful husband, Matt, who always gives me his full support and is a fantastic dad—-fun, thoughtful, and loving. I love being a family with you.

And, of course, to Clare. Being your mom has been the greatest of joys. I love you to the moon and back.

introduction

The vast number of babies being born in Chicago first caught my attention several years ago, shortly after I took a job in the Loop. One summer day, during my walk from the el at Clark and Lake to my office in the Sun Times building, I counted eight pregnant women. That seemed like an awfully high number in just a few short blocks, so I started taking a daily tally. Some days it was as low as six, others as high as ten. It didn't seem to be the same women either; no matter what time I was walking to work, pregnant women were everywhere.

At first I thought it was just me. My husband, Matt, and I were trying to get pregnant, and I had babies on the brain. But when a happily child-free colleague arrived at work exclaiming over the pregnant women everywhere, I knew it wasn't just my imagination. Apparently Chicago was in the midst of a baby boom—and it doesn't seem to have let up since then. While researching this book I interviewed the coordinator of a mom's group in the South Loop, a neighborhood I generally think of as attracting hardcore urbanites, not necessarily parents with young children. But the group has sixty families and some sort of activity or outing nearly every day of the week. Babies, it appears, are everywhere in this city.

I joyfully welcomed my own baby, Clare Mairéad, into the world in February 2000. How I wish City Baby had been around then. While I had a pretty good idea of where I wanted to give birth and who had good quality maternity clothes, I had no idea where to rent a breast pump, how to find a new mom's group, or which neighborhoods had the most kid-friendly parks. As a health writer and syndicated newspaper columnist, I knew how to research a topic upside-down and sideways, but after giving birth, I just didn't have the time or energy to seek out many of the resources I needed.

By picking up a copy of City Baby, you've taken a huge step toward making your life much easier. While there are some excellent resources out there—mainly Chicago Parent magazine and a handful of Chicago-oriented parenting Web sites—there really is nothing that pulls together in one place all the information you might need as a Chicago parent. I took the "ultimate guide" part of my subtitle seriously, and have done my utmost best to give you thoroughly researched information on every topic a city parent might need: how to find an OB or midwife, phone numbers for breastfeeding and postpartum depression hotlines, where to take Mommy and Me classes, who offers great classes for preschoolers, where to throw a terrific first birthday party, which stores sell the coolest maternity clothes, where to find the best resale shops for kids' clothing and furniture…the list goes on and on.

I consider chapter four, "Adjusting to Motherhood," to be one of the most important parts of City Baby. Becoming a parent may be one of the most joyful times of life—but it's also one of the hardest. I've likened it to manic depression: The highs are really high, and the lows are really low.

Most of the moms I know struggled at least a little bit, if not a lot, in making the adjustment to parenthood. I cried every day for two weeks straight after Matt went back to work and my mom went home to Ohio. There I was, tethered to my rocking chair for hours at a time, alone and lonely while I nursed my baby's insatiable hunger and watched more bad TV than I had in my entire thirty-four years combined. I had no idea that what

I was experiencing wasn't that unusual, and I wish I'd known about places like Sweet Pea's Studio and Get Together at the Virginia Frank Child Development Center, where parents can connect with one another and share their experiences. Please take advantage of the parenting resources this city has to offer; at the very least, you'll make some new friends with babies who can relate to the ups and downs of your new life.

As you read this book, keep in mind that while the information was accurate at the time it went to press, stores go out of business, prices tend to go up, and Web sites become defunct. If you want to pass along information and resources for future editions of this book, please contact me, either by writing me in care of my publisher (Universe Publishing, 300 Park Ave. South, New York, NY 10010) or by e-mailing me at karinsull@sbcglobal.net.

You're about to embark upon your greatest adventure, one that will take the rest of your life to complete. Let City Baby help to make these first few years of parenthood easier.

Chapter One

from obstetric care to childbirth

Congratulations! The pregnancy test is positive! Tell the prospective grandparents, aunts, and uncles about the new addition to the clan, then start making the decisions that will keep you busy for the next nine months. First, you will have to consider:

❖ Who will provide you with prenatal care throughout your pregnancy?

❖ Who will deliver your baby?

❖ Where will your baby be born?

Who will look after you and your baby during your pregnancy? Basically, you have two choices: a doctor (who may be the obstetrician/gynecologist you saw in your pre-pregnancy days or another doctor you select at this time) or a midwife. Both of these professionals will essentially perform the same service—meet with you during your pregnancy to monitor your progression and help deliver your baby on the big day.

Where your baby will be born is easy: a hospital or at home. Yes, the occasional Chicago baby has made his or her way into the world via taxi cab, but that is a remote possibility. Chances are, you'll make it to the right place at the right time.

You have had the good sense (or blind luck) to be having a baby in a city that seems to have an obstetrician on every other block and some of the best hospitals in the world. Finding excellent care won't be a problem.

This chapter provides everything you need to know about the birthing business in Chicago—doctors, midwives, hospitals, doulas, childbirth preparation classes, lactation consultants, and more.

Being comfortable with and confident in your birth attendant is the most important part of a positive birth experience. All of the hospitals I list have the qualifications to provide an excellent birthing experience, whether you choose to deliver with an obstetrician or midwife.

the birth attendant

Whether it's an obstetrician or midwife, you should choose this person as soon as you discover you're pregnant.

obstetricians

Most women in Chicago deliver their babies in a hospital under the care of an obstetrician. You probably already have an obstetrician/gynecologist whom you've been seeing for annual checkups, and you may be perfectly happy to continue together throughout your pregnancy. But you may want to find a new doctor for one of several reasons: your current ob/gyn is fine for the routine checkups, but friends have told you about a wonderful new doctor; your ob/gyn is farther away from your apartment than you'd like; your ob/gyn is affiliated with a hospital that doesn't appeal to you; or you may be considered high risk and want an ob/gyn who specializes in high-risk pregnancies.

If you're a high maintenance mom, especially a first-timer, you may want an ob/gyn who is very good at hand-holding, one who gets on the phone to comfort you every time you call, or tells you to come to the office. I had a high-risk pregnancy, and I loved my obstetrician because he understood that I wanted to see actual medical studies on certain topics and asked his staff to send copies to me. If you are more laid back, you might want an ob/gyn more in keeping with that style. If you're comfortable and happy with your current ob/gyn, stick with her. If you would like to find someone else, do so. With the large number of good obstetricians in Chicago, you can afford to pick and choose.

To find an obstetrician:

✳ Ask friends, neighbors, and co-workers who have had babies. A recommendation based on the personal experience of a woman who's already been through what you're just beginning is a good way to go.

✳ Ask your internist or general practitioner to recommend an obstetrician.

✳ Call the hospital where you would like to deliver, and ask for a referral from their obstetrical department. After you check out the hospital chart starting on page 20, you may find a hospital that is especially suited to your needs.

Once you have a candidate or two, call for a consultation. Any doctor should be willing to sit down with you and discuss what you can expect over the next nine months and during the birth. Come for your appointment armed with a list of questions, a pen and pad, and your husband or partner—two listeners are better than one.

After this initial consultation, you should be able to decide whether this is the doctor for you. He or she should listen to you carefully, answer your questions thoroughly, and inspire your trust. You

need to feel confident that this doctor will be there for you any time night or day during your pregnancy. Feeling confident and comfortable with your ob/gyn is the most important thing.

Here are some questions that you should ask:

✳ Are you part of a group practice? If so, will I see the other doctors in the practice? What is the likelihood that you will deliver my baby, rather than one of your colleagues? Ask when the doctor typically takes vacation. You will be able to figure out what month you are delivering, so inquire early on.

✳ How often will I need to have an office visit?

✳ What tests should I expect to have and when?

✳ What is the fee for a vaginal birth? Cesarean birth? What extra charges should I expect? Some doctors now charge the same fee for a vaginal or a cesarean delivery, because they do not want to be accused of performing unnecessary cesareans.

✳ What are your thoughts on natural childbirth, anesthesia, episiotomy, Cesarean section, induction of labor? Ask these and other questions about the doctor's birthing philosophy that are of concern to you.

✳ With which hospital are you affiliated? Does the hospital have birthing rooms; labor, delivery, and recovery rooms; rooming-in for baby and husband or partner; a neonatal intensive care unit?

❊ What do you consider "high risk" birth factors?

❊ How do I get answers to my questions between visits? If you are busy, is there another doctor in the office who will take my call?

❊ Do you have nurses trained to answer basic prenatal questions? Obstetricians spend half their day doing hospital deliveries or patient check-ins, so it is important to know that if your doctor is not there, someone will be available to answer your questions in a timely manner.

While you're at the doctor's office for your consultation, check out the waiting room. If you can, ask one or two of the pregnant women, leafing through the latest Parents magazine, how long they usually wait to see the doctor. Routine visits take about ten or fifteen minutes, and there is nothing more frustrating than waiting an hour for a ten-minute visit. Also, ask whether the doctor works in a collaborative way with patients, making joint decisions, or whether he or she likes to call the shots. Again, the doctor's personality must jibe with yours.

The usual schedule for visiting your ob/gyn in a low-risk, normal pregnancy is every three or four weeks for the first seven months, every two weeks in the eighth month, and every week in the ninth month. Of course, this may vary with different practices, and if your pregnancy is high risk you may see your doctor more often.

Some common tests to expect in the course of your pregnancy are:

❊ **Sonogram.** Typically, a woman has two or three sonograms (ultrasounds) during her pregnancy. The first will be done in the second month (about nine weeks) to date her pregnancy; the second more extensive sonogram will be done in the fifth month (about twenty weeks), sometimes at the hospital, to check the growth and internal organs of the fetus; a third may be done in the ninth month (about thirty-six weeks) to get an idea of the baby's size and position.

❊ **MSAFP (Maternal Serum Alpha-Fetoprotein Screening).** The MSAFP screening is performed in the fourth month (sixteen to eighteen weeks). This simple blood test determines the levels of alpha-fetoprotein (blood protein) present in the mother's blood. High or low levels may indicate serious problems in the development of the fetus. If the MSAFP level comes back either too high or too low, the doctor will probably recommend a second test to confirm the results of the first.

❊ **Amniocentesis.** Known to moms as an amnio, this procedure is performed in the fourth month (sixteen to eighteen weeks) of pregnancy. The technician, guided by an ultrasound image of the uterus, inserts a long hollow needle through the woman's abdominal wall and withdraws a small amount of amniotic fluid. Amniocentesis is recommended for women over thirty-five (although many women over thirty choose to have it performed as well) and in cases in which genetic disorders or chromosomal abnormalities might be suspected.

These tests and procedures are routine, and the obstetrician you choose will have conducted, ordered, or overseen them on hundreds of pregnant women before you. But remember: this is your pregnancy. You should feel perfectly comfortable asking what you think are "dumb questions" about the need for tests and what the results mean.

A number of factors can throw you into the category of high-risk pregnancy. These include maternal age over 35, previous infertility, multiple miscarriages, high blood pressure, diabetes, obesity, and other serious health problems. Make sure your doctor knows your full medical history.

A number of obstetricians specialize in high-risk pregnancies. Your own ob/gyn should refer you to such a specialist if he or she determines you to be high risk. Or call the obstetrical department of any of the hospitals (starting on page 20), and ask for a referral based upon your specific needs.

midwives

A growing number of Chicago moms-to-be opt for a midwife, rather than an obstetrician, to guide them through pregnancy and delivery. A midwife may be a good fit for you if you're low risk, and if you like the idea of working one-on-one. A midwife will likely be more available than an obstetrician to talk with you about the emotional aspects of what you're experiencing, and will probably be more oriented toward natural childbirth.

If this sounds good to you, you will probably want to find a Certified Nurse Midwife (CNM), a registered nurse who has undergone extensive formal training through an accredited nurse-midwifery program. The American College of Nurse Midwives, based in Washington, D.C., provides midwife certification nationally and sets the standards for the practice of nurse-midwifery. Only ACNM-certified midwives are able to practice in hospitals. Midwives can prescribe pain medications for women in labor, and they can call an anesthesiologist to administer an epidural when in a hospital.

Another category of midwife is the direct entry midwife, often referred to as a lay midwife. Lay midwives, trained through a combination of coursework and apprenticeship, are not licensed to practice in Illinois, but do perform or assist at many home births in the Chicago area. Several area doctors also attend home births.

When you choose a CNM, find out about her hospital affiliation. You may prefer to deliver at home, but in the event of a medical complication, it is critical that your practitioner has access to a hospital nearby. Most CNMs in Chicago do practice in hospitals and will deliver your baby in the same birthing rooms that the obstetricians use.

With a CNM, you can expect the same schedule you would have with an obstetrician: a visit every three or four weeks at the beginning of your pregnancy, every three weeks in the seventh month, every two weeks in the eighth month, and every week in the ninth month. Like an obstetrician, the midwife will ask how you are feeling and if you have any questions. She will give you an external exam, take your blood pressure and weight, and listen to the baby's heartbeat.

If you would like to check out midwifery, call any of the names listed here, and set up an appointment for a consultation, just as you would for an obstetrician. Use the list of questions I have provided for choosing an obstetrician (see page 11). In addition, you may be especially interested in learning how the midwife will help you through the stages of labor and delivery, the point at which the practices of CNMs and obstetricians usually differ. Many CNMs are skilled at relaxing and preparing the perineum so that anesthesia and episiotomies are rarely necessary.

The following is a list of Certified Nurse Midwives practices in Chicago. I've divided the list into two categories, those who attend hospital births and those who attend home births (some do both and appear on both lists). I've also included doctors who attend home births.

midwives who attend hospital births

❋ *Advocate Illinois Masonic Medical Center Nurse Midwifery Service*
3000 N. Halsted; Suite 303
773-296-7032

❋ *Nurse Midwifery Group at Swedish Covenant Hospital*
5140 N. California
773-989-6200

❋ *St. Anthony Nurse-Midwifery Service*
2875 W. 19th St.
773-484-4366

❋ *Midwife Associates of Norwegian American Hospital*
1044 N. Mozart
773-292-8200

❋ *University of Illinois Nurse-Midwifery Service*
1740 W. Taylor St.
312-413-7686

❋ *Mt. Sinai Hospital Access Community Health Network*
2720 W. 15th St.; 3rd floor
773-542-2000 ext. 4852

❋ *Chicago Health Outreach*
C.N.M.s attend births at Louis A. Weiss Memorial Hospital
1015 W. Lawrence
773-275-2586

❋ *Northwestern Memorial Physicians Group*
Several C.N.M.s on staff
680 N. Lake Shore Drive; Ste. 810
312-926-8811

❋ *Women's Health Specialists*
C.N.M.s attend births at Weiss Hospital
4646 N. Marine Drive
773-564-6036

❋ *Lorna Davis Midwife Associates*
Attend births at St. Joseph and Advocate Illinois Masonic
3000 N. Halsted St.
773-404-6133

❋ *Erie Family Health Center*
C.N.M.s attend births at Northwestern Memorial

1701 W. Superior
312-666-3488

❊ *UIC/St. Elizabeth's
Nurse-Midwifery Practice*
1431 N. Claremont
773-652-1811

❊ *Female Health Care Associates*
C.N.M.s attend births at Rush
and Northwestern Memorial
201 E. Huron
312-266-2229

❊ *Carol Arthur, C.N.M.*
Attends births at Advocate Illinois Masonic
550 W. Webster, Ste. 304
773-929-4200

❊ *Provident Hospital Midwives*
500 E. 51st St.
312-572-2500

❊ *North Shore Associates in
Gynecology and Obstetrics*
C.N.M.s attend births at Evanston and
St. Francis
2500 Ridge (Evanston)
Evanston
847-475-1224

❊ *Partners in Women Care*
Katherine Puls, C.N.M.
Attends births at Evanston Hospital
1000 Central, Ste. 752 (Evanston)
847-864-1200

❊ *West Suburban Midwife Associates*
C.N.M.s attend births at West Suburban
715 Lake St. (Oak Park)
708-848-3800

Note: You and your doctor or midwife should decide jointly, based on your wishes and her expertise, on a birthing plan for the big day. Sometime after you begin your visits, but well before your due date, decide what will happen regarding anesthesia, IVs, and episiotomies. Your ideal birthing plan (barring any unexpected surprises) should be in writing, in your medical file, and on hand at the hospital when you arrive.

midwives and doctors who attend home births

❊ *Diane Bajus-Abderhalden, C.N.M.*
Authentic Midwifery
630-587-9647
Because Diane is in St. Charles, she first refers patients to colleagues in the city. However, she will attend births in the city herself if a patient wishes.

❊ *Elizabeth Baker, M.D.
George Elvove, M.D.*
847-362-1367
www.elvovemd.com
These nurses and doctors do attend home births in the city, but you will need to travel to their Libertyville office for prenatal care.

❉ *Birth Naturally Inc.*
Kay Furey, C.N.M.
13255 W. Howard (Evanston)
773-764-3780

❉ *Home Birth & Women's Health*
Catherine Craig, C.N.M.
Nancy Derrig, C.N.M.
708-445-8206
www.homebirthandwomenshealth.com
These midwives are based in Lombard but do attend home births in Chicago.

❉ *Homefirst Health Services*
847-679-8336
Six locations with one in the city:
550 W. Webster (in Lincoln Park Hospital)
www.homefirst.com
The largest physician-attended homebirth service in the country, Homefirst has six M.D.s and two C.N.M.s on staff. Homefirst also provides family medicine services.

❉ *Tracey Johnstone, traditional lay midwife*
LifeSpiral Midwifery Services
773-235-4815

❉ *Jennifer Lucchesi, N.D.*
Natural Health Care for Women
847-922-6638
Jenny is the only naturopath-midwife in Chicago, which means that as a naturopathic doctor, she can provide primary care services, treating problems outside the realm of pregnancy with natural methods. Among her areas of expertise are massage therapy, acupuncture, and spinal manipulation. Jenny is based in Elgin but travels to patients' homes for appointments, as well as births.

❉ *Sarah Simmons, C.N.M.*
New Life Midwifery
4140 Maplewood
773-588-MAMA (6262)

doulas

Another type of birth attendant you might consider using is a doula. The main role of the doula is to provide continuous emotional and physical support during labor. A doula will explain your progress during labor, suggest natural ways to ease labor pain, provide encouragement and moral support, use hands-on contact and massage to reduce pain, and advocate on your behalf if necessary. (Some doulas also provide post-partum care; see chapter 3.)

Research has shown that the help of a doula can have a significantly positive effect on birth outcome: Compared to women who didn't use doulas, those who did experienced shorter labors, used less pain medication, and had lower rates of C-section—and furthermore, their husbands offered more support during the birth. Follow-up research at six weeks post-partum found that a greater proportion of doula-supported moms were still breastfeeding, and they also reported less depression.

Because the doula profession is less than ten years old, you'll likely find that even the most seasoned doulas have about 100 hours of experience. Given that there's no licensing for doulas, how do you find a good one? Ask your practitioner, quiz your friends, and check with your childbirth class instructor. One credential to look for is certification by the professional organization Doulas of North America, or DONA, which requires a certain amount of training and experience. Keep in mind, though, the DONA certification process is lengthy and expensive, and some excellent doulas choose not to go through it. Tanya McHale, for instance, is one of the most experienced doulas in the city, with more than 1,000 hours of attending labor—and yet is not DONA-certified. See the resource listing on page 28 for more help in finding a doula.

※ *Doulas of North America (DONA)*
P.O. Box 626
Jasper, IN 47547
888-788-DONA
www.dona.org
DONA's Web site provides a listing of its certified members, including about a dozen in Chicago.

lactation consultants

If you even think you might be interested in breastfeeding, consider contacting a lactation consultant before your first labor pain. As I discovered when my daughter was born, even those of us who are fully committed to breastfeeding (and think we know everything about it!) can have problems and become discouraged once the baby is born. In my case, Clare had trouble latching on; she was several days old before she got the hang of it and I was able to stop pumping milk for bottles. Fortunately, one of my criteria in choosing the hospital where she was born was that it had a staff lactation consultant, or

LC, who was extremely helpful after that tearful first night of unsuccessful nursing attempts.

LCs typically offer services that include prenatal education, postnatal hospital visits, home visits, and rental of hospital-grade electric breast pumps. By getting in touch with a lactation consultant ahead of time, you'll be prepared should you need one. LCs can help with a variety of issues, including:

※ Nipple pain

※ Latch-on problems

※ Low milk supply

※ Slow weight gain

※ Colic

※ Pumping and storing milk, especially helpful if you return to work outside the home

※ Nursing a baby with special needs such as Down's Syndrome or cleft palate

Refer to the chart on page 20 to find out which hospitals include lactation consultants on staff. I also list many independent lactation consultants in the section on breast pump rental in Chapter 4 (page 74). You also can find an International Board Certified Lactation Consultant (IBCLCs) through the International Lactation Consultant Association. IBCLCs have gone through a process that includes at least 30 hours of breastfeeding education.

You also might find it helpful to attend a La Leche League meeting while still pregnant. La Leche

League is the premier breastfeeding support group in the United States; it was founded here in Franklin Park in 1958. By attending a meeting or two before your birth, you can get connected with other nursing moms and find out about helpful resources. I found that after Clare was born I went to La Leche meetings not so much for support—breastfeeding was going well by that time—but as a reason to get out of the house and have some conversation with other grown-ups.

Finally, the free Breastfeeding & Postpartum Help Line at Northwestern's Prentice Women's Hospital is available seven days a week to answer questions regarding feeding and caring for your baby, even if you gave birth elsewhere.

❊ *International Lactation Consultant Association*
1500 Sunday Drive, Suite 102
Raleigh, NC 27607
919-787-5181
www.ilca.org
The Web site includes a referral page for finding an IBCLC in your area.

❊ *La Leche League International*
1400 N. Meacham Road
Schaumburg, IL 60173
847-519-7730
www.lalecheleague.org/home_intro.html
Visit the Web site to find a local meeting; keep in mind the league's site does not necessarily include all meetings. If you don't see a convenient one, call the headquarters or one of the local meeting leaders listed online, who have directories of all meetings in the Chicago

area. La Leche leaders also will provide breastfeeding information and advice free of charge over the phone.

❊ *Northwestern Memorial Hospital Prentice Breastfeeding & Postpartum Help Line*
312-926-7155
Free and available to anyone, regardless of birth place
8 a.m. to 3 p.m., Monday through Friday
8 a.m. to noon, Saturday and Sunday

the birth place
hospitals

All obstetricians are affiliated with a hospital, or maybe two, so once you have selected your obstetrician, you will deliver at her hospital.

If you are still in the process of choosing an obstetrician, you may want to work backward—find the hospital you prefer, and then find an agreeable obstetrician who practices there. Knowing as much as you can about the place your baby will be born is very helpful and comforting.

Here's what's important to know about the hospital: the number of birthing rooms, Cesarean rate, level of care provided in the neonatal unit, policies on husbands/partners in the delivery room, rooming-in (partner and baby staying overnight in your room), and sibling and family visitors. Chicago has many hospitals, but some maternity departments, such as Northwestern's Prentice Women's Hospital, are newer and more comfortable than others. While it may be tempting to choose a hospital based upon decor, trust me when I tell you that once you are in labor, the color of the wallpaper in the labor room will be the last thing on your mind.

The private hospitals in Chicago tend to be similar in many ways. They provide birthing beds, showers, or squatting bars to help your labor and delivery. And in most, if not all, cases, it is your own doctor or midwife—not the hospital or staff—who makes the important decisions concerning your labor.

Other general points to keep in mind:

❋ The hospital should allow you to preregister. This is a good idea, because once you are in labor, you won't want to fill out forms—registering in advance can keep the paperwork to a minimum upon your arrival.

❋ Check your insurance company's policy on length of hospital stay permitted for childbirth. Most insurance companies cover either a twenty-four or forty-eight-hour stay for a vaginal delivery and three to four days for a Cesarean delivery.

❋ Contact your insurance company when you become pregnant so that later there won't be any problems with the forms you submit. Some insurance companies require notification before you check into the hospital.

❋ Private recovery rooms are generally standard at these hospitals. But because semiprivate rooms also are available at some hospitals, the cost of a private room may not be covered by insurance—which could mean your out-of-pocket expenses range from $150 to $300 per night. Check with your insurer ahead of time so you don't get hit with a big bill you didn't expect. Rooming-in for husbands/partners and newborns is permitted in all hospitals in a private room. (In some hospitals it is also permitted in a semiprivate room so long as your roommate doesn't object.)

❋ The hospitals have twenty-four-hour parking lots nearby; ask yours for a list. Find out which hospital entrance to use in case you arrive in the middle of the night.

❋ Most hospitals offer weekly classes for new mothers: bathing the baby, breastfeeding, and basic child-care. If you cannot make it to a class, ask the nurses, who are trained to help. Experience shows you must ask to have these lessons. You are in charge, so speak up about your needs.

❋ Many of the hospitals have extremely generous visiting hours. But keep in mind one experienced nurse's advice: Be selfish and careful about your visitors for your own health and well-being and for that of the baby. Use your hospital stay to get some rest, if possible, and to bond with your baby. There will be plenty of time for visitors when you and your baby get home.

❋ Bring two pillows from home for your postpartum room. You will be a lot more comfortable sleeping on your own pillows, as most hospital pillows are flat as a board. Make sure your pillow cases are any color but white so they don't get mixed in with the hospital laundry.

❋ You should also consider bringing towels from home. If you plan to shower at the hospital, the bath towels are the size of face towels, and can barely fit around a postpartum woman's body!

Here are some of the most common questions you'll hear from expectant parents on hospital tours:

❋ Can we bring music into the delivery room?

❋ Can the baby be wrapped in a receiving blanket that we bring from home instead of a regulation hospital blanket?

❋ Can we dim the lights in the labor room?

❋ Can my husband/partner cut the umbilical cord?

The answer to all these questions is yes—but once labor begins your only concern is delivering that baby any way you can, music or no music.

The following chart provides information to consider while evaluating the hospital in which you will deliver your baby. It includes:

❋ **Hospital:** The name, address, key phone numbers and visiting hours.

❋ **Labor rooms:** The number and type of delivery rooms. In a labor, delivery, and recovery room, known as an LDR room, you will do just that before you are transferred to a postpartum room. An operating room is where Cesareans and complicated vaginal births take place. A labor room is for labor only. A delivery room is where you will be taken when you are ten centimeters dilated and ready to deliver. From delivery you go to a recovery room for one to two hours before going to your own room, where you will stay until you leave the hospital.

❋ **Midwives:** Hospitals with midwives on staff, and those that allow midwives to deliver babies.

❋ **Cesarean birthrate:** Numbers indicate the percentage of births by Cesarean section each year. The percentages listed are the most recent figures available from each hospital. Generally, hospitals with midwives have the lowest rates; hospitals with a large infertility/high-risk patient base have the highest. The national Cesarean rate is nearly 23 percent.

❋ **Nursery level:** In Illinois, neonatal intensive care units are classified in Levels I through III, with Level III being the most advanced. Choosing a hospital with a Level III is recommended, especially for high-risk pregnancies.

❋ **Childbirth classes:** Prenatal classes for women and their husbands or partners, including Lamaze, breastfeeding, and preparation for Cesarean birth. These classes are given at the hospital (unless otherwise noted), and you must sign up in advance. For second time moms, many hospitals offer sibling classes. A number of my friends have taken their children to these classes and have found them to be an excellent way to prepare kids for having a new baby at home.

✳ **Other information:** Any unique features about the hospital.

✳ Advocate Illinois Masonic Medical Center

836 W. Wellington Ave.
773-975-1600 (General)
800-323-8622 (Classes)
773-296-5070 (Patient Info)
Visiting hours:
General: 11 am - 8 pm
Fathers/partners: 24 hours (but no overnight if patient is in a semiprivate room)
Labor Rooms/Other:
8 LDRs (private rooms, unless very busy)
2 operating rooms
Midwives: Yes
Lactation consultants: Yes
Cesarean rate: 25%
Nursery level III
Illinois Masonic was the first hospital in Chicago to offer an alternative birthing center (ABC), though at press time, the center had only one nurse on call for births, and its future was in doubt. Check with the hospital for the ABC's current status.
Classes:
Pregnancy and Beyond
Gamper Childbirth Education
Hypnobirthing

✳ Evanston Hospital

2650 Ridge Ave. (Evanston)
847-570-2000 (General)
Visiting hours:
General: 11 a.m. - 8:30 p.m., but flexible
Fathers/partners: 24 hours
Labor Rooms/Other:
11 LDRs (private, with Jacuzzi tub)
2 operating rooms
Midwives: Yes
Lactation consultants: yes
Cesarean rate: 23%
Nursery level I, but NICU is level III
Evanston is a popular place to give birth and has very high patient satisfaction ratings.
Classes:
Bootcamp for Dads (new in May 2004)
Understanding Your Newborn
Subsequent Pregnancy Support Group
Baby Care Basics
Bereaved Parents Support Group
Multiples
Lamaze
Breastfeeding I and II
Perinatal Loss Support Group
Infant & Child Safety CPR
Car Seat Safety
Prenatal Decisions Support Group
Countdown to Labor and Delivery
Expectant Grandparents
Triplets and More Support Group

❈ Lincoln Park Hospital

550 W. Webster

773-883-2000 (general)

773-883-3540 (patient info)

Visiting hours:

General: 11am-8pm

Fathers/partners: 24 hours

Labor Rooms/Other:

6 LDRs (private)

1 operating room

Midwives: yes

Lactation consultants: no

Cesarean rate: 25%

Nursery level II

Very high patient-to-nurse ratio (often 1-to-1), so laboring moms receive lots of attention.

Classes:

Breastfeeding

Basic Childbirth

Lamaze

Sibling Class

Infant Massage

❈ Mercy Hospital

2525 S. Michigan Ave.

312-567-2000 (General and patient info)

312-567-2441 (The Birth Place and classes)

Visiting hours:

General: 11 am-8 pm

Fathers/partners: 24 hours

Labor Rooms/Other:

9 LDRs (private)

Midwives: yes

Lactation consultants: yes

Cesarean rate: 25%

Nursery level II

Located close to Chinatown, the hospital has staff members who can translate Cantonese and Mandarin Chinese. They also have many staff members who speak Spanish.

Classes:

Parenting

Breastfeeding

❈ Northwestern Memorial Hospital

Prentice Women's Hospital

333 E. Superior St.

312-926-2000 (general)

Visiting hours:

General: 11:00 a.m. - 8:30 p.m.

Fathers/partners and grandparents: 24 hours

Labor Rooms/Other:

25 LDRs (private)

3 Operating rooms

Midwives: Yes

Lactation consultants: Yes

Cesarean rate: 28%

Nursery level III

Northwestern offers the largest ob/gyn program in the Midwest, and is the most popular birthing place in the state. Northwestern offers the city's best selection of pre- and postnatal classes, and is the only place besides West Suburban where you can have a water birth.

Classes:

A Baby? . . . Maybe!

Baby Basics

Breastfeeding: The Best Beginning

Family Matters

Infant/Pediatric CPR and Safety (also offered in Spanish)

Infant Massage

Pediatric Care: Your New Baby

Prenatal Aerobics and Strength

Prenatal Nia

Postnatal Body Sculpting

Postnatal Yoga

Tike Hike

Transitions to Motherhood series

Great Expectations for Parents (also offered in Spanish)

Great expectations refresher

Great Expectations for Teens

Expectant Grandparents

Expectant Fathers

Great Expectations: Preparing for Multiples

Breastfeeding Multiples

Great expectations for multiples refresher

Support Groups:

Together in the Loss of a Child (TLC)

New Mom's Support Group

Endometriosis

Parents of Multiples Club

Support services:

Breastfeeding helpline

❖ Rush University Medical Center

1650 W. Harrison St.

312-942-5000 (General)

312-942-5695 (Patient Info)

312-942-2336 (Classes)

Visiting hours:

General: 11am-8pm

Fathers/partners: 24 hours

Labor Rooms/Other:

8 LDRs (private unless very crowded)

2 operating rooms

Midwives: yes

Lactation consultants: yes

Cesarean rate: 37%

Nursery level III

Typical homelike décor in LDRs. Rush is the regional headquarters for the network of hospitals that serves high-risk mothers and babies.

Classes:

Basic Breastfeeding

Cesarean Birth

Childbirth Education

CPR for Infants and Children

Marvelous Multiples

❖ Saint Francis Hospital

355 Ridge Ave. (Evanston)

847-316-4000 (General)

847-316-6340 (Patient Information)

877-RES-INFO (Classes)

Visiting Hours:

General 8:30am - 10:00pm,

Fathers/partners: 24 hour visitation

Labor Rooms/Other:

12 LDRs (private unless very busy)

2 operating rooms

Midwives: Yes

Lactation consultants: Yes

Cesarean rate: 14%

Nursery level II with extended capabilities

The newly opened maternity suites offer amenities (mini-fridge, CD player, VCR/DVD player) and popular birthing props (hydrotherapy tub, birthing balls, birthing chair, squatting bar). One of the few area hospitals to offer Boot Camp for Expectant Dads.

Classes:

Basics of Newborn Care

Prepared Childbirth and Beyond
Big Brother and Sister
Boot Camp for Expectant Dads
Childbirth Refresher
Grandparents Class
Breastfeeding and Returning to Work

❊ Saint Joseph Hospital

2900 North Lake Shore Drive
773-665-3000 (general)
773-665-3605 (Family Birthing Unit)
773-665-3318 (patient info)
Visiting hours:
General: 10 a.m. - 8:30 p.m.
Fathers/partners: 24 hours
Labor Rooms/Other:
18 LDRs (private)
3 operating rooms
Midwives: yes
Lactation consultants: yes
Cesarean rate: 19%
Nursery level II with extended capabilities
Homey décor, rooms include a refrigerator and entertainment center. Provides a follow-up telephone call and breastfeeding warm-line. The Mom Network, a support group for new mothers, is also available as a resource.
Classes:
Breastfeeding: A Special Time
Prepared Childbirth
Prepared Childbirth (Refresher Class)
Newborn Care
Infant/Child CPR
"Baby and Me" Sibling Class
The Mom Network Support Group
Spanish Prenatal Class

❊ Swedish Covenant Hospital

5145 N. California
773-878-8200 (general)
773-878-1034 (Classes)
773-878-8200 (Patient Info)
Visiting hours:
General: 10 a.m. to 9 p.m.
Mother/Baby Unit: 11 a.m. to 8 p.m.
Fathers/partners: May visit at any time
Labor Rooms/Other:
9 LDRs (private)
2 operating rooms
Midwives: Yes
Lactation consultants: Yes
Cesarean rate: 19%
Nursery level II
Newly renovated LDR suites provide amenities that include a computer hookup (bring your laptop and email the good news right away!). Swedish Covenant is served by board-certified neonatologists and on-site staff from Children's Memorial Hospital. Also has 24-hour high-risk OB services from Northwestern.
Classes:
Prepared Childbirth (English, Spanish, Korean, and Hindi)
Breastfeeding (English and Spanish)
Pre/Post Natal Yoga

❊ University of Chicago Hospitals

5841 S. Maryland Ave.
773-702-1000 (General line)
773-702-6118 (Patient Info line)
773-702-9200 (Classes line)
Visiting hours:
General: 11am to 8 pm

Fathers/partners: 24 hours
Labor Rooms/Other:
9 LDRs (some private)
4 operating rooms
Midwives: no
Lactation consultants: yes
Cesarean rate: 26%
Nursery level III
U of C has one of the largest neonatal intensive care units in the Midwest and cares for more than 1,000 infants a year, including about 120 extremely low birth-weight babies.
Classes Offered:
Beginning Breastfeeding
Boot Camp for Expectant Dads
Infant Care
Infant CPR & Safety
Lamaze Childbirth Preparation
Sibling Preparation

❖ University of Illinois at Chicago Medical Center

1740 W. Taylor St.
312-335-4000 (general)
312-996-4120 (Mother/Baby Unit)
800-842-1002 (appointments)
312-996-4175 (classes)
312-996-9634 (patient info)
Visiting hours:
General: 8am-10pm
Fathers/partners: 24 hours
Labor Rooms/Other:
8 LDRs (private unless very crowded)
2 operating rooms
Midwives: yes
Lactation consultants: yes

Cesarean rate: 18%
Nursery level III
Has a large midwifery practice, as well as extensive facilities for high-tech care. At press time, facilities were under renovation, scheduled to be completed this past spring.
Classes:
Breastfeeding
Baby Care
Care for Mothers after Birth

❖ Weiss Memorial Hospital

4646 N. Marine Drive
773-878-8700 (general)
773-564-5000 (patient info)
Visiting hours:
General: 11 am-8:30 pm
Fathers/partners: 24 hours
Labor Rooms/Other:
11 LDRs (private)
2 operating rooms
Midwives: Yes
Lactation consultants: no
Cesarean rate: 18-20%
Nursery level II
All the LDRs at Weiss feature views of Lake Michigan. Another advantage is a staff of language interpreters, as well as nurses fluent in Spanish, Arabic, French, and Vietnamese.
Classes:
Preparation and childbirth (Lamaze and Bradley)
Baby Care
Breastfeeding

❋ *West Suburban Health Care,
Irvin & Margaret R. Houck Family
Birthing Centre*

3 Erie Court, Oak Park, Il. 60302

708.383.6200

Visiting Hours:

11:00 am to 8:30 pm

LDRP visiting hours for one (1) designated person (father, partner) plus grandparents, 24 hours

Labor Rooms/Other:

22 total mother/baby rooms, all private

8 labor/delivery/recovery rooms

2 operating rooms

Midwives: yes

Lactation Consulting: yes

Cesarean rate: 17% (well below the national average)

Nursery is a Level II

Patients have the option of a variety of alternative birthing methods in the comfort & security of a hospital setting. (also can use verbiage you offered below in addition)

Classes:

Please call for details

Ten Hospital Tips

1. Decide whether you want a private room before you go into labor.

2. Bring a pillow from home. Use a colored pillowcase so it doesn't get mixed up with hospital linens.

3. Bring your own robe and slippers.

4. Bring a bath towel and washcloth. Hospital-issue ones are tiny and thin.

5. Bring sanitary napkins. The hospital will provide them, but they'll charge you a fortune.

6. Bring nutritious snacks: fruit, energy bars, raisins, nuts, and yogurt if your room has a fridge. If you have a midwife, you may be able to eat during labor, and you'll definitely want snacks after the birth. Hospital food is notoriously bad and, ironically, not very healthy.

7. Have a friend or family member be present as much as possible in order to go for drinks, run errands, and get the nurse.

8. Prepare a list of key phone numbers to take with you—friends and family to notify, your postpartum doula, furniture delivery, etc.

9. Call your insurance company as soon as possible after the delivery to add your new dependent.

10. Do what mothers of second children do: Send the baby to the nursery and get as much rest as much as possible. You're not going to get much for the next year or two.

birthing centers

Unlike other states, Illinois does not allow freestanding birthing centers. However, the Chicago area does have two alternative birthing centers (ABCs) attached to hospitals, at Illinois Masonic on the North Side and at West Suburban in Oak Park. The birthing centers provide much more freedom than the standard labor and delivery departments. Because you will not be tethered to a continuous fetal monitor, you can be up moving around, taking advantage of gravity's effects; many women like to get in the shower, which you can't do with a fetal monitor or the also-standard IV.

You can have as many family members, friends, and attendants at the birth as you want, including children. Each room features a queen-size bed for labor and delivery, and at West Suburban you can labor and give birth in a water tub. One caveat though: If you change your mind and want an epidural, you will need to be transferred to the main hospital. Injections of short-acting narcotics are the only pain medications available in the ABCs.

childbirth methods

Once the who and the where of your pregnancy and delivery have been settled, you will start to focus—more and more as you grow and grow—on the how of it all. What are the best, easiest, and most pain-free ways to get that baby out?

As you talk with other pregnant women and new mothers, you will hear about the relative merits of one birthing technique over another. Here is a very short course on four methods.

The Lamaze Method. This method, named after its developer, Dr. Fernand Lamaze, head of an obstetrical clinic in Paris in 1950, is popularly, if not entirely accurately, known as childbirth without pain. The method combines learned breathing techniques (the hoo-hoo-hoo, hee-hee-hee) used during contractions, with relaxation exercises designed to help a woman distract herself from the pain and get through labor as comfortably as possible.

Most hospitals offer Lamaze classes. Couples usually begin Lamaze in the seventh month. Some large obstetrical practices also offer Lamaze or will make referrals to private instructors, so ask your obstetrician or midwife.

the bradley method

This method was developed by Dr. Robert A. Bradley, a Toronto-based obstetrician. The Bradley Method is based on a calming pattern of relaxation, deep abdominal breathing, and close teamwork between a laboring woman and her partner. Bradley's goal is an unmedicated pregnancy, and labor and birth—no epidural block or Pitocin.

With Bradley, the pregnant woman learns various positions for first, second, and third stage labor. She is encouraged to approach her entire pregnancy as training for labor and to prepare her muscles for birth and her breasts for nursing.

Hospitals generally do not offer Bradley instruction. To find the name of a certified Bradley instructor in your area, contact the American Academy of Husband-Coached Childbirth (see page 28).

water labor and water birth

Water birth, popular in Russia since the 1960s, has attracted a small but enthusiastic number of supporters in the United States. Studies have shown that warm water can reduce the hours and stress of labor, offer support to the laboring woman, and help relax blood flow, making the baby's journey into the world easier.

Some women use this method's water-filled tub only as a comfort during labor. Others deliver while still in the tub, and the baby takes his first breaths while most of his body is submerged in water, a gentle and familiar medium from his time in the womb. My friend Nikkola gave birth to her second child in a water tub at West Suburban's ABC and says the water really eased her pain. Should you wish, you can rent a birthing tub and have a water birth at home with the help of a midwife.

hypnobirthing

Begun about 15 years ago, HypnoBirthing involves achieving a state of deep relaxation and focused concentration, where you are able to give yourself messages about what your body is experiencing. The goal is not to deny that pain is occurring but to work with the pain and remain relaxed. Local HypnoBirthing instructor Tanya McHale interviewed one year's worth of her clients—about 60—and found that roughly a third of them said they experienced no pain during labor.

doulas, childbirth educators, classes, and other resources

There are two venues for childbirth education: hospital classes or private instruction, either individually or as part of a group. Hospital classes tend to be offered frequently and typically cost less than those offered by independent instructors. However, keep in mind that in classes underwritten by a hospital, the teacher—generally a nurse who works there— will be limited in the information she can present. Though Lamaze is typically included, natural childbirth methods are not. If you want to try to avoid medication and are seeking alternative methods of pain relief, you'll likely want to seek out an independent teacher. Some independent instructors do rent hospital space for their classes but are not paid by the hospital, and thus are free to design their own curricula.

Here is a list of resources. These private practitioners specialize in a variety of birth-related areas: Lamaze, Bradley, water birth, labor support, and childbirth education. Some practitioners offer more than one kind of service; make some phone calls to find just the right match for you.

Class lengths vary, but most childbirth series cost between $200 to $400 per couple. If you use more than one service from a practitioner, you may be able to negotiate a package deal.

❋ **The American Academy of Husband-Coached Childbirth/The Bradley Method**
P.O. Box 5224
Sherman Oaks, CA 91413
(800) 4-ABIRTH
www.bradleybirth.com
To find a Bradley teacher, call the organization, or fill out and submit the form on the Web site, and you'll be sent the names of teachers nearby.

❋ **Association of Labor Assistants & Childbirth Educators (ALACE)**
P.O. Box 390436
Cambridge, MA 02139
888-222-5223
www.alace.org
ALACE certifies childbirth educators and doulas. Its Web site has a searchable database of local providers; however, BirthLink and DONA have more extensive Chicago listings.

BirthLink
1555 Sherman Ave. (Evanston)
847-733-8050
www.birthlink.com/index.html
Founded in 1996 by doula Jo Anne Lindberg, BirthLink provides free referrals to its extensive listings of local birth professionals, with an emphasis on natural childbirth preparation and labor. The Web site has a listing of resources.

Birthways, Inc.
1484 W. Farragut
773-506-0607
http://www.birthwaysinc.com/index.php
Birthways is a community of about 20 providers and is headed by Karen Laing, previously the director one of the oldest doula services in the Chicago area. Birthways offers labor and postpartum doulas, childbirth education classes, workshops for new parents, and infant massage classes.

Pam Bogda, R.N.
Childbearing Gifts Inc.
312-266-6648
A nurse with extensive experience in labor and delivery and neonatal pediatrics, Pam teaches childbirth preparation, breastfeeding, and infant CPR classes.

Debbie Boucher
Childbirth the Way Nature Intended
Phone: 847-816-4640
www.yourbirth.com
Currently studying to be a midwife, Debbie is a DONA-certified doula and a Bradley instructor. She also teaches a free healthy pregnancy class that focuses on nutrition and exercise, offers a VBAC (vaginal birth after Cesarean) class, and provides assistance in writing a birth plan. Package discounts are available.

Christine Culbert, R.N.
Starbaby Childbirth and Parenting Education
773-381-9728
Christine, who is ALACE certified, worked for ten years as a perinatal nurse and now teaches natural childbirth and parent child classes (see page 63). She also offers private classes if patients wish.

Natalie Evans
Mama Belly Birth Services
773-465-4337
www.mamabellybirth.com
A birth doula and ALACE-certified natural childbirth educator, Natalie teaches at two locations: Sweet Pea's Studio (3717 N. Ravenswood) and Chicago Women's Health Center (3435 N. Sheffield).

Sara Fagan
773-702-5475
Sara is a certified Bradley instructor, teaching in both the Hyde Park and Ravenswood neighborhoods.

Pam Hays
Chicago Doula Care
773-379-2164
A DONA-certified doula, Pam has attended several hundreds of births. She also is an ICEA-

certified natural childbirth educator, and specializes in teaching about VBAC and home and water birth. She teaches at her home and at West Suburban Hospital in Oak Park.

✤ International Childbirth Education Association (ICEA)

P.O. Box 20048
Minneapolis, MN 55420
952-854-8660
www.icea.org
ICEA has 6,000 members worldwide and certifies practioners in a variety of areas: childbirth educators, postnatal educators, perinatal fitness educators, and doulas.

✤ Susan Gallas

Blooming Iris Birth Companion
847-877-6773
A DONA-certified doula, Susan runs a doula service that makes referrals to labor doulas, postpartum doulas, and infant massage therapists. Susan also provides lactation education and transitional adoption care for adoptive parents of infants.

✤ Rhonda Kantor, R.N.

Global Yoga and Wellness Center
1823 W. North Ave.
773-489-1510
www.globalyogacenter.com
The founder and director of Global Yoga in Bucktown, Rhonda is a registered nurse, doula, and yoga instructor for pregnancy women and prenatal teachers-in-training. I took Rhonda's prenatal yoga class and loved it.

✤ Gail Karlovsky

Birth of a Lifetime
630-305-4191
www.birthofalifetime.com
A DONA-certified birth doula who's attended about 40 births, Gail is also working toward certification as a postpartum doula. (Postpartum doulas are harder to find; they offer care for the new mom, sibling care, lactation support, food preparation, and more.) Although she lives in Bolingbrook, she does doula work in the city. She also is a Bradley instructor.

✤ Lamaze International

www.lamaze-childbirth.com
800-368-4404
You can visit the Web site's referral page to find a Lamaze instructor in your area, or call the organization's 800 number.

✤ Abigail Lynn

773-991-7968
Abigail is a former emergency room nursing assistant who now is a doula and certified massage therapist.

✤ Tanya C. McHale, R.N.

708-725-3025
www.tanyamchale.com
Tanya has been a doula since 1989, and has attended about 900 births as a doula. She also is a certified HypnoBirthing instructor, teaching classes at Advocate Illinois Masonic Hospital in the city and West Suburban Midwife Associates in Oak Park. In addition, Tanya sees individual patients to perform hypnotherapy to control nausea and vomiting dur-

ing pregnancy, turn breech babies, and prevent preterm labor.

Jacque Shannon McNulty
Blissful Birth
708-848-0657
Jacque teaches natural childbirth classes that emphasize developing self-confidence, trust, and faith in your ability to give birth. With a background in facilitating support groups for women and children, she also includes information on grieving and healing, for instance, in cases of infertility or miscarriage.

M. Pat Schmidt, R.N.
847-673-2621
Formerly a labor and delivery nurse, Pat is an ICEA-certified doula, Lamaze instructor, and a lactation consultant. She teaches Lamaze and breastfeeding classes throughout Chicago, including private classes in a client's home.

Catherine Willows, R.N., L.C.
773-732-2030
Catherine is a nurse, lactation consultant, and herbalist who has wide experience using natural remedies to treat women's health issues, including pregnancy-related ailments (nausea, allergies and colds, insomnia) and postpartum issues. She uses many flower essences in her practice, which she says can be extremely gentle and helpful in treating children, as well as pregnant and postpartum moms. In addition, she sells a gift basket with a combination of natural products for labor and postpartum, including perineal oil and wash, nipple salve, mother's milk tea, an aromatherapy spritzer, baby massage oil, and flower essences for the whole family; the basket makes a nice shower gift and costs $100.

taking care
of yourself

Once you have assembled your support team, from Lamaze instructor to lactation consultant, and have checked out the hospital room or birthing center in which your baby will first set eyes upon the world, it's time to be good to yourself. Now is the time to pamper and indulge yourself. Take advantage of some of the terrific body-strengthening and spirit-lifting services Chicago has to offer. Treat yourself to a massage when you're in your ninth month and feel as though you can't stand to be pregnant for one more day.

Most importantly, get involved with a physical fitness program early on. It will help you feel your best throughout your pregnancy and prepare you for labor. Check out one or another of the facilities described in this chapter. You'll find information about health clubs, yoga studios, and private practitioners that offer pre- and postnatal exercise classes, fitness training, yoga, and massage, all fine-tuned and appropriate for pregnant women.

exercise

Most experts agree that exercising throughout your pregnancy is safe, healthy, and beneficial to your overall well-being. If your pregnancy is low risk and normal, you can participate in a moderate exercise program throughout your nine months. If you're a longtime jock or have exercised regularly prior to pregnancy (at least three times per week), you should be able to safely maintain that level of activity, with some modifications, throughout pregnancy and postpartum. Of course, check with your obstetrician or midwife before starting or continuing any exercise regimen, whether you are low- or high-risk. Also, be aware of the following recommendations adapted from guidelines issued by the American College of Obstetricians and Gynecologists (ACOG):

❋ Regular exercise (at least three times per week) is preferable to intermittent activity.

❋ Avoid exercise that involves lying flat on your back after the fourth month. Lying on your back is associated with decreased cardiac output in pregnancy. Also avoid prolonged periods of standing.

❋ During pregnancy, you have less oxygen available for aerobic exercise. Modify the intensity of your exercise. Stop exercising when fatigued, and never exercise to the point of exhaustion.

❋ Weight-bearing exercises, such as jogging, may be continued throughout pregnancy, at lower intensities. Nonweight-bearing exercises, such as cycling and swimming, minimize risk of injury.

❋ During exercise, be sure that your heart rate does not exceed 140 beats per minute.

❋ Avoid exercise that could cause you to lose your balance, especially in the third trimester. Avoid any type of exercise with the potential for even mild abdominal trauma.

❋ Be sure to eat enough prior to your workout. Pregnancy requires an additional 300 calories a day just to maintain your weight.

❋ Drink water and wear comfortable clothing to augment heat dissipation during exercise.

Many of the body changes of pregnancy persist four to six weeks postpartum. After your baby is born, resume your pre-pregnancy routines gradually, according to how you feel.

Ten Tips for Prenatal Exercise

1. Consult your obstetrician or midwife before starting any kind of new exercise.
2. Do it!
3. Try as many classes as necessary until you find one you like.
4. Remember to do your Kegels—I didn't and regret it enormously.
5. Don't lie on your back after the fourth month.
6. Drink plenty of water at all times but especially during exercise.
7. Don't exercise on an empty stomach; have a light, nutritious snack first.
8. Exercise with pregnant women; you'll move at the same pace and encourage each other.
9. Try yoga for excellent stretching and relaxation.
10. Don't let your heart rate exceed 140 beats per minute.

fitness/health clubs

If you don't already have an exercise routine and want to get started, walking is a safe way to stay in shape; according to ACOG, swimming, cycling, and even aerobics also are safe for beginning exercisers who are pregnant. For those who desire a more structured workout environment, the following health clubs offer special classes and/or training for pregnant women; I've noted where classes are for members only. Many personal trainers in these health clubs are certified to work with pre- and postnatal women—just inquire. (In many clubs, pregnant women work out right next to their nonpregnant counterparts.)

Private clubs offer pleasant accoutrements: roomy changing areas, lots of towels, and nice snack bars. Check your local Y classes as well. They are the most economical and offer a wide range of classes and equipment.

❋ Bernard Horwich Jewish Community Center

3003 W. Touhy Ave.
773-761-9100
Horwich JCC offers complete workout facilities, including classes, personal training, a steam room, and lounge. Among the classes is a women-only water aerobics class, an especially nice option if you're feeling self-conscious about your expanding body. Various membership packages are available, though you don't have to be a member to take a class. Contact the JCC for specific price information.

❋ Chicago Park District

312-742-PLAY
www.chicagoparkdistrict.com
The park district offers about 50 aquatic exercise classes throughout the city; though not specifically designated as prenatal programs, water fitness classes are an excellent way for pregnant women to stay in shape. You can call the park district or check the

Web site to find out which nearby parks offer water aerobics.

❋ Evanston Athletic Club

1723 Benson Ave. (Evanston)
847-866-6190
www.eaconline.com/index.html
Members only
Evanston Athletic Club offers a huge range of classes, including prenatal yoga, cardio classes, and water aerobics. In addition, it offers a program of pre- and postnatal land and water classes taught by licensed physical therapists from Evanston Northwestern Health. For more information on these classes, call ENH Rehab Services at 847-570-7170.

❋ Galter Life Center

5157 N. Francisco Ave.
773-878-9936
www.galterlifecenter.org
Members only
The only hospital-based fitness center in the city, Galter offers pre- and postnatal exercise classes, as well as various water aerobic classes, which can be ideal as your pregnant body gets bigger.

❋ Halsted Street Multiplex

3228 N. Halsted St.
773-755-3232
Members only
Though there are several Multiplex clubs throughout the city, the Halsted Street location is currently the only one to offer a pregnancy exercise class. Its Prenatal Resist-a-Ball class uses stability balls to focus on strengthening the abdominals, pelvic floor, and lower back muscles.

❋ Lakeshore Athletic Club—Lincoln Park

1320 W. Fullerton
773-477-9888
www.lsac.com/lincolnpark/
Members only
Lakeshore's Lincoln Park location offers the Fit Moms Program, a complete program of prenatal and postnatal exercise. You design your own program; the club recommends two classes a week, one a water aerobics class and the other a "land" class—low-impact cardio, yoga, or ab-strengthening. For postpartum moms there's circuit training and toning, mom and baby yoga, stroller workout, and cardio/sculpting. The program is run by Carrie Poynton, a personal trainer with a background in nutrition.

❋ Lincoln Park Athletic Club

1019 W. Diversey
773-529-2022
www.lpaconline.com
Offers a pre- and postnatal exercise class that uses weights, bands, and balls to strengthen muscles, prevent back pain, and improve posture. Lincoln Park Athletic Club also has a pre- and postnatal yoga class.

❋ Northwestern Memorial Hospital's Prentice Women's Hospital

333 E. Superior St.
877-926-4664

Prentice offers a better variety of classes for pre- and postnatal city moms than just about any of the health clubs. There's Prenatal Nia, a gentle combination of tae kwon do, tai chi, yoga, and modern dance; Prenatal Aerobics and Strength; Postnatal Yoga; and Postnatal Body Sculpting. Sessions are six weeks long, and all classes are $50 for once a week or $95 for twice a week.

✳ *Walk-a-Bye Baby Fitness*
312-829-2229
www.walkabyebaby.com
Walk-a-Bye Baby is a fitness company entirely dedicated to pregnant women and parents of young children. Classes include prenatal fitness, which incorporates strength training, yoga, breathing, and relaxation exercises; half-hour tone-up classes, for the abs and back or legs and rear; circuit training, with a nanny available to watch the kids; mom-and-baby stretching classes; and stroller classes in Wicker Park and at the Lincoln Park Zoo. In good weather, classes are held outdoors at the zoo; in bad weather, they're held at Windy City Fieldhouse (2367 W. Logan Blvd.). Rates vary from $16 for a drop-in ($10 if it's your first time) to $350 for a pass that allows you to attend as many classes as you want per session. Personal training also is available.

✳ *YMCA*
Locations throughout city (see below)
312-932-1200
www.ymcachgo.org
Many of the Ys offer fitness classes appropri-

ate for prenatal and postpartum moms, including water aerobics. You can call the location nearest you, or search the Web site to see the program listings for specific locations.

Austin
501 N. Central Ave.
773-287-9120

Greater Roseland
4 E. 111th St.
773-785-9210

High Ridge
2424 W. Touhy Ave.
773-262-8300

Irving Park
4251 W. Irving Park Road
773-777-7500

Lake View
3333 N. Marshfield Ave.
773-248-3333

McCormick Tribune
1834 N. Lawndale Ave.
773-235-2525

New City
1515 N. Halsted St.
312-440-7272

Pilsen
1608 W. 21st Place
312-738-0282

South Chicago
3039 E. 91st St.
773-721-9100

South Side
6330 Stony Island Ave.
773-947-0700

Wabash
3763 S. Wabash
773-285-0020

yoga

Yoga is great exercise for pregnant women—aiding relaxation, maintaining flexibility, and providing an excellent way to work out without risking injury. Prenatal yoga emphasizes the strengthening of pelvic floor muscles to get them ready for pregnancy and birth. Also, prenatal classes usually allow more time than traditional yoga for resting and relaxation. You'll learn breathing and postures that are helpful for birth and labor.

Many health clubs have yoga classes. If you have taken yoga before your pre-pregnant days and want to continue, do so. Make sure you tell your instructor you are expecting, however, and ask for alternatives that will be safer and more comfortable.

The following studios offer prenatal yoga classes. For a comprehensive listing of the scores of teachers, studios, community colleges, parks, and other places that offer all kinds of yoga, pick up a free copy of YOGA Chicago (generally found in the doorways of bookstores, Whole Foods, and health-oriented businesses throughout the city) or visit its Web site at www.yogachicago.com.

Bubbles Academy
1504 N. Fremont
312-944-7677
www.bubblesacademy.com
Offers Budding Bubbles prenatal yoga classes. Cost is $140 for an eight-week session. You can take a drop-in class for $20, but you must call first to reserve a spot.

Eight Limbs Yoga
4727 N. Damen
773-561-1877
www.eightlimbs.com
Offers prenatal yoga classes. A single class is $15, or you can buy a multiclass pass, ranging from five classes ($60) to twenty classes ($220).

Global Yoga and Wellness Center
1823 W. North Ave.
773-489-1510
www.globalyogacenter.com
Global Yoga is one of two yoga studios in the city that really focus on pregnancy support (the other is Sweet Pea's Studio, below). This is where I took prenatal yoga classes, and the teacher, Rhonda Kantor, also founder and director of the studio, is wonderful. Rhonda is a registered nurse, as well as a doula and Bradley childbirth educator, and she is extremely knowledgeable about how yoga can benefit women during pregnancy and labor. A one-hour prenatal class is $12 per class, or $85 for an eight-class pass. Global Yoga also offers mom and baby yoga, as well as classes in childbirth education, and labor positions and childbirth support.

❋ Priya Yoga

1 E. Oak St.
312-587-7492
www.priyayoga.com

Offers prenatal classes. Drop-in classes are $15, or you can purchase a pass for anywhere from five ($65) to twenty ($200) classes. Also offers a Mommy & Me class for children under 3.

❋ Sweet Pea's Studio

3717 N. Ravenswood, Ste. 213
773-248-YOGA
www.sweetpeasstudio.com

Sweet Pea's Studio is a wonderful place for expecting parents and existing families. In addition to prenatal yoga, it offers couples' massage, birth-education classes, infant massage, parent-baby yoga, kids' yoga, and the postpartum Bouncing Back from Baby massage series. If you're looking for resources on how to take care of yourself as a pregnant woman or new parent, associate director Corrine Peterson, a massage therapist and yoga instructor, is a fount of information. An hour-and-a-half yoga class at the studio is $15 for drop-ins, or $13 per class for a twelve-week series.

❋ Yogaview

2232 N. Clybourn Ave.
773-883-YOGA
www.yogaview.com

Offers prenatal yoga. Single classes are $15, or $65 for a five-class pass. Up to $225 for twenty classes.

massage

Many pregnant women suffer from back pain and strain, especially during the later months. A massage can ease the pain and pamper you at a time when you need it most.

Communication with your therapist is critical. If you feel lightheaded, short of breath, or uncomfortable, let the practitioner know. Many women feel uncomfortable lying on their backs after the fourth month (remember, ACOG recommends that you do not lie on your back after this time), so prenatal massages are often given to a woman as she lies on her side with pillows between her legs. Some therapists even have a special table with a cut-out middle so that you can lie on your stomach when you might be uncomfortable on your side.

A massage therapist should be licensed by the city of Chicago. (Currently, Illinois does not license massage therapists, though the Massage Practice Act signed in 2002 set licensure standards that will take effect in 2005.) Keep in mind that obtaining a city license mainly involves paying the required fee and submitting to a zoning and/or police inspection; it indicates nothing about a person's training and ability to provide a good massage.

You can ask friends and your health-care practitioner for a recommendation for a massage therapist. In lieu of a license, membership in the American Massage Therapy Association (AMTA) is one way to judge that a therapist has achieved a professional level of education and certification. You can find AMTA therapists specializing in pregnancy massage by calling the association (847-864-0123), or by using its easily searchable Web site database (www.amtamassage.org). The Birthlink Web site (www.birthlink.com) has a good listing of practitioners who specialize in pre- and postnatal massage. Some doulas and homebirth midwives also offer massage; check the listings on page 15.

In addition, the spas below offer pregnancy massage—and heck, why not get a facial and pedicure while you're at it?

spas

❈ *Ambra European Day Spa*
1011 N. Rush St., 2nd floor
312-337-5065
A one-hour pregnancy massage is $85.

❈ *Elizabeth Arden Red Door Salon & Spa*
919 N. Michigan Ave.
312-988-9191
www.reddoorsalons.com
Pregnancy massage is $95 for fifty minutes, or $145 for eighty minutes.

❈ *The Peninsula Spa*
108 E. Superior St.
312-573-6860
www.peninsulaspachicago.com/index.php
The prenatal massage here is pricey—$115 for an hour.

❈ *The Quiet Touch*
800-946-2772
www.massageinc.com
The Quiet Touch is a national service that provides an insured and fully equipped massage therapist at your door within a few hours. They have specialists in all types of massage, including prenatal. Massages are $100 per hour (be sure to mention City Baby); membership packages are available for a discounted rate, and there is a 10-percent discount for first-time callers.

❈ *Spa Blue Lakeview*
2915 N. Sheffield
773-525-BLUE
www.salonblue.com/home.htm
A one-hour prenatal massage is $80.

❈ *SpaPURA*
2300 W. Armitage Ave.
773-782-0008
www.spapura.com/spapura.htm
A fifty-minute pregnancy massage is $85.

❈ *Sweet Pea's Studio*
3717 N. Ravenswood, Ste. 213
773-248-YOGA
www.sweetpeasstudio.com
In addition to pregnancy massage, Sweet Pea's offers a wonderful postpartum series called Bouncing Back from Baby. The five two-hour massages focus on different parts of the body to help restore your pre-pregnancy alignment, especially in the pelvis; clients also receive exercises to do between appointments to maintain the massage work. The series can be very healing not only physically but also emotionally, especially for women who've had difficult births or postpartum issues. My friend Judy treated herself to the series and highly recommends it. A one-hour massage is $75, or

$105 for an hour and a half. The Bouncing Back from Baby package is $475. Sweet Pea's also offers infant massage.

Thousand Waves Spa for Women

1212 W. Belmont Ave.

773-549-0700

http://thousandwavesspa.com

Prenatal massage is $45 for a half-hour, or $70 for an hour. This is one of my favorite places to go when I need a respite from the chaos of daily life. Situated as it is in Lakeview, home to a large lesbian community, this is not the kind of body-conscious place where you'll feel you need to drop 20 pounds before you walk in the door; all women are accepted and welcomed. After the baby's born, for just $20 you can treat yourself to three hours in the spa's Jacuzzi, wet and dry steam rooms, and Zen-like relaxation room. A small group of us moms paid a visit to celebrate our friend Michele's birthday and had a wonderfully relaxing afternoon for very little money.

Tiffani Kim Institute

310 W. Superior St.

312-943-8777

www.tiffanikiminstitute.com

Pregnancy massage is $90 for fifty minutes, or $115 for eighty minutes.

Tirra Salon & Spa

375 W. Erie

312-951-8255

www.tirrasalon.com

This Aveda salon charges $75 for a one-hour prenatal massage.

Urban Oasis

Two locations:

12 W. Maple St., 312-587-3500

939 W. North Ave., 312-640-0001

www.urban-oasis.com

A one-hour pregnancy massage is $85. Urban Oasis also offers an infant massage class, which costs $75 for two parents and baby.

Massage Therapists

Ruth Firby Center for Muscle Therapy

1123 Emerson St. (Evanston)

847-869-6869

Ruth is a certified massage therapist who specializes in pregnancy massage; she also teaches infant and child massage.

Susan Gray

Wellspring Integrative Medicine

1565 Sherman Ave. (Evanston)

847-733-9900

Susan is a certified massage therapist who specializes in women's health, especially pregnancy. In addition, she is a birth doula and teaches infant massage, either privately or in groups.

Jo Anne Lindberg

Five Element Shiatsu

847-733-8050

The founder of Birthlink, an incredible pregnancy resource (www.birthlink.com), Jo Anne also is a massage therapist specializing in women's health, from pregnancy to menopause. Jo Anne practices shiatsu, which involves using the hands to apply light to deep pressure on various points of the body.

❊ Abigail Lynn

773-991-7968

A former ER nursing assistant, Abigail is now a certified massage therapist, doula, and infant massage instructor. She makes house calls throughout the Chicago area.

❊ Elizabeth Nostvick

Creating Balance Massage Therapy
3354 N. Paulina
773-758-0607
www.creatingbalancemt.com

The former care coordinator for Birthways doula service, Elizabeth is a certified massage therapist as well as a birth and postpartum doula. She also does some pre- and postnatal exercise therapy.

other health resources

❊ Stacy Bly

Evanston Hospital
1000 Central St., Ste. 101 (Evanston)
847-570-1250

Stacy is a physical therapist who specializes in treating pregnant women, who frequently suffer from low-back and pelvic pain. She also teaches prenatal aerobics at Evanston Athletic Center.

❊ Terri Clemens and Nancy Floy

Heartwood Center for Body, Mind, Spirit
1599 Maple Ave. (Evanston)
847-491-1122

Heartwood is a group of about twenty health-care providers, including massage therapists, psychotherapists, acupuncturists, and reiki and shiatsu practitioners. Terri and Nancy specialize in women's health, including treatment of pregnancy and postpartum ailments.

❊ Bridgid Ellingson

Lakeview Physical Therapy
3548 N. Southport
773-755-9214

Bridgid is a physical therapist whose entire practice is geared toward women, including treatment of pregnancy-related aches and pains.

❊ Laura Olsen

Acuhealth Acupuncture Associates
3723 N. Southport
773-529-3503

Laura specializes in treating women at all stages of conception: infertility, pregnancy, labor, and postpartum. Among the conditions for which she's found acupuncture to be beneficial are pregnancy-related nausea, turning breech babies, labor induction, labor pain, restoring hormonal balance and energy after delivery, and postpartum depression.

❊ Catherine Willows, R.N., L.C.

773-732-2030

Catherine is a nurse, lactation consultant, and herbalist who has wide experience using natural remedies to treat women's health issues, including pregnancy-related ailments (nausea, allergies and colds, insomnia) and postpartum issues. She uses many flower essences in her practice, which she says can be extremely gentle and helpful in treating children, as well as pregnant and postpartum moms.

nutrition

You know that good nutrition is a critical part of producing a healthy baby, and there are many books available addressing this subject. One of the most popular is What to Expect When You're Expecting, the pregnant woman's bible that has a section called the "Best Odds Diet," with guidelines on how to eat every day. While these nutrition guidelines are certainly sound and represent the ideal way to eat for two, I find the authors too rigid and judgmental in their advice—and I've been a health-conscious vegetarian for nearly 20 years, including during my pregnancy. Your baby is not going to lose IQ points if you eat a few hot fudge sundaes. As a pregnant woman, you'd be wise to follow the Best Odds Diet as closely as you can, but recognize that you're human and don't beat yourself up if you break down and eat a bag of potato chips. Enjoy them fully, then try to eat more healthfully tomorrow.

If you are underweight, overweight, diabetic, or need extra help managing what you eat, consult a nutritionist to set up a diet that meets your needs. Weight Watchers also offers a healthy plan for overweight pregnant women. You might want to keep them in mind for after the pregnancy, too. I have a number of friends who have gone to Weight Watchers and achieved post-baby bodies that are even more svelte than before pregnancy. My friend Claire, who has two preschoolers 15 months apart, lost more than 70 pounds on Weight Watchers.

eating right while you're pregnant

What you should know about nutrition and pregnancy:

✳ Eat regularly and well. This is no time to diet. You will gain weight, and most obstetricians today say a gain of 25 to 35 pounds or more is normal. Increase your calorie intake by about 300 calories a day during the last two trimesters, as you will need more energy during this time.

✳ Eat healthful foods. That means ample daily servings of grains (cereal, whole grain bread, crackers), fruits, vegetables (steamed are best), protein (eggs, meat, fish, peanut butter, tofu), and calcium (milk, cheese, yogurt).

✳ Avoid junk food. When you want sugar, reach for fresh fruit, which will also help you avoid the ubiquitous affliction of pregnancy: constipation. I've also found that eating ample protein assuages sugar cravings.

✳ Drink water. Your core body temperature is higher than normal when you are pregnant and you need to take in at least two quarts of liquid a day, especially before, during, and after exercise.

✳ Do not drink alcohol.

✳ Don't drink caffeinated beverages (coffee, tea, colas) during your first trimester, and restrict intake to one cup a day after that. Caffeine reaches the baby through the placenta.

✳ Listen to your body. Those infamous cravings for pickles and Taco Bell may have a basis in physiology. Your body may need a little extra salt.

Many hospitals, as well some health clubs, have nutritionists on staff, and you can ask your OB or midwife for a referral. The following nutritionists are members of the American Dietetic Association and have expertise in working with pregnant women. Initial consultations cost around $100 to $150, with follow-up visits about half that.

✳ *Roberta Clarke Jenero, M.S., R.D., L.D.*
1250 N. Dearborn St.
312-335-9850
In addition to doing individual counseling, Roberta has a very useful nutrition Web site: www.figurefacts.com. For $10 a month, you can use the interactive database to create a personalized nutritional-needs profile, fill in a daily food diary that tracks your caloric and nutrient intake, and access educational tips and tools.

✳ *Eileen Corrigan, R.D., L.D.*
708-535-3358

✳ *Carla R. Heiser, M.S., R.D., L.D.*
Advocate Illinois Masonic Integrative Medicine Center
3000 N. Halsted St.
773-296-8410

✳ *Monique C. Ryan, M.S., R.D.*
847-864-8689
Sees clients at locations in Chicago and Evanston.

from health care
to day care

Sometime toward the end of your pregnancy, you should begin searching for the people who will help care for your little one. This is a toughie. The very idea of entrusting your baby to another person can be terrifying. You'll feel more comfortable with the idea if you take the time to do the necessary research—scout around, ask questions, make phone calls, pay visits.

First, you will need to find a pediatrician. Your goal is to find one you and your husband or partner connect with and who can provide your baby with the best available medical care. But, that is just the beginning. You may wish to hire a baby nurse or doula (see page 48) to help out in your home the first few days or weeks after your baby is born. After that, your childcare needs depend on what else is going on in your life. If you are returning to a job after a maternity leave, you will probably require full-time help, either in your home or elsewhere. If you work at home or are involved in activities that will take you away from your child for a period of time each day or week, you will need childcare part-time. Also, if you simply want to get out of the house now and then, sans baby, you should have one or two reliable baby-sitters to call upon. If you have family nearby, you may be lucky enough to have occasional free baby-sitting come your way.

pediatricians

You should begin looking for a pediatrician during the last few months of your pregnancy. Your baby's doctor will be noted on the record form that your obstetrician will send to the hospital about a month prior to your due date; in many cases—especially if your pediatrician's practice is affiliated with the hospital where you give birth—the pediatrician you've chosen will then come by the hospital to examine your baby before the two of you are released.

Here's how to find one, and what you should look for:

❋ Ask your obstetrician or midwife for a recommendation. If your practitioner lives in the city, whom does she use for her own children? My midwife gave me the name of our pediatrician, and we've been really happy with her.

❋ Ask relatives, neighbors, and friends about pediatricians they use.

❋ Call any of the hospitals in the city, and ask for a referral from the pediatric department.

❋ Go to the Chicago Public Library and look up listings in the American Academy of Pediatrics Directory.

❋ Consider location. Your newborn will be going to the doctor often, and having a pediatrician with an office near your home is practical, especially during an emergency or nasty weather.

❋ Consider whether you place importance on the doctor's age, type of practice (group, partnership, or solo practitioner), or gender (I like having a woman pediatrician as an example of professional achievement for my daughter).

Once you have the names of two or three pediatricians who sound promising, set up a consultation.

Most will agree to make appointments in the early evening after regular office hours. Good doctors should be willing to take the time to meet with you and your husband or partner. One mom I know of requested consultations with five pediatricians. One did not conduct prenatal interviews; the other four were happy to meet with her and her husband to answer their questions and give them a brief office tour. It was time-consuming, but the mom has been very happy with the pediatrician she chose, and has never had to change. (If your prospective pediatrician is part of a group practice, it's a good idea to meet with most of the doctors; chances are each will be treating your child at one time or another.)

Prepare a list of questions in advance and write down the doctors' answers. That way, you can compare pediatricians and discuss everything with your partner if he or she can't be with you at each consultation. And while you are waiting, take a look around the waiting room.

* Is it child-friendly, with enough toys, pictures, and books to keep a baby or toddler busy during the wait to see the doctor?

* Is the receptionist friendly, or does she seem curt and harried?

* If you're visiting during office hours, ask parents in the waiting room about their experiences with the doctor; have they been positive?

* Find out how long they typically wait to see the doctor. A forty-five-minute wait with a sick toddler is no fun.

* Do sick and healthy children wait in the same waiting room? Many practices have a separate sick bay to reduce the spread of illness.

* Is there an on-site lab for quick blood tests, ear-wave sonograms, etc.?

When you sit down with the doctor, ask:

* How does the doctor answer parents' non-emergency calls throughout the day? Is there a call-in hour or does the doctor take calls all day and return them intermittently between patients? Is there a nurse who can answer questions?

* How are emergencies handled? Is the doctor affiliated with a nearby hospital? Is the practice affiliated with more than one hospital? Some pediatricians will meet you at the hospital or have a specialist meet you there in case of an emergency.

* How does the pediatrician feel about breast-feeding? Whether or not you choose to breast-feed, you will want a pediatrician who is supportive and encouraging of your decision.

* What are the pediatrician's views on circumcision, nutrition, immunizations, and preventive medicine? It is important that you and your doctor are in sync on most of these issues.

* If the pediatrician is a solo practitioner, who handles phone calls when she is on vacation?

If you don't feel rushed during the consultation, and the pediatrician is patient with you, these are good indicators of how the doctor will be with your baby. Again, don't be afraid to ask any questions. Even after you select a pediatrician don't be afraid to change. There are hundreds of pediatricians in Chicago, so just persevere. Like all aspects of child-care, the right one for you is out there.

baby nurses/doulas

Immediately after the birth of your baby, you may wish to have a baby nurse or doula.

A baby nurse usually comes the day you bring the baby home. She cares for the baby, and if you hire her for nighttime work she will get up in the middle of the night to change and feed him or bring him to you for breastfeeding, and generally allow you to sleep late and rest up. Only one of the nursing agencies in Chicago—Relief Medical Service—hires out R.N.s for baby care, so you may want to call nanny agencies to find live-in or nighttime care for your newborn.

A postpartum doula is more than an extra set of hands; she's specially trained to care for the new mother and her family both physically and emotion-ally. She comes to your home for a few hours each day—in some cases at night if you prefer—and almost always lives out. She helps and pampers you: She does the grocery shopping, laundry, and fixes meals, so you have more time with your baby. She also will assist you in taking care of your baby by bathing and changing him, and she should be able to answer questions regarding breastfeeding and any parenting concerns you have. Postpartum doulas can help take care of older siblings and address their emotional needs as they adjust to the new baby. Many postpartum doulas also are trained to recognize a new mom's possible mood disorders and make referrals.

When you hire a doula, typically you buy a set block of visits or hours; Birthways has a four-hour minimum, and you can schedule just one shift if that's all you need. A postpartum doula costs approximately $20 to $25 an hour, though some may charge as much as $30.

One of the best ways to find a baby nurse or doula is through a trusted friend who has used one herself. Or call one of the many agencies below. Baby nurses/nannies and postpartum doulas get booked way in advance, so plan early; Birthways rec-ommends calling by the twenty-seventh week of your pregnancy. Postpartum doulas generally also work as birth doulas, so they in particular need plen-ty of notice to block off a chunk of time when they don't have other clients with due dates.

Of course, your mother or mother-in-law may offer to come stay with you. If you feel comfortable with a family member living in and helping out, great. However, we've found that many new parents prefer to hire short-term professional help which allows them to get the rest they need without hav-ing to impose on—or be nice to—a relative.

The following is a list of baby nurse and doula agencies, as well as individual postpartum doulas, in the Chicago area. All of the doulas listed do work in the city, though some live rather far out in the suburbs.

✳ *American Registry for Nannies & Sitters, Inc.*
866-626-6939
www.american-registry.com
Provides nighttime nannies.

❋ **Birthways**
1484 W. Farragut
773-506-0607
www.birthwaysinc.com
An agency for a group of about twenty doulas that provide labor support and postpartum doula services.

❋ **Gail Bowker**
847-475-5562
Gail works within forty-five minutes of Evanston and is willing to consider nights.

❋ **Susan Diamond-Tsingos**
815-765-1765
Susan specializes in overnight care and has experience with premature infants, babies on apnea monitors, multiples, children with special needs, and postpartum mood disorders.

❋ **Rachel Dolan-Wickersham**
West Suburban Doula Care
630-832-3556
Rachel, who trains doulas, works throughout Chicago and the suburbs and will consider some nighttime care.

❋ **Peggy Healy**
A Mother is Born
773-774-9705
Peggy is a doula with a masters in counseling—a nice qualification for providing emotional support—and is studying to be a lactation consultant. With five children of her own, she does not work nights.

❋ **Susan Krojniewski**
773-677-2252
Susan is a doula who also has worked as a nanny; she is willing to work nights and weekends.

❋ **Carol Montgomery, R.N.**
773-626-6299
Carol, the mother of six children, is an R.N. and doula who will do nights and multiples.

❋ **Relief Medical Service**
312-266-1486
www.reliefmed.com
This nursing agency has R.N.s available for newborn care.

❋ **Ellen Richter**
BirthRight Doula Services
847-639-4604
Ellen, who also is a lactation educator, serves the northern part of the city and north suburbs and will do occasional night work.

❋ **Julie Schlachter**
773-764-1474
Julie is a doula with a background in lay midwifery and has some knowledge of homeopathic and herbal medicine. She will consider some nighttime work.

❋ **Debra Siegel, R.N.**
847-559-1084
Debra has worked as a postpartum nurse at Evanston Hospital since 1991. She works primarily in the northern part of the city, as well as the north suburbs, and does not do nights.

nannies

Hiring someone to look after your child while you're at work or away is stressful and nerve-racking. You want someone who is good, kind, smart, honest, sober, and reliable, loves kids, knows infant CPR, bakes cookies, and is going to think your baby is the most adorable child she's ever seen. You want another you.

Of course, you won't find another you, but if you're determined and keep your ears open, you will locate someone who will be an affectionate, caring, responsible childcare provider for your youngster.

You may want a nanny who lives with you or one who comes to your home each morning and leaves each evening. You may need this person's help on a part-time or full-time basis. There are several ways to go about finding her. As is true for so many services, word of mouth is the best place to start. Ask friends who have childcare whether their nannies have friends looking for work. You can stop nannies in the park, talk to mothers and nannies at the classes you take with your child, and look at bulletin board notices in child- and religious-oriented institutions and at pediatricians' offices. Many schools also post nanny information on their bulletin boards.

If you get nowhere by word of mouth, try the newspapers. Many parents have successfully found childcare by advertising in newspapers or by answering an ad. I'll show you how to do that shortly. Finally, a number of agencies specialize in nanny placement. I list those agencies below.

I cannot sufficiently stress the importance of checking references and thoroughly questioning candidates. We've all heard stories of falsified references in which nannies listed friends or relatives instead of former employers. Toward the end of this section, I'll give you a list of some of the most important questions to ask your future nanny. You may also want to read How to Hire a Nanny by Elaine S. Pelletier. This step-by-step guide helps you through the nanny search. Another excellent resource, written by two experienced British moms is The Good Nanny Guide by Charlotte Breese and Hilaire Gomer. Although geared to the English nanny system, it is full of practical advice and guidelines.

Full-time (five days a week), live-out nannies usually cost about $400 to $600 per week. A live-in nanny commands a similar salary, but you also provide room and board. Prices vary according to experience, education, checkable references, and legal status.

newspaper advertisements

Placing a classified ad can be an excellent way to find a nanny. A number of newspapers are published for various nationalities and many nannies look in them for jobs. Explore them if you would prefer a nanny from a specific country, would like your child to learn a foreign language, or if your spouse is from another country.

When you place an ad, be as specific as possible. If you must have a nonsmoker, live-in help, or someone with a driver's license, say so. If you need someone to work on Saturdays or stay late in the evening, state it. Check the classified sections to see examples of help-wanted ads, or follow this example:

❋ **North Side Nanny Needed.**
Live-in nanny needed for a two-year-old boy.
Light housekeeping, shopping, and errands.
Must have two years' experience with toddlers
and excellent checkable Chicago references.

Nonsmoker. Must swim, drive, and cook. Must have legal working papers. Willing to travel with family. M-F, weekends off. Own room, TV-VCR, A/C. Call 773-555-5555.

Interview candidates on the phone before you bring them to your home. Tell them about the job, find out what they are looking for, and ask about their past work experience. Screen them carefully; it will save you time later. For instance, if you need a caregiver who can work on Saturdays and travel with the family, you can eliminate candidates who cannot fill those requirements over the phone.

Make a list of the three most appealing and the three least appealing aspects of the position you're offering. Discuss them with the applicant over the phone. Start with the three worst aspects: She must arrive at 7:30 every morning, she must baby-sit three nights a week, and she will be expected to work on Saturdays. If the applicant is still interested and if you are pleased with her responses to your key questions, proceed from there with an interview in your home or office.

The following four newspapers are good bets for finding domestic help. When you call, double-check their deadlines. Ads can be phoned or faxed, and can be paid for with a credit card.

❖ The Chicago Tribune

435 N. Michigan Ave.
Chicago, IL 60611
312-222-2222
fax: 312-222-4014
www.chicagotribune.com/classified
A classified ad in the Tribune can run in one Sunday paper only ($174 for three lines and $31 for each additional line), two consecutive Sundays ($286, $46.50 each additional), a consecutive Sunday-Wednesday-Sunday ($306, $51.50 each additional), or for eight consecutive days beginning on a Sunday ($322, $55.50 each additional). "Childcare needed" ads that run on Sunday also appear online at chicagotribune.com for one week starting that same Sunday. The deadline for Sunday ads is the preceding Friday at 5 p.m.

❖ Irish American News

7115 W. North Ave., Suite 327
Oak Park, IL 60302
708-445-0700
fax: 708-445-2003
e-mail: ads@irishamericannews.com
The Irish American News comes out once a month. A classified ad is $15 for thirty words, and $10 for each additional increment of thirty words. Submit your ad by the 20th of the month before you want the ad to run.

❖ La Raza Newspaper

6001 N. Clark St.
Chicago, IL 60660
773-273-2001
La Raza is Chicago's Spanish-language weekly; it comes out on Sundays. A twenty-word classified costs $32, thirty words cost $48, and forty words cost $64. Deadline is the Wednesday before you want the ad to run.

❖ The Polish Daily News

5711 N. Milwaukee Ave.
Chicago, IL 60646

773-763-3343

fax: 773-763-3825, att'n: Classified

This Polish-language daily will run your ad either in Polish or English. Ads must be submitted by 2 p.m. two days before you want it to run. An ad with up to twenty words costs $10.50 for one day; you can run the ad for a week for $26.25.

agencies

On one hand, good word-of-mouth and a sterling reputation keeps a service business alive. On the other hand, the more people they place, the more money agencies make; high turnover is oddly beneficial to their business. This is contrary to what you are looking for—someone who will stay with you a long time. So, a few words of caution when using an agency. Although agencies claim they check references, many have been known to send a candidate on an interview with skimpy or weak references. Some have never even met the candidate face to face. Be on guard if, for example, a nanny's previous employer has moved and now has an unlisted phone number somewhere in Florida, or if the applicant hands you a hand-written letter of reference with grammatically incorrect sentences and misspelled words.

❋ *American Registry for Nannies & Sitters, Inc.*
866-626-6939
www.american-registry.com

❋ *Best Nannies*
1925 Richmond Court (Schaumburg)

847-882-9844
www.bestnanniesinc.com

❋ *Childminders*
4350 Oakton (Skokie)
847-673-8998
www.childmindersinc.com

❋ *Family Perfect Care, Inc.*
4112 W. Henderson St.
773-545-5352

❋ *Family Home Help Service, Inc.*
5415 W. Higgins Ave.
773-286-9170

❋ *4Nannies.com, Inc.*
800-810-2611
www.4nannies.com

❋ *Gold Coast Domestic Employment*
820 W. Belle Plaine Ave.
773-525-4273

❋ *Lakeview Domestic Agency, Inc.*
3166 N. Lincoln Ave.
773-404-8452

❋ *Nanny Resource*
4006 N. Milwaukee Ave.
773-736-3173

❋ *Nanny Sitters Inc.*
200 W. Higgins Road (Schaumburg)
847-885-1700

Sandy's Nannies & More, Inc.

847-679-7766

www.sandysnannies.com

Traycee Nannies

448 Sheridan Road (Highwood)

847-432-6111

http://traycee.com/tray03.htm

TeacherCare

1701 W. Woodfield Road, Ste. 700

(Schaumburg)

312-214-6411

www.teachercare.com

This online matching service places nursery and preschool teachers in private homes to provide daily care and do planned activities (kind of like nursery school). The providers may live out and come just during the day, or live in as a nanny.

the interview

Nothing is as important as the interview to determine whether a candidate is the right person to take care of your little one. Be conscious of the atmosphere you create. Are you interviewing potential nannies at your office, in your formal living room, in the playroom, family room, or at the kitchen table? Are you looking for someone to join the family, or will this person be more of an employee with a formal working arrangement?

It can be a good idea to interview nannies with your partner present. It's useful to get a second opinion, and to have another person asking questions you might forget to ask. It's also good to have your child nearby so you can see how the potential candidate interacts with him or her.

Here's a suggested list of interview questions:

* Tell me about yourself. Where are you from? Where did you grow up? How many brothers and sisters do you have? Did your mom and dad work?

* Why do you want to be a nanny? What is it you like about being a nanny?

* What previous childcare experiences do you have? Tell me about those jobs.

* What was a typical day like? What did your duties/responsibilities include? (Look for someone who has held a childcare position similar to the one you are offering. If she cooked and cleaned on the last job and you are looking for light cooking and cleaning, she probably won't be upset if you ask her to grill a chicken breast or wipe off the kitchen counter.)

* How many children did you take care of in your previous positions? How old were they?

* Do you have children of your own?

* What did you like best about your previous jobs? What did you like least?

* Why did you leave your last job(s)?

* Did Mrs. X work? How did you two interact on a daily basis?

* Do you smoke?

- Do you have CPR or first-aid training?
- Can you stay late during the week or work on weekends if necessary?
- Describe an emergency or stressful situation in your past job? How did you handle it?
- What are your child-rearing philosophies or views on discipline? Do you believe in spanking and time-outs?
- What are your interests? What do you like to do when you're not working?
- Do you have any health restrictions or dietary preferences I should know about?
- What are you looking for in a family?
- Would you travel with the family if needed?
- Do you know your way around the city?
- Do you drive, swim, bicycle, or (whatever else is important to you)?
- Do you like to read? What is your favorite children's book? (Some nannies can't read well in English.)
- When could you start? What are your salary requirements?

checking references

Checking references with previous employers can be one of the most challenging parts of finding childcare. Who are you calling? How can you be sure the name you have been given is not a candidate's friend or relative? And then, some people just aren't very talkative on the telephone. They reveal very little that can help you reach a decision.

Use your common sense and intuition; be open and friendly; and identify yourself in detail. For example: "Hello Mrs. X, this is Mrs. Y, and I am calling to check a reference on Carmen Martinez, who told me she worked for you. My husband and I live in Chicago on Armitage and we have a three-year-old daughter." Tell her a little about your family. This will help break the ice and allow you to ask about her family and work situations. It's important to know the kind of household in which your potential nanny has worked, because it may be very different from your own. If Mrs. X had a staff of three, and Carmen had no household duties, she may not be happy in your home if you ask her to cook, clean, and do the laundry. Be realistic.

Here are some questions you may want to ask:

- How did you meet Carmen? (agency, friend, ad?)
- How long was Carmen with you?
- Why did she leave?
- How many children do you have? How old are they?

✲ Do you work? What do you do? Were either you or your husband home during the day or was Carmen pretty much on her own?

✲ What were Carmen's responsibilities?

✲ What were her hours?

✲ Was there ever an emergency or difficult situation that Carmen had to handle on her own?

✲ How would you describe her overall personality and attitude?

✲ Was it easy to communicate with her? Did she give you daily feedback on your children? Did she take direction/instruction well?

✲ Did she cook, clean, drive, run errands, swim, iron (or whatever you need most)?

✲ Did you trust her? Did you find her reliable and honest?

✲ How did your children like her? Did you like her?

✲ Would you hire her again?

Several agencies verify references on nannies. One is U.S. Information Search (800-596-4327; www.usinformationsearch.com/nannycheck.html), which charges $49 for a basic background check that includes a check of the social security number, criminal records, and use of any aliases. With a credit check added on the total is $65; that plus a driving record check the total is $84. You also can request an international criminal check for no charge, and a drug screening for $44.

when the nanny starts

After you have found the right person, it is important to watch how she and your baby and/or children interact in order to make sure they are comfortable with each other. It's a good idea to have prepared a typewritten list of duties as well as what is expected of the nanny on a daily basis aside from childcare, such as cooking, cleaning, laundry and grocery shopping. Be specific. Sit down and go over everything again within the first few days to make sure she understands and accepts the responsibilities of the job. Set a date for a follow-up meeting in two weeks to discuss how things are going, what's working well, and what is not.

Consider giving the nanny a "trial" period. Try her out for a week or so and see if it's a match before hiring her full-time. If you are going back to work, it is a good idea to have your new nanny begin at least two weeks before you start. This will give you an opportunity to observe her with your baby and to show her around your neighborhood.

Take her to your supermarket, dry cleaner's (or to whatever other places she may need to visit while working for your family), as well as to the pediatrician's office so that she can feel comfortable going there without you if necessary.

Inquire about your nanny's health and vaccinations. Depending on where your nanny is from and how long she has been in this country, she may not be vaccinated against measles, mumps and rubella, or chicken pox. If she's not, arrange with your doctor for her to get these shots.

Once a nanny is on the job, you may want to monitor her activities in your absence. Parents who have had to hire a caregiver very quickly and have little time to train and supervise may find that this service provides peace of mind.

Babywatch is a nationwide service founded in 1992; you've probably seen its nanny surveillance systems featured on Oprah and ABC's Primetime. In some cities, Babywatch has representatives who rent out the company's sophisticated surveillance equipment, though at press time, no reps were available in Chicago. However, for $499—a little more than some of its rental rates—Babywatch sells an observation camera disguised as a clock radio. Richard Heilweil, vice-president of Babywatch, told me that 70 percent of parents who said they felt good about their caregivers before using Babywatch ended up firing their nanny based on what they observed; the most common reason was not outright abuse but neglect. You can find Babywatch at www.babywatch.com or 800-558-5669.

A wide variety of surveillance cameras disguised as such everyday objects as a smoke detector, clock radio, silk plant, and even a teddy bear is available at online vendors, starting at about $300.

taxes and insurance

Remember that once you hire a nanny, you have become an employer, and you need to be sure you abide by IRS regulations regarding household employees. According to the IRS, as an employer, you need to:

- Apply for an employer identification number using Form SS-4.

- Withhold 7.65 percent from each payment to your nanny (6.2 percent for social security tax and 1.45 percent for Medicare tax) if you pay her cash wages above $1,400 per year. Then you must send this amount to the IRS with a matching amount for your share of the taxes.

- Obtain Form W-4, Employee's Withholding Allowance Certificate, and Circular E, Employer's Tax Guide, which has tax withholding tables, if you agree to withhold federal taxes for your nanny.

- File Form W-2 at the end of the year if you withhold or pay social security and Medicare taxes for your nanny. You will also need a Form W-3.

- Pay federal unemployment tax on a certain amount of the wages you pay to your nanny. In 2003, that amount was the first $7,000 of the wages paid to the nanny.

- File a Schedule H, Household Employment Taxes, with your individual income tax return if you file Form W–2 or pay federal unemployment tax. (You can obtain state unemployment tax forms from the Illinois Department of Labor.)

Downloadable tax forms and further information on employment taxes for nannies are available from the IRS at www.irs.gov/individuals/household/index.html. The IRS also publishes a booklet to help employers through this maze: "Household Employer's Tax Guide" (Book 926). You can download the booklet at the Web address above, or call the IRS at (800) 462-8100.

Other areas of concern are health insurance and compensation and disability policies. If you employ a childcare provider for more than forty hours a week, you should buy a workers' compensation and disability policy. Call the National Council of Compensation Insurance (800-622-4123) for information on rates. You'd be wise to consult an accountant on all these matters as well.

au pairs

Hiring an au pair is a childcare option many parents find practical and economical; au pairs live in and earn about $250 per week. The Au Pair Program is administered by the U.S. Department of State and is an educational and cultural exchange program with a strong childcare component. Au pairs come to the United States from various countries, but they are usually European. They can remain in this country legally for one year and may work for their host family for up to ten hours a day and no more than forty-five hours per week. An au pair must take six hours of academic coursework here before returning home. Generally, an au pair has a weeklong orientation just after she arrives in this country, and is provided with support counselors and a health plan by her sponsoring organization.

Au pairs tend to be young and inexperienced childcare providers. Typically their main goal is to experience the life of a young person in the States, and being an au pair is a means to that end, not necessarily their calling. Also keep in mind au pairs are not allowed to remain alone with children overnight, so they're not a good option for parents who travel.

For further information on the Au Pair Program, go to the U.S. Department of State Web site (http://state.gov) and search the term "au pair"; you also can contact DOS Exchange Visitor Program staff at 202-401-9810.

Au pair sponsoring agencies are the ones who handle the day-to-day operation of the program and screen, select, and match au pairs with host families. Always interview a prospective au pair over the phone or in person if possible. Most agencies provide background information on several candidates. If you are interested in an au pair, here are some sponsoring agencies to contact:

* ❋ *Au Pair in America*
  River Plaza
  9 W. Broad St.
  Stamford, CT 06902
  800-928-7247
  www.aupairinamerica.com

* ❋ *Cultural Care Au Pair*
  One Education St.
  Cambridge, MA 02141
  800-333-6056
  www.culturalcare.com

* ❋ *Au Pair USA/InterExchange Inc.*
  161 Sixth Ave.
  New York, NY 10013
  212-924-0446
  www.aupairusa.org

Top Ten Things to Look for in a Caregiver

1. Track record and references—strong ones. How long does she stay at a job?

2. The ability to speak and read English or your native language.

3. Personality. It's hard to be around someone who never smiles.

4. Experience, especially with children the same age as your own.

5. Honesty. This is fundamental to any relationship between employer and employee, and particularly in regard to someone hired to watch your children.

6. Patience.

7. Positive attitude.

8. Nice appearance.

9. Reliability and responsibility.

10. Instinct: Trust your gut.

day care centers

According to the Day Care Action Council of Illinois, Cook County has more than 2,000 day care centers; this includes not only programs where you can bring your child each morning and pick him up in the evening, typically by 6 p.m., but also preschools, before- and after-school centers, Head Start pre-kindergarten, and special needs programs. Centers must meet rigid requirements in order to be licensed by the state of Illinois. In addition, there are more than 3,200 in-home care centers or family day care providers in the city and Cook County suburbs. In family day care, an individual takes care of a few children (by law, no more than eight, or twelve with an assistant) in her home. Make sure the provider is licensed by Illinois State. Even if it is, be cautious. Pay a personal visit to the center, speak with other parents, and trust your instincts.

Investigate options offered by your employer. More and more companies are offering on-site day care, or are willing to contribute to day care costs.

For more information contact the following:

❋ *Illinois Department of Children and Family Services*
This state agency regulates daycare in Illinois. You can gather information online at www.state.il.us/dcfs/daycare/index.shtml, or call the DCFS Daycare Information Hotline at 877-746-0829.

❋ *The Day Care Action Council of Illinois*
www.daycareaction.org
The Day Care Action Council of Illinois (DCAC) is an alliance of individuals and groups dedicated to helping Illinois parents find high-quality childcare. When you call one of the programs below, you'll get connected with an experienced childcare consultant who can help identify your family's needs, explain licensing, list indicators of a quality program, and provide referrals. DCAC does not endorse or regulate childcare programs, but it's the best resource for making informed choices.

DCAC provides information and referrals through the following programs:

❋ *Cook County Child Care Resource and Referral Service*
(773) 769-8000
Monday–Thursday, 8:30 a.m.–4:30 p.m., and

Friday, 8:30 a.m.–12:30 p.m.

childcare@daycareaction.org

One year of service/referrals costs $0—$30, depending on family size and income

Any parent in Cook County may call the referral line and speak to a consultant, who will complete a family intake, give you a list of childcare providers who meet your family's needs, and send you information to help make an educated selection.

❋ *Teen Parent Project*

(773) 769-8027

Monday–Friday, 8:30 a.m.–4:45 p.m.

www.teenparent@daycareaction.org

This free program provides specialized services for teen parents (19 years and younger), so that they can find childcare to allow them to complete their education. In addition to identifying a family's childcare needs and providing education about quality care, the consultant actually will call appropriate providers who have space available. Also, the consultant will remain in contact with the teen until an acceptable childcare arrangement has been made.

hotel baby-sitters

If you have out-of-town family or friends visiting with their children, they may want to take advantage of two local services that provide baby-sitting in downtown hotels. The first two companies charge $16.50 per hour with a four-hour minimum, plus a $10 transportation fee. Treasured Offspring charges between $15 and $20 an hour, depending on the number of children, with a four-hour minimum.

❋ *American Childcare Service*

312-644-7300

www.americanchildcare.com

❋ *American Family Childcare Service*

312-482-9300

www.trustamerican.com

baby-sitting co-ops

As a stay-at-home parent, I had a really hard time finding baby-sitting during the day; teenagers and college students were in school, and as the anxious parent of a newborn, I probably wouldn't have trusted them anyway. I found an older woman who was wonderful, but because we had gone down to one income, I couldn't afford to pay her $10 an hour very often. Joining a baby-sitting co-op turned out to be the solution to my problem.

A baby-sitting co-op is a group of parents who sit each other's children in exchange for baby-sitting time of their own. Our co-op has 25 families. Each month one of the members acts as secretary; anyone who wants to request a sit calls the secretary, who then calls other members to find someone to do the sit. After a sit, the person who did the baby-sitting calls it in to the secretary, who keeps track of everyone's hours for the month. For one child, the sitter earns one hour for every hour of sitting; for two children she earns 1.5 hours for every hour of sitting, and for each additional child, she earns an additional quarter-hour per child (1.75 hours per hour of sitting for three children, two hours per hour of sitting four children, etc.). At the end of the month, each member gives the secretary an hour from her bank—or 24 hours total—for her work.

To join our co-op, you need to be sponsored by a member who's known you for at least a year, or by two members who've known you at least six months. We have a pretty extensive list of bylaws that have been developed over the years, to govern things like last-minute cancellations, amount of time needed to request a sit, quarterly meetings, and so forth. We also do not permit anyone with guns in their home to join the co-op.

The co-op has been a great thing for my family. I've made connections with local parents I wouldn't have met otherwise, I know that my daughter is always being cared for by another parent, and I never have to pay for sitting with anything but my time (or, even better, my husband's!). For more specifics on how a co-op operates, you can check out the rules of the Northside Parents Network (www.northsideparents.org); if you join the network, you're eligible to join their co-op. Or try forming your own co-op. It can work perfectly well with a small group of families, but a larger group makes it more likely you'll be able to find a sit whenever you need one. If you do a Google search for "baby-sitting co-ops," you'll find lots of online information and tips on how to make a co-op work.

adjusting
to motherhood

After you bring your newborn home, your bulging belly won't be the only thing missing— all semblance of control over your life will have vanished too . . . but that's OK.

The first few weeks at home are going to be turbulent. Many new mothers feel blue or depressed. Having a baby is an emotionally draining experience. The week before the birth, you may have been closing a big deal with a new client; now, you're still in your bathrobe at three in the afternoon. To complicate things, those hormones really kick in after the birth. You may feel tired all day. Life will seem to be reduced to baby feedings, diaper changing, and laundry, laundry, laundry. The state of your apartment will deteriorate right before your very eyes.

My advice? Try to remind yourself that your life won't always be like this, no matter how interminable a difficult day may seem. Your new identity as a mom will one day feel normal, and you will be able to restore some order to your life. But for now, cut yourself a lot of slack. The best advice I got was to sleep when the baby did. I found this recommendation incredibly hard to follow—after all, that was the only time I had my hands free to do some chores—but when I did, I felt so much more sane. Keep in mind that although it may not feel like it, you are accomplishing a major achievement every day: You are sustaining another human life—no wonder you're tired!

If you actually cook, forget about it now. Order in. Chicago is take-out heaven, and there is wonderful prepared food within a mile or two. Have groceries, diapers, and baby supplies delivered from Peapod, the online grocery shopping and delivery service (800-5-PEAPOD or www.peapod.com). Let the place get messy. Allow willing friends and grandparents to throw in a load of laundry for you. Ask your mate to run some errands, even if you're the one home all day. The way I look at it, if your partner gets home and the baby is alive and healthy, you've done your job.

In the following pages you'll find suggestions on places to connect with other new mothers and learn from the experts. I can't say enough about forming or joining a playgroup, or a group of moms with babies who are the same age as your own. Playgroups usually meet once a week in rotating homes. If you don't have friends with babies your age, don't worry, you'll meet some. Take a Walk-a-Bye Baby class, visit a drop-in discussion-and-play program, sign up for a hospital class—before you know it, you will have friends all over town.

Joining a playgroup was a good experience for me. My only at-home mom friends lived on the other side of the city, and talking to them on the phone just wasn't as satisfying as being in the same room with other sleep-deprived moms and new babies. An acquaintance told me about Debra Rosenberg, a social worker who leads new-moms discussion groups in River Forest. After the group wrapped up, five of us continued meeting in each other's homes for a year, before things like going back to school and work interfered; to this day, one of the original babies in the group is a favorite play date of my daughter.

A playgroup typically has four to six moms and babies and meets at a specific time each week. You can serve lunch, or just cold drinks, and let the babies do their thing while the moms discuss everything from breastfeeding to sleep deprivation and more. These get-togethers become vital to a new mother's sanity, and will become one of the highlights of your week.

new mother classes

Once your baby is a few weeks old and you have settled into something of a routine, you'll enjoy swapping baby stories with other mothers and sharing advice on how to care best for your infant.

hospital classes

Some of the area hospitals offer classes you can attend with your baby. They provide an opportunity to hear from pediatricians, child psychologists, child-safety experts, and other skilled professionals. Plus, you'll be able to ask questions and meet other new parents. Fees vary from hospital to hospital and change frequently; most range from $15 to $50 for one-time classes or workshops, and $100 to $200 for a series of classes or new mother support group meetings. Most hospital classes and support groups are open to all women, not just those who delivered at that hospital.

❋ **Advocate Christ Medical Center (Oak Lawn)**
4440 W. 95th St.
708-425-8000 (general)
708-346-3300 (classes)
Christ offers classes in breastfeeding and new baby care.

❋ **Advocate Illinois Masonic Medical Center**
836 W. Wellington Ave.
773-975-1600 (general)
800-323-8622 (classes)
Offers classes in breastfeeding, infant and children's CPR, and postnatal exercise.

❋ **Northwestern Memorial Hospital's Prentice Women's Hospital**
333 E. Superior St.
312-926-2000 (general)
877-926-4664 (classes)
Northwestern has more classes for new parents than any other hospital in the city, offering classes on breastfeeding, infant and pediatric CPR (also offered in Spanish), postnatal exercise, infant massage, and new-baby care. The Transitions to Motherhood Series for moms with one- to six-month-old babies is a program of lectures that covers feeding and sleeping issues, handling your difficult emotions, the impact of a new baby on your marriage, positive and negative coping skills, and returning to work. The six-week series is $60. Northwestern also offers a New Mom's Support Group, which is more loosely structured, with a psychiatric nurse available to answer any questions you might have. Attending the group costs $120 for six weeks.

❋ **Rush University Medical Center**
1650 W. Harrison St.
312-942-5000 (general)
312-942-2336 (classes)
Offers classes on breastfeeding and CPR for infants and children.

❋ **Swedish Covenant Hospital**
5145 N. California
773-878-8200 (general)
773-878-1304 (classes)
Offers a breastfeeding class.

❋ University of Chicago Hospitals

5841 S. Maryland Ave.

773-702-1000 (general)

773-702-3925 (classes)

U. of C. offers classes on breastfeeding, infant care, and infant CPR. It's also one of the few area hospitals to offer Boot Camp for Expectant Dads, a men-only class that covers birth and bonding, caring for the new baby and mother, and adjusting to fatherhood. The three-hour class is $15 per person.

❋ University of Illinois at Chicago Medical Center

1740 W. Taylor St.

800-842-1002 (appointments)

312-413-7501 (classes)

Offers classes in breastfeeding and infant parenting.

❋ West Suburban Hospital (Oak Park)

3 Erie Court

708-383-6200 (general)

708-763-3274 (classes)

Offers classes on breastfeeding and infant care.

other classes, groups, and seminars

It's easy to find mommy-and-me classes where you can have fun with your baby and meet other parents; finding groups that focus on your personal development as a parent can be a bit more challenging. Fortunately, there are some excellent support and discussion groups throughout the city, and the number seems to be growing, thanks to rela-tively new places like Smart Love Parenting Center and Sweet Pea's Studio.

Keep in mind that schedules and fees are always subject to change. Call for the most up-to-date information.

❋ Buzz Café

905 S. Lombard Ave. (Oak Park)

708-524-2899

Thanks to the efforts of owner Laura Maychruk, mother of two young daughters, the Buzz Café, a coffeehouse and restaurant, is an extremely family-friendly place. Tuesday evening is Family Dinner Night, when in addition to the regular menu there's a special that has home-cooked, comfort-food appeal; the café also has a baby-food menu and a cozy nook in the back with couches, a kid-size table, and children's books and toys. Laura has made an effort to create a business that's also a community-building hub. At 7 p.m. on the first Thursday of every month, the Buzz hosts a birth-oriented discussion group, typically led by a midwife. Topics have included homebirth, the Birthing from Within program, breastfeeding, and post-partum depression. At 7 p.m. on the third Thursday of the month, a parenting book group meets to discuss a particular parenting book, such as The Discipline Book, by William and Martha Sears. The groups are free, but call ahead to reserve your spot.

❋ Fussy Baby Network

Erikson Institute

420 N. Wabash Ave., 6th floor

888-431-BABY (2229)

www.fussybabynetwork.org

Based on focus groups of parents, the Erikson Institute, a graduate school in child development, created the Fussy Baby Network for families with children from newborn through twelve months old. The network helps parents cope with issues of crying, sleeping, and feeding through a program of telephone support (no cost), home visits (offered on a sliding scale of no cost to $50 per visit), and parent classes and groups (cost varies). In addition, the network's Web site features message boards so parents can communicate with others experiencing the same stress.

❊ *MOPS (Mothers of Preschoolers)*

2370 S. Trenton Way
Denver, CO 80231
800-929-1287
www.gospelcom.net/mops/index.shtml
MOPS is a Christian-based nonprofit mothers' organization with more than 2,700 local chapters meeting throughout the world. Groups get together in local churches on a regular basis, and have anywhere from 10 to 200 members. Meeting formats vary from group to group but typically involve group discussion, a lecture, or a creative activity. Four local MOPS groups meet in the city:

❊ *Moody Church*

1630 N. Clark St.
312-943-0466

❊ *Beverly Evangelical Covenant*

10545 S. Claremont
773-445-4319

❊ *Christ Evangelical Lutheran Church*

3253 W. Wilson Ave.
773-478-7941

❊ *Christian Fellowship Free Church*

3425 N. Damen
773-348-3450

❊ *Mother-Infant Connection*

Karen Benson, M.E.D.
Family and Child Development Center of the Juvenile Protective Association
1707 N. Halsted St.
312-440-1203
Karen Benson, a child-development specialist, leads this support group for first-time mothers whose children are less than a year old. The groups run in five- or six-week sessions, with four to six moms getting together to discuss questions about their children's development and their own transition to motherhood. The Mother-Infant Connection is for the general public (as opposed to clients of JPA). A session costs $50 or $60, depending on its length; a sliding fee scale is available.

❊ *Mothers and More*

P.O. Box 31
Elmhurst, IL 60126
630-941-3553
www.mothersandmore.org
Mothers and More is a national organization for women aimed at improving the daily lives of mothers, whether they are at home with children full-time or struggling to balance the demands of family and paid work. Meetings tend to feature

speakers and discussions, on topics that range widely and might include keeping your résumé up to date, friendships before and after children, personal finance, and anger management.

More than 7,500 members participate in local chapters across the country. Currently, there are no chapters right in the city. However, two chapters in the suburbs do include city moms on their membership rolls: The near west suburban chapter meets at the LaGrange Park Library (555 N. LaGrange Road) on the second Tuesday and fourth Thursday of the month from 7 to 9 p.m. A Chicago/near north suburban chapter meets at Patten House in Glenview (939 Harlem Ave.) on the third Thursday of the month from 7:30 to 9:30 p.m. Leadership changes each year, so contact the number above for further information. A one-year membership is $45.

❊ New City YMCA Drop-In Program
1515 N. Halsted St.
312-440-7272 (YMCA)
312-440-1203 (Karen Benson)
Karen Benson of the Mother-Infant Connection (page 65) co-leads this drop-in play group program with a social worker. The program runs on Thursdays from 1:30 to 3:00 p.m., and is open to parents with children from birth to age four. The kids play while parents talk and get parenting questions answered. The cost is $5 per session; a sliding scale is available.

❊ Northside Parents Network
1218 W. Addison
312-409-2233
www.northsideparents.org/index.asp

The Northside Parents Network is a tremendous resource for families on the North Side. An all-volunteer nonprofit organization, it comprises more than 1,000 members and offers a wealth of activities and resources, including:

❊ A newsletter

❊ New moms' groups

❊ A single moms' group

❊ A baby-sitting co-op

❊ A cooperative morning-out program, where parents rotate watching children in order to have a morning off

❊ Age-based playgroups

❊ A nanny-share service, to make finding a part-time nanny easier

❊ A speaker program

❊ Social events

❊ A resource booklet of North Side preschools and elementary schools

❊ Discussion boards on the Web site

Membership is $30 per year, and because it is an all-volunteer effort, families are expected to contribute a few hours per year working on one of the group's projects or programs.

❋ Parenthesis Morning Drop-in Program

405 S. Euclid Ave. (Oak Park)

708-848-2227

The Morning Drop-in Program at Parenthesis saved my life—it's where I finally met other stay-at-home parents in the area and found a community of friendship and support that I expect will be life long. The Morning Program is open to parents and children ages newborn through kindergarten Monday through Thursday from 9:30 a.m. to 12:30 p.m. (Hours are reduced in the summer, however.) You settle your children in one of the four age-appropriate playrooms, where the excellent staff cares for them. Parents then go to the Parent Parlor, where you can work at long tables in the back or socialize with other parents on the couches; parenting workshops also are available. An area with little tables allows parents to feed kids lunch. Cost of the program is $11 per family per day; coupons for several visits are available at a reduced rate, or you can pay by the month on a sliding scale. Parenthesis also runs evening programs for single parents and teen parents once a week.

❋ ParentPrep

773-454-9535

www.parentprep.net

Founded by Amy Tardio, a licensed clinical social worker and life coach who organizes discussion groups for new mothers, ParentPrep is a collective of professionals that provides enrichment seminars for moms on topics such as life coaching, nutrition, financial planning, and fitness. Amy also publishes a life-coaching e-newsletter called Messages for Moms.

❋ Parents Support Network of Hyde Park

First Unitarian Church of Chicago

5650 S. Woodlawn Ave.

773-324-4100

When the weather dips below about 60 degrees, the Parents Support Network opens its volunteer-run, nondenominational, drop-in playroom at First Unitarian. The program runs from approximately September to May on Tuesday through Thursday from 9 a.m. to 1 p.m., and on Friday from 9 a.m. to 3 p.m. The group asks for a contribution of $75 for the year, though a sliding scale is available. Once you've paid the fee, you'll also receive the group's quarterly newsletter and can join its e-mail list. Currently the list has about 90 members from Hyde Park and the South Shore; parents say they love the community of support they've found through the list.

❋ Smart Love Parenting Center

Carolyn Stolper Friedman, executive director

1422 W. Wolfram St.

773-665-8052

Smart Love is a new parenting center based on the work of Martha Heineman Pieper, Ph.D., and William J. Pieper, M.D., child development professionals who co-authored the book Smart Love: The Compassionate Alternative to Discipline That Will Make You a Better Parent and Your Child a Better Person and who write a monthly column in Chicago Parent magazine.

The center takes a warm, compassionate approach to helping parents better understand their children's behavior from a developmental perspective, which in turn increases parents' enjoyment of their children. The center runs an eight-week discussion group for parents of babies six weeks to six months old; topics include how to have fun during the time you spend with your baby, helping your baby fall asleep on her own, building self-esteem, and understanding your changing relationship with your mate. The series costs $200. Future plans for the center include parent workshops, playgroups, a parent cooperative child care, and private consultation for parents.

Debra Rosenberg

708-366-9000 (West Suburban Temple)

For fifteen years, Debra, a licensed clinical social worker and the author of The New Mom's Companion: Care for Yourself While You Care for Your Newborn, has been leading new mom's discussion groups at West Suburban Temple in River Forest (1040 N. Harlem Ave.). Her series may be a bit too far for anyone but moms on the western edges of the city, but I include her here because I attended one of her groups and found it to be an enormously helpful source of support. Groups generally include about a half-dozen moms with babies in tow, and each week the discussion centers on a different topic, such as your changing relationship with your partner and making the decision to go back to work. The six-week series costs $75.

Virginia Frank Child Development Center

3033 W. Touhy Ave.

773-761-4550

The Virginia Frank Child Development Center provides counseling services for families with young children as well as a therapeutic nursery/kindergarten. In addition, Robin Davis, the center's human development family life educator and consultant, runs a variety of programs for parents. Get Together is a drop-in program for parents with children ages newborn to four years; children play and listen to a story while parents socialize or take the opportunity to discuss parenting issues with any of the three professionals on hand. The program is an hour-and-a-half long three mornings and afternoons a week; the cost is $5 per family per session, with a sliding scale available. Additionally, Robin organizes discussion groups based on need, such as first-time mothers, sibling rivalry, and toilet training. The center also hosts a single-parents dinner several times a year. All programs, including the drop-in, require registration or reservations.

Sweet Pea's Studio, A Mecca for New Parents

3717 N. Ravenswood, Ste. 213

773-248-YOGA

www.sweetpeasstudio.com

Of all the resources I encountered in writing this book, none seems to nurture the body, mind, and spirit of new parents like Sweet Pea's Studio. Not only does Sweet Pea's offer prenatal and postpartum massage, couples massage, prenatal yoga for mothers and couples, mommy-and-baby yoga, child-birth education, and infant massage; it also is home to Women to Women: Nurturing Ourselves As New Mothers, an eight-session discussion group led by Ann Tharayil and Lauren Goffen, clinical social workers and moms who founded the group to relieve stress and isolation and provide emotional support as new mothers embrace their changing identity. Each session focuses on a specific topic, such as adjusting to and enjoying your new routine, balancing partnership and parenthood, and tending to your body, mind, and spirit while also caring for your baby. Babies three weeks to crawling are welcome at the hour-and-a-half long sessions; the series is $120.

Besides offering formal classes, Sweet Pea's also is open to suggestions for family-friendly programs. For instance, one mom's group held a "spa playgroup" in the studio; the children played while the moms took turns receiving 20-minute chair massages from founder Jennifer Baron Fishman. Now that's a playgroup we could all use every week!

therapists

If you decide you need one-on-one help, several therapists specialize in working with women who are dealing with issues related to pregnancy, parenting, and postpartum depression.

❋ *Andrea Harris Alpert, L.C.S.W.*
  30 N. Michigan Ave.
  3166 N. Lincoln Ave.
  312-409-7272

❋ *Kim Richardson, L.C.P.C.*
  180 N. Michigan Ave., Ste. 2200
  Also practices in Wilmette
  847-207-9970
  www.radiantmother.com

❋ *Colleen Roney, L.C.S.W.*
  435 W. Diversey Parkway
  773-680-2868

❋ *Mara Tesler Stein, Psy.D.*
  4801 W. Peterson
  773-338-2980
  Mara, the mother of twins and co-author of Parenting Your Premature Baby and Child: The Emotional Journey, also specializes in issues of birth trauma and loss, such as infertility, premature birth, miscarriage, and multiple gestations.

hotlines, warmlines, and other special help

There may be times during your baby's first few weeks or months when you need more specialized help or support than your pediatrician, mother, or friend can provide.

During these weeks it is a good idea to keep handy the telephone number of the nursery of the hospital in which you delivered. Often, the nurses can easily answer your questions and help you through a minor crisis. Some hospitals also have special telephone numbers set up to assist new moms.

Inquire about your hospital's policy for new mother call-ins. Following are a variety of additional support groups and referral programs, as well as some important numbers to have in case of an emergency.

adoption

❋ *Adoptive Families Today*
847-382-0858
www.adoptivefamiliestoday.org
Provides information and resources, holds parent-child play groups, sponsors adult social activities, hosts parent discussion groups as well as an annual conference, and publishes a newsletter for Chicago-area adoptive families.

❋ *National Adoption Information Clearinghouse*
888-251-0075
A comprehensive resource on all matters relating to adoption: legal matters, adoption databases, publications, statistics, conferences, etc.

❋ *At-Home Parents*
National Association of At-Home Mothers
www.athomemothers.com
Publishes a quarterly magazine.

❋ *National Association of Mothers' Centers*
800-645-3828
These moms' groups are dedicated to breaking the isolation of motherhood and advancing maternal health and well-being. Currently, there are no centers in Illinois, but the organization provides information on to mothers who

wish to create a group, which is how other groups around the country got started.

breastfeeding

❋ *Breastfeeding Warmline at Highland Park Hospital*
847-480-3702
Free breastfeeding help. Leave a message and a lactation consultant will call back within two hours during normal business hours.

❋ *La Leche League*
847-519-7730
www.lalecheleague.org
A worldwide volunteer organization founded by a group of mothers to support other moms who chose to breastfeed their babies. La Leche's services are free, nonsectarian, and supported by membership fees ($36 per year). La Leche has group leaders in various parts of Chicago who run monthly meetings to discuss breastfeeding. They also provide a valuable telephone help service.

❋ *Medela Electric Breast Pump Rental*
800-835-5968
Provides a complete listing of where to find Medela breastfeeding pumps and specialists in your area.

❋ *Prentice Women's Hospital Breastfeeding & Postpartum Line*
312-926-7155
Free and available to anyone, regardless of birth place. Operates 8 a.m. to 3 p.m. Monday

through Friday, and 8 a.m. to noon, Saturday and Sunday.

child abuse

❊ *Child Abuse Prevention Services (CAPS)*
800-4-A-CHILD
National hotline for reporting suspected cases of child abuse.

❊ *Illinois Child Abuse Hotline*
800-252-2873
Part of Child Abuse Prevention Services (CAPS). Hotline for reporting suspected cases of child abuse.

depression

❊ *Depression After Delivery*
800-944-4PPD
Provides a free information packet and referrals to local professionals and support groups.

❊ *National Institute of Mental Health Publications Ordering Line*
800-421-4211
National campaign to increase awareness and education on depression and anxiety. Provides free brochures and publications.

❊ *Postpartum Depression Illinois Alliance*
847-205-4455
Voicemail for those experiencing postpartum depression.

❊ *Northwestern Memorial Outpatient Psychiatry Treatment Center*
312-926-8100
Ask for an intake worker, who will provide counseling and resources for postpartum depression and other crises.

gay and lesbian parents

❊ *Family Pride Coalition*
202-331-5015
Provides advocacy, information, support, events, and parent groups for gay, lesbian, bisexual, and transgender parents.

grief and loss

❊ *The Compassionate Friends*
877-969-0010
National support group for parents who have lost a child. Provides information and referrals to local chapters.

❊ *SHARE Pregnancy & Infant Loss Support, Inc.*
800-821-6819
Provides information and referrals to support groups nationwide.

❊ *The Sudden Infant Death Syndrome (SIDS) Alliance*
800-221-7437 (SIDS)
Provides support to SIDS families, as well as education and research.

mixed race families

❋ Biracial Family Network
773-288-3644

A family support and educational group that offers resources, meetings, activities, and a newsletter.

parenting support

❋ The Parental Stress Line
800-632-8188

A 24-hour service offering crisis intervention or simply someone to talk to about parental stress.

❋ Parent's Resource Network
847-675-3555

This warmline is available to parents who have nonmedical, child-rearing questions about children ages newborn through eight, or who just need to talk to someone about parenting stress.

premature infants

The best place to get advice and counseling or to find out about support groups for parents of premature babies is through your hospital's Neonatal Intensive Care Unit. Many NICUs automatically provide such support. If yours does not, ask the staff to direct you to a group in your area.

safety

❋ Illinois Poison Center
800-942-5969

Hotline for questions, advice, and referrals in cases of poisoning.

❋ U.S. Consumer Products Safety Commission
800-638-2772

Provides information on product safety. Also takes consumer complaints about product safety.

single parents

❋ National Organization for Single Mothers
704-888-KIDS

Provides information and support to single mothers. Helps establish local support groups and publishes an award-winning newsletter, SingleMOTHER.

❋ Parents without Partners
800-637-7974

Provides advice and support for single parents, as well as referrals to local chapters.

special needs

❋ Child Find/Look What I Can Do
800-851-6197

Part of the State of Illinois Department of Human Services. Provides information and literature for families with children with special needs, ages newborn to 21.

❋ Cystic Fibrosis Foundation
800-344-4823

A foundation providing advice, counseling, and hospital referrals for families of children with Cystic Fibrosis.

❋ **Equip for Equality**

312-341-0022

Provides advocacy assistance for parents of children with disabilities, legal representation, and educational seminars.

❋ **Family Resource Center on Disabilities**

312-939-3513

Provides information, support, and free seminars for families.

❋ **National Dissemination Center for Children with Disabilities**

800-695-0285

Provides information on specific disabilities, early intervention services for infants and toddlers, special education services for school-age children, parent materials, and resources in each state.

❋ **Jewish Family & Community Services**

773-761-4550

Includes Virginia Frank Child Development Center, which offers a therapeutic nursery school and kindergarten, social services, education, and training.

❋ **Lighthouse International**

800-829-0500

Provides comprehensive services and resources for the blind.

❋ **National Association for Down Syndrome**

630-325-9112

Provides information and support to Chicago-area families with children with Down syndrome. Also has information on playgroups.

❋ **National Down Syndrome Society**

800-221-4602

Provides information and support.

❋ **United Cerebral Palsy of Greater Chicago**

312-368-0380

This organization offers comprehensive services for children and their families, beginning at infancy.

❋ **Spina Bifida Association of America**

(800) 621-3141

twins or more

❋ **M.O.S.T. (Mothers Of Super Twins)**

631-859-1110

A support group for parents of triplets, quadruplets, or quintuplets.

❋ **National Organization of Mothers of Twins Clubs, Inc.**

877-540-2200

This club provides information on local twin, triplet, and quadruplet (or more) support groups.

diaper service

If you're looking for cloth diaper delivery service, there's really just one choice: Bottoms Up Dy-Dee Wash Diaper, based in Waukeegan; the number is 847-336-0040. Bottoms Up delivers to the city as far south as 120th Street, and will deliver to many out-lying suburbs as well. A week's supply of eighty new-born diapers is $16.45. Bottoms Up also sells diaper pails for $13.95, and diaper covers for $7.

Diapers & More (219) 944-0778, is a Gary, Ind.-based delivery service that sells Huggies and Cuties disposable diapers at a significant discount. A case of 288 newborn diapers, for instance, is $39.99, plus a $7 to $10 delivery fee, depending on where you live.

breast pumps

For breastfeeding working moms or other women who would like their husbands or caregivers to feed baby an occasional bottle of breast milk, an electric breast pump is a wonderful convenience. Electric pumps are faster and easier to use than manual or battery-operated pumps. If you plan to breastfeed for three months or less, I recommend renting an electric, hospital-grade pump; if you're going to be pumping for a longer period of time, or plan to have more children, purchasing one is probably more economical.

Try to rent or purchase your breast pump from a lactation consultant if you can. Although pumps are available at many pharmacies, the staff there won't be able to give you the same support as a lac-tation consultant, who can show you how to use the pump properly, keep the attachments sanitary, store your milk safely, and answer any questions you have about pumping and nursing.

Pumps generally are rented by month. They also can be purchased through One Step Ahead catalog (www.onestepahead.com/index.jsp; 800-274-8440). The Medela Lactina or Pump in Style are good ones to rent or purchase. For the nearest outlet, call Medela at: (800) TELL-YOU. A local La Leche League leader 800-LALECHE can also help you locate a breast pump. Prices for pump rental range from $50 to $80 per month. Most places sell an accompanying kit that contains sanitary accessories to be used with the pump. The kit is priced at about $50, for the dou-ble pump, and a little less for the single pump. The single pump allows you to pump milk from one breast, and the double from both breasts at the same time; I found the double saved time.

Breast pumps can be rented at the following locations:

northside

❋ *Ballin Pharmacy*
   3330 N. Lincoln Ave.
   773-348-0027
   Ballin also does a lovely job of fitting nursing bras, which is not an easy service to find in Chicago.

❋ *Becker Professional Pharmacy*
   4744 N. Western Ave.
   773-561-4486

❋ *Braun Drug*
   2075 N. Lincoln
   773-549-0634

✳ Chicago Maternity Gift Shop
Prentice Women's Hospital
333 E. Superior St.
312-926-7648

✳ Cynthia Guzman, I.B.C.L.C., R.L.C.
The Art of Breastfeeding
Home delivery
773-745-0992

✳ Home Care Plus
2808 W. Foster
773-784-7848

✳ Angela Jacobi, R.N., I.B.C.L.C.
773-274-0643

✳ Peg Janssen, R.N., I.B.C.L.C.
Nursing Care of Newborns
847-853-1285
Peg has about ten lactation consultants working for her, so you should be able to find help quickly here.

✳ Martha Johnson, R.N., B.C.L.C.
773-267-0816

✳ Kosirog Pharmacy
1000 N. Western Ave.
773-486-3998

✳ Parkway Drugs
2346 N. Clark St., 773-549-2720
680 N. Lake Shore Drive, 312-943-2224

✳ Pat Schmidt, R.N.
Breastfeeding Support of Evanston
847-675-2964

✳ Melanie Silverman, R.D., L.D.
Feeding Philosophies
Specialist in pediatric nutrition and lactation support
773-525-0292

south side

✳ Sylvia Davis, R.N., I.B.C.L.C.
Sylvia's Lactation Service
Home delivery
773-844-3392

✳ Debra Nawracaj, R.N., I.B.C.L.C.
Go with the Flow
773-927-9114

✳ Barbara Hardin, R.N., I.B.C.L.C.
The Mother's Milk Company (Cicero)
708-652-0060

✳ Brady's Home Med Health
3235 W. 111th St.
773-238-6686

✳ Katsaros Pharmacy
1521 E. 53rd
773-288-8700

✳ Little Company of Mary
5610 W. 95th St. (Oak Lawn)
708-499-0071

✳ *Noreen Shilney, R.N., I.B.C.L.C.*
Breastpumps Plus (Oak Lawn)
708-424-9976

✳ *Sinai Community Pharmacy*
California Avenue at 15th Street
773-257-6900

✳ *University of Chicago Hospital*
58th and Maryland
773-702-3925

✳ *Women's Resource Center*
Christ Hospital and Medical Center (Oak Lawn)
4440 W. 95th St.
708-346-3300

Ten Things to Keep You Sane with a Newborn

1. Before the baby is born, stock the freezer with lasagne, casseroles, soup, and other easy-to-prepare meals.

2. Don't be afraid to ask for help if possible from your mother and mother-in-law, sister, friends, or babysitters. Someday when your life is more settled you'll pass the favor along to another new mom.

3. Sleep when the baby sleeps. I repeat: Sleep when the baby sleeps. Chores can wait.

4. Budget ahead of time to order takeout the first few weeks. Cooking is a big job you don't need right now.

5. Buy in bulk and have it delivered if possible. A case of diapers and several packages of baby wipes on hand will make life much easier.

6. Open up charge accounts at stores in the neighborhood that will deliver.

7. Let the house get messy. It's not forever.

8. Make friends with other new moms and call them to commiserate.

9. Try to get outside for at least a few minutes every day.

10. While you're nursing or feeding a bottle, read Anne Lamott's Operating Instructions. It's her true, hilarious, heartbreaking account of life as a single mom during her son's first year. Just when you think you're going to lose your mind, Annie lets you know you're not alone.

Chapter Five

entertainment for kids and moms

Congratulations, you've survived the first couple of months! You have packing the diaper bag down to a science, you know how to do just about everything one-handed, and you've accepted sleep deprivation as a way of life—it's now time to venture out with your little one, meet other parents, and have some fun.

You and your baby can take yoga together at Bubbles Academy, learn infant massage at Sweet Pea's Studios, make music at the Old Town School of Folk Music, or take an exercise class at Walk-a-Bye Baby.

In this chapter, I'll give you a rundown of the Mommy and Me classes and activities available in the city. (Unless otherwise indicated, caregivers, dads, and grandparents are also welcome to take their young charges to these classes.) Then we'll turn to Chicago's playgrounds and parks, museums, child-friendly restaurants, and other special spaces where you and your baby can have a good time.

First, though, a few thoughts on monitoring your child's schedule. It's easy to overdo the classes, especially with a first child. You're eager to get out of the house, and engaging with your baby in new, creative ways is a lot of fun. If you're not careful, though, you can find yourself signed up for music, art, gym, storytime, yoga—you name it. You get the idea; it's easy to become overbooked. Playgroups and time with mom in the park are just as valuable as Gymboree. You may even find it pays to wait until your child is a year old or so to sign up for classes, because she'll likely be able to engage and enjoy it much more then than at three or six months.

mommy and me classes and programs

As your child grows, she is going to learn to run, jump, tumble, sing songs, and scribble pictures all on her own. But classes can help her develop social skills, learn discipline, and acquire a host of other skills. Above all, children enjoy themselves in these programs, and it's nice to have some places to go during our looong winters by the lake.

The following places and programs offer classes for children age three and under. Some take babies as young as three months. However, you and your child will find an organized class much more enjoyable if he's able to sit up on his own, so it's a good idea to wait until your baby is six to nine months old before signing up.

Here are some guidelines to follow as you check out these programs:

❋ Take a trial class or attend an open house before you sign up. You may have to pay for it, but you'll have a better sense of what you are getting into.

❋ Look for classes with children the same age as your own.

❋ Look for big, open, clean rooms with plenty of space and light, accessible by elevator or ramp. You should not have to walk up five flights of stairs carrying your baby, diaper bag, and stroller.

❋ Equipment should be scaled down to small-child size, and any gymnastic-type facilities should include lots of mats and other safety features.

❋ Small- to medium-size classes are best. Do not be too concerned if a class is very big on the first day, because everyone is not there every week. Illnesses, naps, and vacations normally account for a quarter of a class being absent in any given week.

❋ The teacher makes all the difference; some are better than others. The other children and their mothers and nannies also can affect the atmosphere of a class. If you are the only mom in attendance, for example, you may feel awkward spending time with ten nannies every Thursday afternoon at two o'clock. (You can always ask to switch to a class with more moms.)

❋ Location is important. Enroll in a class near your home. If you can push your baby in a stroller less than ten blocks, you will be more likely to attend and to make it there on time.

Prices and schedules change almost every semester, so call ahead for the latest information. Classes often run in sessions of ten to twenty weeks; prices vary widely, from free storytimes to nearly $1,000 for a full semester at Language Stars. Remember, what's important is spending time together, not spending a ton of money to turn your baby into the next Einstein.

infant massage

Scientific research has found many benefits to infant massage: It improves bonding between parent and baby, promotes deeper sleep, alleviates colic and gas, reduces episodes of breathing cessation (which can cause sudden infant death syndrome), and increases weight gain in premature infants. Plus, it's simply a wonderful way to spend some quiet, relaxing time with your baby.

Here are some resources for learning infant massage:

❋ *Center for Muscle Therapy*
1123 Emerson, Ste. 200 (Evanston)
847-869-6869
Three therapists work at this practice that specializes in pregnancy, infant, and child massage therapy and instruction.

❋ *Susan Gray*
Wellspring Integrative Medicine
1565 Sherman Ave. (Evanston)
773-710-9219
Susie is a massage therapist and birth doula who specializes in women's health, especially pregnancy. She also teaches infant massage, either privately in your home or in a larger class.

❋ *Abigail Lynn*
773-991-7968
Abigail is a former emergency room nursing assistant who now is a doula and certified massage therapist. She teaches infant massage and makes house calls throughout the Chicago area.

❋ Northwestern Memorial Hospital's Prentice Women's Hospital

333 E. Superior St.

877-926-4664

Prentice offers a three-part series on infant massage for parents and babies up to five months old. The series is $75; private instruction is available for $60 per hour.

❋ Sweet Pea's Studio

3717 N. Ravenswood, Ste. 213

773-248-YOGA

www.sweetpeasstudio.com

This mecca for pregnant women and new parents offers instruction in baby massage; two classes are $60.

❋ Urban Oasis

Two locations:

12 W. Maple St.; 312-587-3500

939 W. North Ave.; 312-640-0001

www.urban-oasis.com

Urban Oasis is a full-service spa that also offers an infant massage class, which costs $75 for two parents and baby.

storytimes

❋ Barbara's Bookstore

1350 N. Wells

312-642-5044

Storytime for children under age five on Saturdays at 10 a.m.

❋ Barnes & Noble Booksellers

1130 N. State St.

312-280-8155

Storytime on Tuesdays and Thursdays at 11 a.m. Stories are geared toward children five and under.

1441 W. Webster

773-871-3610

With one of the largest children's sections in the city, this Barnes & Noble has a plethora of activities for young children and their parents. The Monday storytime at 10 a.m. is aimed at toddlers and preschoolers. Books for the storytimes on Thursday at 4 p.m. and Saturday at 11 a.m. are chosen based on who shows up, with an age spread of anywhere from two to eight years old. The fourth Friday of the month it's Pajamarama Storytime at 7 p.m., when kids show up in their jammies to hear bedtime stories—the reader dons p.j.s, too. And once a month, except during November and December, children can hear stories read by a favorite costumed character, such as Cat in the Hat, Curious George, Angelina Ballerina, and Clifford; call for a specific month's character and time.

❋ Borders Books & Music

830 N. Michigan Ave.; 312-573-0564

Storytime for young children on Tuesdays at 11 a.m.

2210 W. 95th St.; 773-445-5471

At the weekly Pajama Party on Fridays at 7 p.m., kids come dressed in their pajamas to hear bedtime stories.

Children in Paradise

909 N. Rush St.

312-951-5437

This gorgeous store, owned by my former editor colleague Jodi Block, is Chicago's only exclusively children's bookstore. Children in Paradise hosts storytime on Tuesdays and Wednesdays at 10:30 a.m.

57th Street Books

1301 E. 57th St.

773-684-1300

Hosts storytime on Mondays and Wednesdays at 10:30 a.m.

Women & Children First

5233 N. Clark St.

773-769-9299

Hosts a half-hour storytime on Wednesdays at 10:30 a.m. The recommended age is 18 months and up.

the arts: music, movement, and crafts

Beverly Arts Center

2407 W. 111th St.

773-445-3838

www.beverlyartcenter.org/index.html

Ages: Birth and up

This vibrant arts center offers a wealth of classes for both children and adults. Parent-child classes include Music Together (newborn to age five, divided by age) and Family Circle Art, a wide-ranging, hands-on program for parents and children ages two to three. A 10-week session is $180 ($162 for members) for Music Together, and $100 ($90 for members) for Family Circle Art.

Chicago Waldorf School

1300 W. Loyola Ave.

773-465-8630

www.chicagowaldorf.org

Ages: Infant through high school

sThe largest independent, nondenominational school movement in the world, Waldorf education places a strong emphasis on learning through the arts and being in tune with the natural world. The Chicago Waldorf School, which serves children through grade 12, offers a 10- to 14-week parent-child series for infants through three-year-olds. Parents engage in crafts or homelike activities, like making bread, while children help or play nearby. Circle time, creative play, snack, and storytime are all part of the class. My friend Judy loves the program so much that her older son has continued on to the Waldorf preschool. Prices vary, depending on your child's age, number of classes per week, and length of the session; call for further information.

Gymboree Play and Music

3158 N. Lincoln Ave.; 773-296-4550

www.playandmusic.com/b2c/customer/home.jsp

Ages: Newborn to 5 years

These popular, organized playgroups are the original "mommy and me" classes. Gymboree, which runs a chain of kids' clothing stores, also offers a wide variety of music, art, and play classes that combine the arts with physical movement and imaginative storytelling and play. Each class is broken down by age, with music classes covering smaller age spreads (for instance, newborn to 6 months) than the art programs (18 months to 2-1/2 years, and 2-1/2 to 5 years). Two mobile siblings can take the Gym Pairs class. Music and play classes run $195 for 12 weeks; art classes are $279 for 12 weeks. Visit the Web site and print out a coupon to take a free introductory course.

❖ Hands On Children's Art Museum

1800 W. 103rd St.

773-233-9933

www.handsonart.org/index.php

Ages: 1-1/2 to 4 years

This relatively new art center in the historic Beverly neighborhood offers Culture Bugs, a class where toddlers and preschoolers can experiment with paint, texture, shape, and color in a creative environment that also includes songs and storytelling. Classes are divided by age into 18 to 30 months and 2-1/2 to 4 years; a six-week session runs $85. In addition, the museum has a wonderful variety of permanent open-art studios, where children can drop in and paint, play with Colorforms material, sculpt with clay, make prints, weave on a loom, put on puppet shows, and dress up.

❖ Happy Child Studios

741 Main St. (Evanston)

847-733-9545

www.happychildstudios.com

Ages: Newborn and up

Founded by Julie Frost, award-winning producer of children's music, Happy Child Studios offers a unique variety of fun, creative classes for the entire family. You can take a one-on-one music class with your child, or bring the whole gang to Happy Family Music, which also is offered in Spanish. (Chicago Happy Family Music classes take place at St. Michael's Church, 1744 N. Cleveland.) Book Boogie Babes combines stories, movement, and live music for one- to three-year-olds; yoga classes are available for toddlers on up; and moms with babies in tow can take belly dancing and salsa dancing. Happy Child Studios also hosts a variety of concerts and other family events throughout the year, such as a Crayon-a-thon-a-rama, where dozens of kids create a work of art together, and a Winter Holiday Picnic Party, where everyone dresses up in summerwear for an indoor party. Call the studios or visit the Web site for a schedule and prices.

❖ Hyde Park Art Center

5307 S. Hyde Park Blvd.

773-324-5520

www.hydeparkart.org

Ages: 2 years and up

The Hyde Park Art Center is a nonprofit organization that presents exhibits, mainly by Chicagoland artists, and holds classes for everyone from preschoolers to adults. Multimedia classes for children two to five are generally held in the late afternoon and change on a quarterly basis. At the time of this writing, for instance, the center was offering a preschool class called People Pictures, where children use various media to draw, paint, mold, and construct images of people. The 10-week course is $110 for members and $130 for nonmembers; a one-year family membership is $50 and entitles the holder to a $20 discount on all classes.

❖ Jewish Community Center

North Side: 524 W. Melrose Ave.; 773-871-6780

Hyde Park: 5200 S. Hyde Park Blvd.; 773-753-3080

Ages: Newborn to 32 months

Better known as the JCC, the Jewish Community Center offers several different music classes for little ones. Infants Hour serves babies up to 12 months, and Child's Play involves toddlers from 12 to 26 months. Both classes are 55 minutes and take a multisensory approach, using songs, instruments, scarves, and more; the older class also has a snack. You and Me classes, which last an hour and 15 minutes, are offered to parents and children 20 to 32 months and go beyond music to incorporate art and free play too. Costs vary depending on the class and length of the session. Members get about a $50 price break per class—and you don't have to be Jewish to join.

❖ Kindermusik

www.kindermusik.com

Locations in the city:

Portage Park Center for the Arts, 5801 W. Dakin St.; 773-205-0151

Sweet Pea's Studios, 3717 N. Ravenswood; 773-248-YOGA

Ages: Newborn and up

Started in Germany in the 1960s, Kindermusik now has more than 5,000 teachers worldwide. A Kindermusik class will get kids singing, chanting, dancing, and playing simple instruments like rhythm sticks, bells, and drums. The sessions are 45 minutes to an hour long, and children can participate with either a parent or caregiver. Use the Web site's class locator to find a teacher near you, or call one of the local phone numbers above.

❖ Music Together

Sherwood Conservatory of Music, 1312 S. Michigan Ave.; 312-427-6267

Merit School of Music, 47 W. Polk St.; 312-786-9428

Marsha's Music Together (at Joan's Studio for the Performing Arts), 1438 E. 57th St.; 773-288-3815

Merry Music Makers (classes in Andersonville and Edgebrook); 773-209-8083

Music Together of Lakeview, 3047 N. Lincoln Ave.; 773-975-9874

www.musictogether.com

Ages: Birth to 4 years

Music Together is a 45-minute class for parents or caregivers and children, where they sing, dance, chant, and play with various instruments. At the beginning of the program, parents receive a cassette tape, a CD, and a charming illustrated songbook. They are encouraged to play the tape at home and children come to know and love the songs. Music

Together has 10 to 12 children per class. There are classes for babies and toddlers separately and classes for infants and toddlers mixed together. Prices vary, depending on location, but a 10-week series is about $150; some locations offer financial aid. Instructors vary with location, so see if you can take a trial class before signing up. Use the Web site's class locator to find a teacher near you, or call one of the local phone numbers above.

❊ Lookingglass Theatre
2936 N. Southport Ave.
773-477-9257, ext. 193
www.lookingglasstheatre.org/index.html
Ages: 1 year and up
PLAYtime classes for one- to two-year-olds combine high-energy warm-ups, games, sing-a-longs, and storytelling, encouraging toddlers to use their budding imaginations. Dance with Me, for two- to three-year-olds, incorporates structured and creative games with an emphasis on rhythm, stretching, and fun. Both classes are $130 for a 10-week session.

❊ Old Town School of Folk Music
4544 N. Lincoln Ave. and 909 W. Armitage Ave.
773-728-6000
www.oldtownschool.org
Ages: 6 months to 3 years
Arguably the best-known kids' music class in the city, Wiggleworms is where children and their parents sing, play finger games, dance, and bang instruments made especially for little hands. Classes are divided by age: 6 to 12

months, 12 to 24 months, 24 to 36 months, and a sibling class for siblings six months to five years old. A 16-week session is $210. For children ages one to three, Wiggleworms is available in a bilingual Spanish or German class, and children one to five can take it in French. These 16-week sessions are $215, which includes a take-home songbook to practice. Old Town also offers art classes (I love the names—Scribble, Squeeze and Pound) for toddlers.

❊ Portage Park Center for the Arts
5801 Dakin St.
773-205-0151
Ages: All
The Portage Park Center for the Arts offers a wide variety of classes for everyone in the family, including adults. Circle Time brings together parents and children 18 months to three years old for an hour of music, fingerplay, storytelling, and a snack. A four-week session is $40. The center also offers Creativity Corner, a multisensory art class for two- to six-year-olds that incorporates games, puzzles, music, and more. A four-week session is $40.

❊ Reel Moms
Loews Cineplex
600 N. Michigan Ave.
312-255-9347
Every Tuesday at 11 a.m. the Loews theater on Michigan Avenue shows a current film for moms with children under two in tow. The film is not necessarily rated G—in fact, some have been rated R—so this outing is mainly suited to moms with babes in arms; you probably

wouldn't get to watch the movie with a toddler to chase anyway. Doors open at 10 a.m. for socializing and settling in. Cost is $6.00 per adult; free for babies.

❋ Sing 'n' Dance

2632 Halsted St.
773-528-7464
www.singndance.com
Ages: Newborn through 36 months
You'll find a variety of hour-long parent-child programs at Sing 'n' Dance. For infant classes, which are divided into ages 8 weeks through 4 months, 5 through 10 months, and 11 through 17 months, the focus is on rhythmic music and movement, with some baby massage, too. A lively parent discussion follows, with parents sharing their experiences and new-parenting tips. Toddler classes involve songs, rhythmic games and dancing, puppet stories, hands-on play with a variety of instruments, and active play on climbers, ramps, and tunnels. Classes wrap up with snacks and parent conversation. A 12-week session is $180 up to nine months, and $216 from nine to 36 months.

❋ Starbaby Childbirth and Parenting Education

Christine Culbert
1220 W. Glenlake Ave.
773-381-9728
www.starbabybirthandparenting.com
Ages: Newborn to 1 year
Christine is a former labor and postpartum nurse who now teaches childbirth education and parent-child classes. She offers two class-es for parents and babies: A Star Is Born (birth to crawling) and Twinkle Twinkle Little Star (crawling to age one). Classes include parenting support, information on development, play, song, and rhyme. A 10-week session costs $150.

❋ The Suzuki-Orff School for Young Musicians

1148 W. Chicago Ave.
312-738-2646
www.suzukiorff.org/index.html
Ages: 6 months through 4 years
The Suzuki-Orff School offers a Baby STEPS movement-and-music program that aims to foster social interaction in a relaxed atmosphere. Classes are divided into four different age groups: Twinkle Tots (6 to 18 months), Learning Explorers I (1-1/2 to 2-1/2 years), Learning Explorers II (2-1/2 to 3-1/2 years), and Steppin' into Orff (3-1/2 to 4-1/2 years). Babies through preschoolers build a repertoire of songs, rhythms, and rhymes, and make their own music, while the class for the oldest children prepares them to begin more formal study of musical instruments. Depending on the class, a 17-week session runs from $204 to $385, plus a $28 registration fee.

❋ Ukrainian Village Children's Center

918 N. Damen
773-342-7415
http://uvcc.home.mindspring.com/
Ages: 2 years and up
The Ukrainian Village Children's Center is a wonderfully homey, colorful place where small

groups of children create art projects with paint, beads, shells, clay, and other materials. The kids also have free time to play with the center's handmade furniture, including a play kitchen, a dollhouse, and sand and water tables. The center offers daily two-hour classes in the morning, and a Saturday afternoon drop-in arts class for preschoolers through second graders. Classes cost $10; parents of older children may drop them off, while parents of preschoolers must stay.

❊ World Folk Music Company

1808 W. 103rd St.

773-779-7059

www.worldfolkmusiccompany.com

Ages: 6 months and up

Founded by Irish and American folk musician John Devens, the World Folk Music Company offers a multitude of classes and private lessons taught by multi-talented Chicago folk musicians. The Infant and Toddler class for children six months to three years is designed to teach them melody and rhythm in a social setting. An eight-week session is $60.

physical activities

❊ Bubbles Academy

1504 N. Fremont

312-944-7677

www.bubblesacademy.com

Ages: Infant through 7 years

The Blossom Bubbles class for moms and babies helps new mothers rebuild their abdominal and pelvic muscles, while babies

enjoy baby yoga, music, and infant massage. Classes are $140 for an eight-week session.

❊ Corner Playroom

2121 N. Clybourn Ave.

773-388-2121

www.cornerplayroom.com

Ages: 1 to 5 years

If you're going bonkers cooped up at home, head for the Corner Playroom, where parents and kids have fun together in a very social setting. This huge indoor play space offers something for just about every kid's interest: play houses and kitchens, slides, climbers, dollhouses, balls, and more. You can drop in just for the day ($15 for the first child, $9 for each additional), or buy a membership ($80 for one month, with price breaks for multiple months; membership is about $20 less in the summer). The playroom also offers a music class several mornings a week for parents and children three and under; a 12-week session is $190 for members and $220 for nonmembers. Finally, kids two to five can be dropped off at the playroom's summer camp two, three, or four days a week for one to 13 weeks; call for prices. Note that the playroom is closed on weekends, when it's booked for birthday parties.

❊ Global Yoga and Wellness Center

1823 W. North Ave.

773-489-1510

www.globalyogacenter.com

Ages: Newborn to 1 year

Global Yoga offers a mom and baby class for infants up to one year. The restorative and strengthening class focuses on body alignment and muscle strength, targeting abdominals, hips, legs, back muscles, and the pelvic floor. A one-hour class is $12, or $85 for an eight-class pass.

✳ Happy Child Studios
741 Main St. (Evanston)
847-733-9545
www.happychildstudios.com
Ages: Newborn and up
Book Boogie Babes combines stories, movement, and live music for one- to three-year-olds, yoga classes are available for toddlers on up, or moms with babies in tow can take belly dancing and salsa dancing.

✳ Lakeshore Academy
937 W. Chestnut
312-563-9400
Ages: 6 months and up
Lakeshore Academy offers a variety of parent-tot movement classes, starting at age six months through three years. Children three and up can enroll in tumbling classes that set the stage for more serious study of gymnastics, which can continue at the academy through adulthood. An eight-week session costs $135 for members and $180 for nonmembers for a one-hour class; a one-year membership is $100, and there are price breaks for enrolling more than one child in classes.

✳ The Little Gym of Chicago
3216 N. Lincoln Ave.
773-525-5750
www.tlgchicagoil.com

Ages: 4 months to 12 years
The Little Gym offers a parent-child class for children four months to three years old. Motor development activities are combined with music, ball play, group activities, and bubbles.

✳ My Gym Chicago
1880 W. Fullerton Ave.
773-645-9600
Ages: 3 months to 9 years
My Gym offers a series of parent-child gymnastics and movement classes on custom-designed equipment that changes every week, just to keep things interesting. Classes include Tiny Tykes (3 to 11 months), Waddlers (11 to 18 months), Gymsters (19 months to 2-1/2 years), and Terrific Tots (2-1/2 to 3-1/2 years). Parent involvement is gradually decreased in Terrific Tots, to get kids ready for the next, parent-free level. The 10-week classes are $160 for children three to 18 months, and $170 for ages 19 months and up. Also, your first class requires a $50 lifetime membership fee.

✳ Old Town School of Folk Music
4544 N. Lincoln Ave. and 909 W. Armitage Ave.
773-728-6000
www.oldtownschool.org
Ages: 6 weeks to 3 years
Old Town's Yogamotion classes for infants and toddlers are a fun introduction to yoga. The infant class also includes some infant massage. An eight-week class is $105.

✼ Partners in Play

In United Lutheran Church, 409 Greenfield St. (Oak Park)
708-386-2788
Ages: Newborn and up
This program of parent-child physical and creative activities has been going strong for more than twenty years. You can take a mother-baby exercise class up until your child starts crawling, then move on to parent-child gym classes. Partners in Play also offers parent-child music and art classes, and four- to six-year-olds can take acting, art, and music classes on their own. Matt and Clare have taken Saturday art and gym classes and really enjoyed them—and I liked getting a break. Prices are among the cheapest around: $48 for an eight-week session.

✼ Priya Yoga

1 E. Oak St.
312-587-7492
www.priyayoga.com
Ages: Infant to 3 years
Priya offers a Mommy & Me class for children under 3. Drop-in classes are $15, or you can purchase a pass for anywhere from five ($65) to twenty ($200) classes.

✼ Satchidananda Yoga Center

1521 Chicago Ave. (Evanston)
888-900-YOGA
www.specialyoga.com
Ages: Birth and up
Satchidananda Yoga Center doesn't offer parent-tot classes—preschool classes start at age three—but I mention the center here because it is home to Yoga for the Special Child, a unique program for children with special needs, including Down's syndrome, cerebral palsy, microcephaly, autism, and attention deficit disorder. Satchidananda recommends beginning Yoga for the Special Child as soon as possible after birth. If your child has special needs, he or she needs to be evaluated before signing up for a class, which costs $50 for a half-hour session.

✼ Sweet Pea's Studio

3717 N. Ravenswood
773-248-YOGA
www.sweetpeasstudio.com
Ages: Infants to 12 months
Sweet Pea's offers a mom-and-baby yoga class for infants up to 12 months. The one-hour class is $13 for drop-ins, or $11 per class for a 12-week series.

✼ Yoga Bound

1753 N. Damen
773-395-2929
www.yogaboundchicago.com/default.asp
Ages: 3 months and up
Yoga Bound offers several mom-and-baby classes: for three to twelve months, one to two years, and two to three years. Single classes are $15, a five-class pass is $65, and a ten-class pass is $120.

✼ Walk-a-Bye Baby Fitness

www.walkabyebaby.com
312-829-2229

Walk-a-Bye Baby is a fitness company entirely dedicated to pregnant women and parents of young children. Mom-and-tot classes include circuit training, with a nanny available to watch the kids; mom-and-baby stretching and yoga classes; and stroller classes in Wicker Park and at the Lincoln Park Zoo. In good weather, classes are held outdoors at the zoo; in bad weather, they're held at Windy City Fieldhouse (2367 W. Logan Blvd.). Rates vary from $16 for a drop-in ($10 if it's your first time) to $370 for a pass that allows you to attend as many classes as you want per session.

other programs

❋ Lake Shore Preparatory School

300 W. Hill St.

312-266-2020

Ages: 3 months to 3 years

For parents and young children, this private school offers the Beginnings Program, a series of multisensory classes that's divided into three age categories. Teeter Tots, for ages 3 to 18 months, involves music, parachute games, puppets, and bubbles. Tots, for ages 1-1/2 to 2 years, offers arts and crafts, circle time, snack time, dramatic play and gym, musical instruments, and group play. Both of these once-a-week classes are an hour long. Transition, for two- to three-year-olds, is a "first time alone class" that helps get children ready for preschool; parents remain on-site but not in the class. Transition runs twice a week for an hour and a half. Parents can use the school's atrium lounge before or after class to enjoy a snack or socialize with other parents.

Prices vary, so call for a brochure; there's free parking with a sticker.

❋ Language Stars

1777 N. Clybourn

312-587-8795

www.languagestars.com/index.html

Ages: 12 months to 3 years

Very young children are uniquely able to pick up foreign languages, and Language Stars capitalizes on this ability with its FunImmersion classes, taught by native speakers of each language. One-hour Parents & Tots classes are divided into two ages (12 to 24 months, and 2 to 3 years) and combine movement, songs, puppet shows, arts and crafts, and other activities. Classes are available in Spanish, French, German, and Italian—and they aren't cheap: A 20-week session runs $570 for once a week, and $995 for twice a week. Classes also are available for older children; see page 108.

❋ The Parent/Toddler Nursery School

940 West Weed Street

773-528-7464

Ages: 17 through 36 months

Classes at the Parent/Toddler Nursery School provide a fun and safe environment to help toddlers begin making the transition to preschool. During the hour-and-fifteen-minute classes children engage in gym play; choose activities at creative-play stations (sand table, arts and crafts, puzzles, reading, dress-up, etc.); have a snack; then join in circle time—all the activities you'd typically find in preschool, but here the parents are present. A 19-class session is $418.

chicago museum passports

The Chicago Public Library has a fantastic program where any adult with a valid Chicago library card can check out a Chicago Museum Passport, good for free admission to one of eleven city museums. You can check out one passport per loan period and keep it for one week; passports cannot be renewed or reserved. Keep in mind that each library has a limited number of passports for each of the museums, so it helps if you can be flexible in your plans.

Passports are available for the following museums:

- Adler Planetarium
- The Art Institute of Chicago
- Chicago Children's Museum
- Chicago Historical Society
- DuSable Museum of African American History
- The Field Museum
- The John G. Shedd Aquarium
- Mexican Fine Arts Center Museum
- Museum of Contemporary Art
- Museum of Science and Industry
- Peggy Notebaert Nature Museum

In addition, the Museum Campus Passport will gain you admission to all three museums on the campus: Adler Planetarium, the Field Museum, and Shedd Aquarium.

See page 110 for information on early-childhood programs at area museums.

public libraries

chicago public library

www.chipublib.org/cpl.html
With seventy-five branches throughout the city, the Chicago Public Library has a location in your neighborhood. You can find the one nearest you, as well as its hours and special services, by visiting the Web site.

Central location:

- *Harold Washington Library Center/ Thomas Hughes Children's Library*
  400 S. State St.
  773-LIBRARY (main number)
  312-747-4200 (registration)
  The Thomas Hughes Children's Library at the Harold Washington Library Center hosts a half-hour lapsit storytime series where parents and babies 6 to 23 months share books, fingerplay, and songs. Registration is required, and the series tends to fill up early. The children's library also hosts a wealth of other family-oriented activities throughout the year, including puppet shows, musical performances, video nights, arts and crafts, author appearances, and more. Check the Web site for a complete listing.

Regional branches:

❋ *Sulzer Regional Library*
4455 N. Lincoln Ave.
312-744-7616
Sulzer offers preschool storytimes, as well as various family activities. Some events are drop-in, but most require registration.

❋ *Woodson Regional Library*
9525 S. Halsted St.
312-747-6900
Woodson offers preschool storytimes, as well as various family activities. Some events are drop-in, but most require registration.

parks and playgrounds

Chicago's parks and playgrounds provide just about every activity you can think of. The park is a great place for your baby or toddler to explore, swing, slide, and climb, and for you to meet other parents with children close in age to yours. And when the weather's nice, you'll love going out, enjoying a change of scenery, and taking in some fresh air.

With 552 parks—not to mention beaches, lagoons, nature preserves, and more—the Chicago Park District is the largest park system in the nation. No matter where you live, there is most definitely a park, or at least a tot lot, within walking distance. In recent years the park district has been in the midst of a major renovation project, and many city parks now have special age-appropriate areas (making it

easier to watch your little ones) and spray parks with soft rubber mat surfaces and water sprayers.

To get the lowdown on great parks for babies to preschoolers, I talked to parents, as well as park district employees, from all over the city for their recommendations. Here are some of the best parks to take your kids.

north

❋ *Adams Park*
(1919 N. Seminary Ave.)
Adams is a clean, big park with a popular sprayer park and sliding tube. One mom says she would rather go there than to the pool any day.

❋ *Albion Play Lot*
(1754 W. Albion Ave.)
This park is small but sweet. Shady, quiet, and rarely busy, this is a good alternative to Loyola Park when it's overrun with day camps and older kids.

❋ *Fellger Park*
(2000 W. Belmont)
This fenced-in park keeps the kids contained, making it so much easier to keep an eye on toddlers. Fellger has two age-appropriate play areas, and a water play area right next to a grassy spread, so you can sit under a tree and still keep an eye on the kids if you don't feel like getting wet yourself. It's also a good spot for a picnic.

❄ Indian Boundary Park

(2500 W. Lunt)

A gem of the Northwest Side, this is a thriving park that features one of the best playgrounds in the city, with a castle structure, a boat and train, bars to hang on, three slides, a sandpit, and swings. You also can feed the ducks at the lagoon; visit the small zoo with Beth the cow, a llama, goats, deer, and sheep; play in the water at the spray park; then take a break with a treat from one of the popsicle vendors.

❄ Lincoln Park

Without question the city's most famous green space, Lincoln Park extends five miles along the lakefront, from Oak Street Beach on the south end to Foster Avenue Beach on the north. Lincoln Park boasts the nation's oldest, free public zoo (Lincoln Park Zoo), the world-renowned Lincoln Park Conservatory, lakefront bike and walking paths, paddle boats on South Pond (at Stockton and Armitage), and literally miles of open space for running, picnicking, and relaxing. For many residents, knowing that the expanse and lake views of Lincoln Park are practically out their back door is what makes the urban jungle of Chicago inhabitable.

❄ Loyola Park

(1230 W. Greenleaf)

Despite being a city with 29 miles of shoreline, Chicago actually has very few playgrounds right on the lake. Loyola is one of the nicest, with a climbing structure, a boat, and big and little slides. Be sure to take your sand toys.

❄ Oz Park

(2021 N. Burling St.)

Named after Wizard of Oz because its author Frank Baum settled in the area in 1891. Oz Park is big and spacious, with lovely landscaping and a huge grassy field where kids can run around and kick a ball, as well as a playground for climbing and swinging. Look for the Tin Man statue, sculpted from old car bumpers.

❄ Portage Park

(4100 N. Long)

There's loads going on at this huge park that is so beautiful that many people hold outdoor weddings here. Features include an Olympic-size pool, a smaller heated pool, an interactive spray park with a slide, tennis courts, two playgrounds, a bike path, a nature walk, baseball and soccer fields, and a cultural arts building.

south

❄ Hale Park

(6258 W. 62nd St.)

Hale has a nice playground for little ones as well as a spray park.

❄ Harold Washington Park

(5200 S. Hyde Park Blvd.)

Named best playground in the city by New City, this park has a spray park, pirate ship, sandbox, swings, and more.

❄ Jackson Park

(6401 S. Stony Island Ave.)

Laid out by the same designers who did New

York's Central Park, Jackson Park's rolling parkland is one of the treasures of the South Side. Its Wooded Island is on the migratory bird flyway and provides ample opportunity to enjoy nature, including the lovely, restful Osaka Garden. A terrific spray park and sports fields give the kids chance to blow off steam.

❋ Promontory Point

(55th Street and the lake)
Accessible from the 55th Street underpass, the point has a large grassy area for picnicking and running around, with beautiful lake views from three directions.

west

❋ Holstein Park

(2200 N. Oakley)
Parents recommend Bucktown's Holstein Park for its great outdoor pool. I was there on a hot Sunday in August, and it wasn't even crowded—and, like other park district pools, it's free.

❋ Walsh Playground Park

(1722 N. Ashland Ave.)
The equipment here is tailored to younger children, and there's a big field for running or playing catch. A paved basketball area is great for riding toys and bikes. And an adjacent, contained dog run keeps the animals off your kids while providing lots of free entertainment.

Ten Things to Do with Your Family on the Weekend

1. Pay a visit to your neighborhood fire station. City moms say they've had great experiences with friendly firefighters showing kids around and letting them sit in the trucks.
2. Use your Chicago library card to check out a pass to visit one of eleven local museums at no cost.
3. Visit the Lincoln Park or Garfield Park conservatories, especially in the winter, when you need to see some green and smell the earth.
4. Shop at a farmers' market during the summer. More than a dozen are held around the city on the weekends.
5. Hook up the Burley or bike seat and take a bike ride along the lakefront.
6. Hop on the Blue Line and ride the train out to O'Hare Airport. Choose a seat at the front of the first car so the kids can get a good view.
7. Feed the ducks and geese at the lagoon by the Lincoln Park Zoo; they're there in the winter, too.
8. Invite some other families to a potluck picnic in a nearby park.
9. Form a dads' playgroup. The fathers get to bond with other dads and children, and you get some much-needed time off.
10. Visit one of the more than three dozen Chicago Park District facilities with indoor pools for a family swim.

Chapter Six

activities
for preschoolers

Preschoolers are tremendously curious about the world and have a great capacity for learning. Today many children ages three to five are enrolled in programs designed to expand creativity, enhance social skills, and improve fitness. They might take violin lessons, attempt computer games, or plunge into the muddy delights of clay. Many preschoolers enjoy tumbling or the challenge of martial arts classes, while others study languages, take ballet, and learn to swim.

Never before have there been so many choices for your child. But a word of caution: Beware of overscheduling. Every city baby, no matter how bright, needs free time to play with friends or simply to be alone.

choosing a program

The hardest part of choosing a program is determining the best, most wonderful activity for your child when there are so many great options available. It's easy to become overzealous in your approach to your child's happiness and wellbeing, but you have to keep your perspective. Remember to be light-hearted about your child's free time. You're not sending him off to become a neurosurgeon or a master violinist, but rather, you're exposing him to activities that may or may not become large parts of his life. Finding a program ultimately should be a child-directed process. Ideally, you want your child to experiment and learn, and have a great time, too!

Most classes are offered once a week on a yearlong, semester-long, or per-class basis. A more intensive class, like a violin class, might meet twice a week. Some kids may enjoy taking up to three or four classes per week, but don't push; you don't want to force anything, or you'll end up making a chore out of what should be a fun, passion-driven experience. In this chapter you'll find classes in art, dance, music, and theater, as well as a number of sports and personal enrichment programs.

Whatever you choose, be sure to take convenience into account. Particularly if you don't have a car, try to choose classes within ten blocks of your home.

Here are a few more things to think about when choosing a class or program:

❋ How long has the school/gym/academy been in business?

❋ How large are classes?

❋ How many teachers/coaches are there?

❋ Must you commit to a full year, by the semester, or by the class?

To make the process as easy as possible for you, I've listed classes by subject. Be sure to check out each program carefully yourself. Notice how the class is structured, and how the teachers interact with the children. Time and day can be important factors, too. My four-year-old daughter's generally ready for anything on Mondays, but after a busy week of preschool, a couple of play dates, some errands, and maybe a trip to the zoo or library, by Friday afternoon she's not in the mood for much besides PBS Kids.

one-stop shopping: after-school institutions

❋ Chicago Park District

312-742-PLAY

www.chicagoparkdistrict.com

Ages: All

With 552 parks—not to mention beaches, lagoons, conservatories, and wildlife gardens—Chicago has the largest park system of any city in the country. The array of programs offered at Chicago parks is staggering: Search the district's Web site for preschool classes alone, and you'll get more than 850 listings. Young children can take acting, arts and crafts, ballet, basketball, ceramics, computers, cooking, floor hockey, gymnastics, ice hockey, ice skating, indoor and outdoor soccer, indoor and outdoor tennis, swim lessons, music and movement, family swim, percussion, piano, play group, preschool, reading, tumbling, self-defense (yes, you read that correctly), story telling, tap, tennis, violin, voice, woodcraft, and yoga.

The park district no longer mails out catalogs to all residents, so to see what programs are offered at a park near you, you can search class listings at the park district's Web site using various criteria, such as specific park, ZIP code, or type of facility. If you aren't sure which parks are closest to you, call 312-742-PLAY and an operator can give you that information based on your address. In my experience, the quality of classes can really vary from park to park and depends a lot on the facility and the enthusiasm of the staff. If you're unhappy with a class at one park, it may pay to try the same class at another location.

❋ Jewish Community Centers of Chicago

Several locations:

Florence G. Heller JCC, 524 W. Melrose Place; 773-871-6780

Bernard Horwich JCC, 3003 W. Touhy; 773-761-9100

Hyde Park JCC, 5200 S. Hyde Park Blvd.; 773-753-3080

Ages: Newborn and up

I have wonderful childhood memories of going to the JCC, where I hung out and played bingo with my friends (and a lot of older women!). The JCC is a great family-oriented center—and you don't have to be Jewish to take classes there. The three JCCs in the city offer a variety of classes for kids ages three to five, including Iddy Biddy Sports, Tumble Tots, Young Artists, Alphabet Soup (a multimedia intro to letter recognition), Petite Chefs, Music Mania, Super Science, Dramarama, and Hola Amigos (introduction to Spanish). Classes vary by location, so check with the one nearest you for specifics. In addition, kids can take swim lessons year-round at Horwich JCC, and during the summer at the Horwich, Heller, and Apachi Chicago at UIC summer day camps. (For information on Apachi day camp, call Heller JCC.)

❋ The Menomonee Club

244 W. Willow St.

312-664-4631

www.menomoneeclub.org

Ages: Junior kindergarten (age 4 by September 1) through grade 6

A North Side institution, the Menomonee Club is a nonprofit organization whose goal is to improve the life of city kids through a program of physical activities, arts classes, and social gatherings. The club's programs vary from season to season. Among the typical offerings for preschoolers are tumbling, introduction to sports, creative movement, tap, jazz dancing, art, cooking, drama, chess, game time, and movie nights. Annual membership is $35 for four-year-olds, and $60 for older children, through grade six. Additional fees for specific classes range from about $70 to $120 for members, more for nonmembers. In keeping with Menomonee's mission to serve all children regardless of economic status, financial assistance is available.

✳ YMCA

Locations throughout city
312-932-1200
www.ymcachgo.org
Ages: All

The YMCAs in Chicago offer a huge variety of early-childhood and family activities, including daycare and preschool, day camp, swim lessons, arts and crafts, soccer, baseball, basketball, gym activities, music, science programs, and outdoor play. Once a month YMCAs throughout the city host Family Night, when facilities and activities are open to the community at no charge. Offerings vary, so call or visit the Web site to see the program listings for specific locations.

The following locations offer activities for children and families:

Austin
501 N. Central Ave.
773-287-9120

Duncan YMCA Chernin Center for the Arts
1001 Roosevelt Road
312-421-7800

Greater Roseland Family
4 E. 111th St.
773-785-9210

High Ridge
2424 W. Touhy Ave.
773-262-8300

Irving Park
4251 W. Irving Park Road
773-777-7500

Lake View
3333 N. Marshfield Ave.
773-248-3333

McCormick Tribune
1834 N. Lawndale Ave.
773-235-2525

New City
1515 N. Halsted St.
312-440-7272

Pilsen
1608 W. 21st Place
312-738-0282

South Chicago
3039 E. 91st St.
773-721-9100

South Side
6330 Stony Island Ave.
773-947-0700

Wabash
3763 S. Wabash
773-285-0020

the arts

multi-arts centers

❉ *Beverly Arts Center*
2407 W. 111th St.
773-445-3838
www.beverlyartcenter.org/index.html
Ages: Birth and up
This vibrant arts center offers a wealth of classes for both children and adults. Among the early-childhood programs are:

  ❉ Creative Movement, for three- to
    five-year-olds

  ❉ Pre-Dance, for five-year-olds with previous
    dance experience

❉ Songbirds, an introductory singing class
  for five- and six-year-olds

❉ Music Together, for parents with children
  from newborn to age five

❉ Keyboard Kapers, an introductory
  keyboard class for five- and six-year-olds

❉ Percussion for Kids, for four- to
  six-year-olds

❉ Family Circle Art, a wide-ranging, hands-
  on program for parents and children ages
  two to three

❉ Budding Artists, for ages three to five

❉ Beginning Drawing, ages five and up

❉ Painter's Studio, ages five and up

Prices vary from about $90 to $180, and session lengths vary too, so call the center for specifics. The new second-floor gallery hosts a rotating series of free contemporary art shows, so stop in and get some culture while your kids are in class. Afterward, the whole family can grab a bite to eat in the center's Café Odyssey, which features a delectable menu of soups, sandwiches, pizzas, and desserts, designed by local food artist Peggy Mikros.

❉ *Old Town School of Folk Music*
4544 N. Lincoln Ave. and 909 W. Armitage Ave.
773-728-6000

www.oldtownschool.org

Ages: 6 months and up

You may know it as the place to take Wiggleworms with your baby or hear a concert with your mate, but Old Town has more to offer, including classes in art, dance, yoga, and acting, as well as private music instruction. Wigglegrads and Little Drummers show children how to have fun playing percussion instruments; Jitterbugs, Kangaroos, and Tap classes teach different forms of dance; and Yoga for Kids encourages kids to do yoga poses that mimic animals. The school also offers frequent musical performances and family events.

art classes

❊ Bubbles Academy

1504 N. Fremont

312-944-7677

www.bubblesacademy.com

Ages: Infant and up

This new art, music, and yoga center for kids offers Brushin' Bubbles, an art class for ages two to seven, and Boogie Bubbles, a movement and music class for children from walking through age five. (Classes generally break down by two-year age increments.) An eight-week session of classes is $140. Parents rave about the beautiful space at Bubbles, where the green carpet merges into the landscape murals on the walls, making you feel as if you're out in nature.

❊ Gymboree Play and Music

3158 N. Lincoln Ave.

773-296-4550

www.playandmusic.com/b2c/customer/home.jsp

Ages: Newborn to 5

At Gymboree's GymARTS II class, 2-1/2- to 5-year-olds paint, make crafts, play dress-up, listen to stories, and engage in movement activities. (GymARTS I is offered for children 18 months to 2-1/2 years.) Art classes are $279 for 12 weeks. Visit the Web site and print out a coupon to take a free introductory course.

❊ Hands On Children's Art Museum

1800 W. 103rd St.

773-233-9933

www.handsonart.org/index.php

Ages: 1-1/2 to 4 years

This relatively new art center in the historic Beverly neighborhood offers Culture Bugs, a class where toddlers and preschoolers can experiment with paint, texture, shape, and color in a creative environment that also includes songs and storytelling. Classes are divided by age into 18 to 30 months and 2-1/2 to 4 years; a six-week session runs $85. In addition, the museum has a wonderful variety of permanent open-art studios, where children can drop in and paint, play with Colorforms material, sculpt with clay, make prints, weave on a loom, put on puppet shows, and dress up.

❊ Hyde Park Art Center

5307 S. Hyde Park Blvd.

773-324-5520

www.hydeparkart.org

Ages: 2 years and up

The Hyde Park Art Center is a nonprofit organization that presents exhibits, mainly by Chicagoland artists, and holds classes for everyone from preschoolers to adults. Multimedia classes for children ages two to five are generally held in the late afternoon and change on a quarterly basis. At the time of this writing, for instance, the center was offering a preschool class called People Pictures, where children use various materials to draw, paint, mold, and construct images of people. The 10-week course is $110 for members and $130 for nonmembers; a one-year family membership is $50 and entitles the holder to a $20 discount on all classes.

Lillstreet Art Center

4401 N. Ravenswood

773-769-4226

www.lillstreet.com/index.html

Ages: 2 years and up

After two decades as a Lincoln Park institution, Lillstreet Art Center last year opened in beautiful, spacious new digs in Ravenswood. At the new center, preschoolers can take a variety of classes, including Toddler Clay (ages 2 to 4, with parent); Clay, Song, and Stories (ages 2-1/2 to 4, with parent); Kinder Clay (ages 4 to 6); Multi-Media Art (ages 3-1/2 to 5); and Hairy Potter (ages 4 to 6), which combines fiber and clay. A ten-week session costs $140 or $150. In addition, families can drop in for a one-hour Toddle-In Saturdays class (ages 2 to 4 with parent) and create works of clay together; cost is $20 for one class, or $150 for a 10-week session.

School of the Art Institute

37 S. Wabash

312-899-5100

www.artic.edu/saic/

Ages: 3 years and up

The Young Artists' Studios offers kids the chance to be creative in an engaging and fun environment. During Open Studio Exploration (ages 3 to 6), children visit work stations that offer various sensory experiences; children with special needs are welcome to attend. In Exploring the Arts, for ages four to five, children create individual and group projects, learn to respect others' creativity, and take trips into the museum for observation assignments. A 14-week class runs $400 ($360 for Art Institute members).

Ukrainian Village Children's Center

918 N. Damen

773-342-7415

http://uvcc.home.mindspring.com/

Ages: 2 years and up

The Ukrainian Village Children's Center is a wonderfully cozy, colorful place where small groups of children create art projects with paint, beads, shells, clay, and other materials. The kids also have free time to play with the center's handmade furniture, including a play kitchen, a dollhouse, and sand and water tables. In addition to weekday classes, a Saturday afternoon drop-in arts class is offered for preschoolers through second graders. Classes are two hours and cost $10; parents of older children may drop them off, while parents of very young children must stay.

dance classes

With several dozen schools of dance throughout Chicago, your child has numerous opportunities to take a class. I recommend asking if you can take a trial class before signing up for a full session, however. As a three-year-old, my daughter was crazy about Angelina Ballerina and couldn't wait to take a ballet class herself. Unfortunately, I signed her up for a three-month program, then had to pull her out after she spent several classes lying on the mat whining for me; she just wasn't ready.

Here's a sampling that includes the more popular schools.

❋ Ballet Chicago

218 S. Wabash
312-251-8838
www.balletchicago.org/index.html
Ages: 3 years and up
Based on the methods of famous choreographer George Balanchine, preparatory division classes at the School of Ballet Chicago lay the foundation for preschoolers to go on to more formal study of ballet. Three- and four-year-olds take Creative Movement I, five-year-olds take Creative Movement II, and six-year-olds are ready for Introduction to Ballet. Classes are $256.50 for a 19-week session. Or, for about $30 more, children can take classes at two satellite centers: Creative Movement at Menomonee Center (940 W. Weed St.) and Pre-Ballet at Alphonsus Academy/Center for the Arts (1439 W. Wellington).

❋ Chicago School of Ballet

2635 W. Grand Ave.
312-243-1160
www.chicagoschoolofballet.com/index.htm
Ages: 4 years and up
The school's Pre-Ballet class uses creative movement to introduce very young children (generally ages four and five) to ballet, while the Pre-Primary class for five- and six-year-olds begins the school's 10-level formal study of ballet, based on the curriculum of London's Royal Academy of Dancing. Pre-Ballet and Pre-Primary are $80 per session.

❋ Hyde Park School of Ballet

5650 S. Woodlawn Ave.
773-493-8498
www.hydeparkschoolofballet.org
Ages: 3 years and up
Three-year-olds begin their study of ballet with the Creative Movement class ($120 for a 20-week session), then move on to Pre-Ballet I ($175), where children ages four and five begin studying specific dance positions and steps. The school recommends that three- and four-year-olds sign up for a single trial class ($15) before committing to a full session. HPSB also offers classes in modern dance, tap, jazz, and flamenco for four- to six-year-olds ($200).

❋ Joel Hall Dance Center

1511 W. Berwyn Ave.
773-293-0900
www.joelhall.org/
Ages: 3 years and up

The largest dance instructional facility in Chicago, Joel Hall Dance Center has worked hard to become a model of cultural diversity, both in its faculty and the students it serves. Three- to five-year-olds can take Creative Movement, then move on to the classes for five and up, including ballet, tap, and creative storytelling. Prices vary from $150 to $687, depending on the number of classes per week; a session is approximately five months long. Children also can take a single Creative Movement class for just $10.

❋ *Trinity Academy of Irish Dance*

2936 N. Southport
773-774-5961, ext. 11
www.trinity-dancers.com/
Ages: 4 years and up
Sparked by the U.S. tour of Riverdance in the 1990s, interest in Irish dancing reached a fever pitch, and it continues to be popular here in Chicago. Trinity Academy's Trinity Tots class introduces four- and five-year-olds to the storytelling, singing, stretching, and drills that lay the foundation for Irish dancing. The Introductory class, for children five to twelve, moves on to specific dances, concentrating on proper positions and movements, as well as stage presence. Classes meet once a week and cost $48 per month for Trinity Tots and $51 per month for the Introductory class. Classes are offered at several locations in northern Chicago and southern Wisconsin, including the Irish Heritage Center (4626 N. Knox) and Alphonsus Academy/Center for the Arts (1439 W. Wellington).

music classes

❋ *Chicago Center for the Performing Arts*

777 N. Green St.
312-327-2000
www.theaterland.com/index.html
Ages: Walking to 5 years
The center's EarlyBirds! class uses music, movement, and hands-on instrument play to teach kids the fundamentals of music. Each 45-minute class begins with a brief period of free play, when children get comfortable by playing with toys or reading books while the teacher plays songs for the class. The more structured portion of the class focuses on 12 songs chosen for the quarter, which are in harmony with the events of that particular season. Cost of a 12-week session is $225 and includes a CD of songs for the class.

❋ *Gymboree Play and Music*

3158 N. Lincoln Ave.; 773-296-4550
www.playandmusic.com/b2c/customer/home.jsp
Ages: Newborn to 5 years
Gymboree's Whole Notes music class is designed for children ages 2-1/2 to five. (Other music classes are offered for younger children; see page 81.) Kids sing, play instruments, chant, and play finger games. Music classes run $195 for 12 weeks. Visit the Web site and print out a coupon to take a free introductory course.

❋ Happy Child Studios

741 Main St. (Evanston)

847-733-9545

www.happychildstudios.com

Ages: Newborn and up

Founded by Julie Frost, award-winning producer of children's music, Happy Child Studios offers a unique variety of fun, creative classes for the entire family. You can take a one-on-one music class with your child, or bring the whole gang to Happy Family Music, which also is offered in Spanish. (Chicago Happy Family Music classes take place at St. Michael's Church, 1744 N. Cleveland.) Happy Child Studios also hosts a variety of concerts and other family events throughout the year, such as a Crayon-a-thon-a-rama, where dozens of kids create a work of art together, and a Winter Holiday Picnic Party, where everyone dresses up in summerwear for an indoor party. Call the studios or visit the Web site for a schedule and prices.

❋ Kindermusik

www.kindermusik.com

Locations in the city:

Portage Park Center for the Arts, 5801 W. Dakin St.; 773-205-0151

Sweet Pea's Studios, 3717 N. Ravenswood; 773-248-YOGA

Ages: Newborn and up

Started in Germany in the 1960s, Kindermusik now has more than 5,000 teachers worldwide. A Kindermusik class will get kids singing, chanting, dancing, and playing simple instruments like rhythm sticks, bells, and drums. The sessions are 45 minutes to an hour long, and children can participate with either a parent or caregiver.

❋ The Suzuki-Orff School for Young Musicians

1148 W. Chicago Ave.

312-738-2646

www.suzukiorff.org/index.html

Ages: 6 months and up

Beginning at age four, the Suzuki-Orff School offers its more formal program of music study. Orff Instruction uses rhythm, movement, and singing to prepare children for the next stage, note reading. Parents attend Orff classes with their children to observe and take notes that will help them further the child's learning at home. After a semester of Orff Instruction, the school recommends adding Suzuki Instruction courses, which focus on learning technique for violin, viola, cello, guitar, flute, or piano. A semester of Orff Instruction costs $198; if, as the school suggests, you add two Suzuki classes—one individual lesson and one group class—the total for three weekly classes is $613 for a 17-week semester.

❋ World Folk Music Company

1808 W. 103rd St.

773-779-7059

www.worldfolkmusiccompany.com

Ages: 6 months and up

Founded by Irish and American folk musician John Devens, the World Folk Music Company offers a multitude of classes and private lessons taught by multi-talented Chicago folk musicians. Preschoolers (ages 4 to 6) can take the Music Class for Young Beginners, which involves drumming and dance, as well as drawing and skits. An eight-week session is $80. In Children's Introduction to Baritone Ukelele, kids get comfortable on an instrument that's just the right size for little hands; all the chords, notes, and songs learned here eventually can be applied to full-size guitar. An eight-week session is $125; in addition, each child must have a ukelele, which can be rented or purchased at the company's shop.

theater

* ### Emerald City Theatre Company
2936 N. Southport Ave.
773-529-2690
www.emeraldcitytheatre.com
Ages: 3 years and up
Emerald City Theatre is known for being Chicago's preeminent theater company dedicated entirely to putting on productions aimed at families. The Theater Fun and Games class brings out the natural thespian in three- to five-year-olds by engaging them in movement, song, and acting. The eight-week class costs $100 and concludes with an informal recital held on the historic Apollo Theater stage. (Classes take place at the Apollo, 2540 N. Lincoln Ave.)

* ### Lookingglass Theatre
2936 N. Southport Ave.
773-477-9257, ext. 193
www.lookingglasstheatre.org/index.html
Ages: 1 year and up
Famous for being the theater company of

"Friends" star David Schwimmer and his Northwestern University pals, Lookingglass offers several fun classes for three- to five-year-olds. Bodies in Motion uses structured games to teach dance skills, Picture This! employs various materials to create costumes and props, Team Players introduces budding actors to the concept of improvisation, and Imaginastics (ages four to five) combines drama and tumbling. Eleven-week sessions cost $130 to $140.

sports

* ### East Bank Club
500 N. Kingsbury
312-527-5801
www.eastbankclub.com
The East Bank Club offers Pee Wee Sports for ages three to five ($10 per class) and Junior Tennis Clinics for ages three to 14. Also, members of the club can take Preschool Tumbling (ages 3 to 5), Little Listeners Book Club (ages 3 to 5), Creativity and Motion (ages 3 to 5), and summer camps (ages 3 to 7).

* ### Galter Life Center
5157 N. Francisco Ave.
773-878-9936
www.galterlifecenter.org
The only hospital-based fitness center in the city, Galter is affiliated with Swedish Covenant Hospital on the Northwest Side. Galter offers swim lessons for children 4 to 11; the cost for

a six-week session is $35 for members and $50 for nonmembers.

❖ Lakeshore Athletic Club

Several locations:

Downtown: 441 N. Wabash; 312-644-4880

Illinois Center: 211 N. Stetson; 312-616-9000

Lincoln Park, 1320 W. Fullerton; 773-477-9888

www.lsac.com

Children's swim lessons are offered for members and non members at the downtown, Illinois Center, and Lincoln Park locations. Lincoln Park also offers lots more kids classes, including Toddler Time (gym class), Short Sports (intro to various sports), tennis, ballet, creative movement, martial arts, tumbling, art, piano, and Spanish.

❖ Lincoln Park Athletic Club

1019 W. Diversey

773-529-2022

www.lpaconline.com

Ages: 4 months and up

Lincoln Park Athletic Club is a full-service club that, in addition to workout facilities and classes, offers fitness testing, personal training, nutrition counseling, massage, and childcare while you exercise. Kids' classes include parent-toddler swim (for members only) swim lessons (starting at 3-1/2 years), yoga, climbing (ages 5 to 9), creative movement, ballet, and karate. Kids' classes are generally members-only, though nonmembers can take swim lessons, creative movement, ballet, and yoga for a higher fee.

❖ Windy City Field House

2367 W. Logan Blvd.

773-486-7300

www.windycityfieldhouse.com

Ages: 3 years and up

With a facility the size of a football field, Windy City Field House has the capacity to offer a multitude of sports classes for both children and adults. Programs for preschoolers include Pee Wee Basketball, Lunch & Play (bring your own lunch and come for an introduction to various sports), Tiny Tots Sports (fundamentals of various sports), Pee-Wee Soccer, Parent/Tot Sports, and Youth Tae Kwon Do. Prices vary by class and length of session but generally run about $175 and up for a 10-week session.

gymnastics

❖ Lakeshore Academy

937 W. Chestnut

312-563-9400

www.lakeshoreacademy.com

Ages: Infant and up

Known as the training ground for some of the top gymnasts in the state, Lakeshore Academy offers a number of gymnastics classes for preschoolers, as well as rock-climbing and karate for slightly older kids. Despite Lakeshore's record of success with team gymnastics, the young children's classes encourage kids to participate in the sport for the sheer joy of it, without necessarily aiming for competition. An eight-week session of classes costs $180 for nonmembers and $135 for members.

The Little Gym of Chicago

3216 N. Lincoln Ave.

773-525-5750

www.tlgchicagoil.com

Ages: 4 months to 12 years

The Little Gym offers a fun, noncompetitive approach to gymnastics for children up to 12 years old. The Pre-School/Kindergarten classes for children ages three to six teach basic gym apparatus skills, tumbling, and group games. For precocious youngsters there are Invitation-Only Team classes, which feature an accelerated curriculum in a team environment. The Little Gym also offers a Sports Skills class, where preschoolers (ages 3 up to 8) can learn the fundamentals of soccer, basketball, football, and volleyball, in combination with gymnastics. Classes are broken down into one-year age spreads, so you don't have three-year-olds and six-year-olds mixed together. Classes are an hour long and cost $300 for a 20-week session.

My Gym Chicago

1880 W. Fullerton Ave.

773-645-9600

www.my-gym.com

Ages: 3 months to 9 years

My Gym offers a series of gymnastics classes on custom-designed equipment that changes every week, just to keep things interesting. Mighty Mites (ages 3-1/2 to 4-1/2) is the first independent class without parents and teaches self-reliance and following directions through relays, games, and specific gymnastics skills. Whiz Kids (ages 4-1/2 to 5-1/2) moves on to more complex gymnastics and emphasizes

group cooperation. Champions (5-1/2 to 7) gets serious about the sport with advanced techniques and tumbling skills. Children can continue their studies here through age 9. The 10-week classes are $160 for children three to 18 months, and $170 for ages 19 months and up. Also, your first class requires a $50 lifetime membership fee.

yoga

Bubbles Academy

1504 N. Fremont

312-944-7677

www.bubblesacademy.com

Ages: Infant and up

Bubbles is a huge space gorgeously painted with landscape murals that make you feel as if you're actually out in nature. The Yogini Bubbles class is offered for children ages crawling through seven; parents must stay with kids through age three or four. (Classes generally break down by two-year age increments.) The focus is on poses that stretch arms and legs; classes end with relaxation time, teaching children how to calm their minds and their bodies. Classes are $140 for an eight-week session.

Enso Yoga & Martial Arts Studio

1329 S. Michigan Ave.

312-427-3676

www.ensostudio.com

Ages: 3 years and up

Enso's Radiant Child Yoga classes are offered for kids 4 to 12 years old; children's classes are generally divided by two-year increments (for instance, ages 4 to 6). Enso also offers Kinder Karate for 3- to 5-year-olds, which focuses on running, balancing, and jumping, as well as the basics of karate. Bodies in Motion is the studio's summer day camp program for kids 5 to 12, and exposes participants to martial arts, tumbling, dance, and yoga. Karate and yoga classes are $50 per month for once-a-week classes, plus a one-time registration fee of $25. One week of day camp is $150 (three hours each day), or sign up for two weeks for $275.

❊ Happy Child Studios

741 Main St. (Evanston)
847-733-9545
www.happychildstudios.com
Ages: Newborn and up

One of the main reasons the studio was founded was to teach kids' yoga, and Julie Frost does it with unique style, incorporating music with yoga poses. Yoga La-La is offered for three- to six-year-olds and costs $106 for an eight-week session. Happy Family Yoga costs $120 for one child and one adult together, up to $200 for three children and one adult. Drop-ins are welcome, but you need to call ahead.

❊ Satchidananda Yoga Center

1521 Chicago Ave. (Evanston)
888-900-YOGA
www.specialyoga.com
Ages: 3 years and up

In addition to offering kids' classes, Satchidananda Yoga Center is home to Yoga for the Special Child, a unique program for children with special needs, including Down's syndrome, cerebral palsy, microcephaly, autism, and attention deficit disorder. Regular Hatha Yoga classes are offered for children from ages 3 and up. Single classes are $15; multi-class packages range from $65 for five classes to $225 for 20 classes. If your child has special needs, he or she needs to be evaluated before signing up for a Yoga for the Special Child class, which costs $50 for a half-hour session.

❊ Yoga Bound

1753 N. Damen
773-395-2929
www.yogaboundchicago.com/default.asp
Ages: 3 years and up

Yoga for Kids, ages three to six, introduces kids to various yoga concepts, interspersed with activities—running like butterflies, for instance—geared to their short attention spans. Single classes are $15, a five-class pass is $65, and a 10-class pass is $120.

language classes

❊ Language Stars

1777 N. Clybourn
312-587-8795
www.languagestars.com/index.html
Ages: 12 months to 10 years

As with its parent-child classes (see page 89), Language Stars offers older children classes based on the FunImmersion technique, taught by native speakers of each language. Classes use movement, songs, puppet shows, arts and crafts, cooking, and other fun activities to teach kids Spanish, French, German, and Italian. A 20-week session runs $570 for once a week, and $995 for twice a week for classes that run one-and-a-quarter hours. Longer classes also are available, as well as a summer camp.

nature classes

✳ Garfield Park Conservatory
300 N. Central Park Ave.
312-746-5100
www.garfield-conservatory.org/gpca_visitor.htm
Ages: All

Thousands of people discovered this city gem in 2002, thanks to the fantastic Chihuly glass-art exhibit, and it is most definitely worth a trek to the west side. The plant rooms are enormous and lush. I especially love taking Clare there in the winter, when we're desperate to see some green and breathe in the scent of soil.

To be perfectly honest, the conservatory's Elizabeth Morse Genius Children's Garden could be a lot more compelling; there's one rather lame sculpture of a sprouting seed, a slide, and a tiny toddler play corral. However, the Children's Activity Hour offered every Saturday from 1 to 2 p.m. can be a lot of fun. Geared for children ages four and up, the structured activities include plantings, story-telling, arts and crafts, and music, all with a plant-based theme. And from noon to 3 p.m. on Saturdays and Sundays, the Discovery Area is open so children can explore the soil table, sensory cart, insect puzzles, and more. The conservatory is open 365 days a year; admission and the activity hour are free.

✳ North Park Village Nature Center
5801 N. Pulaski Road
312-744-5472
www.ci.chi.il.us/Environment/NaturalResources/NorthParkVillage.html

My family and I recently discovered the nature center on the recommendation of a friend, and we're so glad we did. Easy walking trails criss-cross the 46 acres of woodlands, wetlands, prairie, and savanna; take a hike, look for wildlife, and you'll soon forget you're smack in the middle of an urban area.

A variety of classes are offered throughout the year for children ages three to six, accompanied by a parent; recent programs have included How to Succeed as a Seed, Snow and Tell (outdoor winter games), and Flickers, Sapsuckers, and Other Woodpeckers. The center also offers family programs throughout the year, including the Harvest Festival in October, the Maple Syrup Festival in March, and periodic storytelling festivals. Festivals are free; call the center or visit its Web site for class times and prices.

public libraries

chicago public library

www.chipublib.org/cpl.html
With 75 branches throughout the city, the Chicago Public Library has a location in your neighborhood. You can find the one nearest you, as well as its hours and special services, by visiting the Web site above.

Central location:

❋ Harold Washington Library Center/ Thomas Hughes Children's Library

400 S. State St.
773-LIBRARY (main number)
312-747-4200 (registration)
The Thomas Hughes Children's Library at the Harold Washington Library Center frequently hosts storytimes for preschoolers, as well as a wealth of other family-oriented activities throughout the year, including puppet shows, musical performances, video nights, arts and crafts, author appearances, and more. Check the Web site for a complete listing.

Regional branches:

❋ Sulzer Regional Library

4455 N. Lincoln Ave.
312-744-7616
Sulzer offers preschool storytimes, as well as various family activities. Some events are drop-in, but most require registration.

❋ Woodson Regional Library

9525 S. Halsted St.
312-747-6900
Woodson offers preschool storytimes, as well as various family activities. Some events are drop-in, but most require registration.

museum programs

The Chicago Public Library has a fantastic program where any adult with a valid Chicago library card can check out a Chicago Museum Passport, good for free admission to one of eleven city museums. See page 90 for more information.

❋ Adler Planetarium

1300 S. Lake Shore Drive
312-922-STAR
www.adlerplanetarium.org
Ages: All
Get a different perspective when you explore the planetarium at night on Far Out Fridays, held from 5 to 10 p.m. the first Friday of every month. With an emphasis on family activities, Far Out Fridays include telescope viewing, shows in the Sky and StarRider theaters, talks by Adler astronomers, special demonstrations, and Doane Observatory tours. Cost is $15 for adults and $12 for children over four, or $45 for a family of four.

❋ The Art Institute of Chicago

111 S. Michigan Ave.
312-443-3600
www.artic.edu/aic/visitor_info/index.html
Ages: All
The Kraft Education Center, on the lower level

of the Art Institute, is a wonderful, hands-on space where kids and their parents can explore the arts together. The center regularly hosts family drop-in programs that are free with your paid admission (which is voluntary). Recent programs for four- to six-year-olds have included Bon Voyage! Journeys by Sea, a multimedia class focused on making nautical-themed projects; Gifts in Art, where participants made decorative paperweights; and Art Goes Pop, which involved a visit to the galleries to see works from the 1960s, followed by time to create a multimedia work of Pop art. The center also puts on a variety of all-ages family festivals throughout the year.

❋ Chicago Children's Museum

700 E. Grand Ave. at Navy Pier
312-527-1000
www.chichildrensmuseum.org/index.cfm
Ages: All
The Chicago Children's Museum offers a wide and ever-changing variety of activities for young children. The Art Studio offers a schedule of workshops for ages four and up. Past offerings have included Alphabet Art, Papermaking, and Native American Arts & Crafts. To attend one of the free-with-admission studio workshops, you need only pick up a studio pass an hour before the program's start time. The museum also features other early-childhood activities virtually every day. Selections might include Kids of All Colors, a celebration of diversity; Movers & Shakers, a creative movement class for ages three and up; and Super Sprouts, an all-ages weekly drop-in program with various multi-sen-

sory activities. During Kraft Family Free night, Thursdays from 5 to 8 p.m., there is no admission charge, and family-friendly activities are always offered. Check the museum's Web site for a complete listing of activities.

❋ DuSable Museum of African American History

740 E. 56th Place
773-947-0600
www.dusablemuseum.org
Ages: Preschool and up
The museum periodically offers onetime programs appropriate for preschoolers. Offerings have included Babies of the Blues, a hands-on musical workshop on the blues; a performance of African folktales; and Wild about Learning, an introduction to the alphabet using jungle animal puppets. Call the museum or visit its Web site for current offerings.

❋ The Field Museum

1400 S. Lake Shore Drive
312-665-7400 (public programs)
www.fieldmuseum.org
Ages: Preschool and up
On Saturdays and Sundays at 1:30 p.m., visit the Mammals of Asia exhibit where preschoolers and their families can hear a story, sing songs, and make a project—all in 20 minutes. The Field Museum also offers an ongoing program of family-oriented events, some of them appealing to children as young as four. Call the museum or visit its Web site for a current schedule.

❋ Museum of Science and Industry

57th Street and Lake Shore Drive
773-684-1414
www.msichicago.org
Ages: Infant and up

Though it isn't a structured program, so many of my sources mentioned how much their kids love the Museum of Science and Industry's Idea Factory that I've included it here. The centerpiece of the museum's Imagination Station, The Idea Factory is aimed at infants to 10-year-olds and is a learning-through-play exhibit that gives young children the chance to explore scientific principles through hands-on activities. Using just four basic objects—a cube, sphere, tetrahedron, and cylinder—children can experiment with construction, light, color, magnetism, balance, air, and water. Especially popular is the electromagnetic construction crane that kids can use to retrieve and move objects.

❋ Peggy Notebaert Nature Museum

2430 N. Cannon Drive
773-755-5100
www.chias.org
Ages: 3 to 7 years

On Tuesday afternoons, from 2:30 to 3:30 p.m., the Nature Museum hosts classes for caregivers and children ages three to seven. Recently, for instance, a series of classes focused on the places that different animals call home. The classes are free, but pre-registration is required (773-755-5111, ext. 6). In addition, museum educators also periodically teach workshops for classes of preschoolers and kindergarteners; check the Web site for current listings.

❋ Shedd Aquarium

1200 S. Lake Shore Drive
312-939-2438
www.sheddaquarium.org
Ages: Preschool and up

Each week Shedd offers Tots on Tuesdays, an all-day program of story times, crafts, animal touch programs, videos, costumed characters, dancing and singing, all based on a theme that changes every eight weeks. Activities are designed for children ages three to five; check the listing in the main foyer to find activity locations.

Shedd also offers an ongoing series of classes geared for preschoolers and their caregivers. Recent classes have included Swimming for Supper, where kids figure out whether sea animals are chompers, slurpers, or gulpers; Neighboring Nurseries, an exploration of how coral reefs provide safe haven for baby sea creatures; and From Puddles to Ponds, a close-up look at the creatures in the Shedd's pond. A one-hour-fifteen-minute class costs $20 for one child and parent.

concerts and shows

❋ Puppet Parlor

1922 W. Montose
773-774-2919
Ages: All

The Puppet Parlor puts on full-length feature productions, as well as highlights from operas, for kids and adults.

Rhythm Revolution Chicago Drumming Circle

Green Briar Park, 2650 W. Peterson
312-742-7888
www.drummingcircle.com
Ages: All

If you're up for a noisy good time, drop by Green Briar Park on Friday nights, where John Yost, a Chicago Park District music instructor, leads a drum circle for everyone from babies to old pros. Bring a drum, or borrow one of Yost's few loaners, then drum, dance, meditate, or just watch. The drum circle is from 7:30 to 9:45 p.m., year round; in the winter it moves to the park fieldhouse.

The following theater companies put on performances for children and families:

Chicago Kids Company

Puts on plays at four area locations
773-205-9600
www.chicagokidscompany.com

Chicago Playworks

Performs at DePaul University's Merle Reskin Theater
60 W. Balbo Drive
312-922-1999
http://theatreschool.depaul.edu/perform/play works.php3

Emerald City Theatre Company

2936 N. Southport Ave.
773-529-2690
www.emeraldcitytheatre.com

Lifeline Theatre

6912 N. Glenwood Ave.
773-761-4477
www.lifelinetheatre.com

Raven Theatre Company

6157 N. Clark St.
773-338-2177
www.raventheatre.com/index.htm

kid-friendly
restaurants

Yes, dining out with your new baby or toddler actually can be an enjoyable experience; you just have to remember that the choice of restaurant is critical and must meet your needs. They are as follows:

❋ When your child is still an infant, under one year, you want a restaurant that provides stroller or carriage space and a staff that doesn't mind babies.

❋ When your child is a toddler, an understanding staff is even more important since your youngster may knock over a glass of water, rip up the sugar packets, or throw silverware on the floor. Also, the restaurant should provide adequate booster seats and quick service so you can be in and out of the restaurant in an hour.

Certainly, if you have favorite neighborhood spots with food you already love, you can always look around to see if children are dining there and whether there is adequate space next to tables for a stroller holding a sleeping infant.

But what do you do when you are in an unfamiliar neighborhood? Look for kid-friendly clues: paper rather than cloth table covering, crayons, children's menus, booster seats, highchairs, and interesting sights such as fish tanks, rock pools, gardens, shopping areas, and the like. Chicago's ethnic restaurants can be wonderful for children. The owners often like kids, waiters will bring them something to eat right away, and these places can be quite flexible about menu offerings. Coffee shops are good, too, but not necessarily during a frantic lunch hour.

But what about the food? I'm not a restaurant critic, but my friends and I do know what we like where family dining is concerned. Good food for everyone is integral to the dining experience. Out of two zillion options for you to dine en famille, I'm including personal favorites as well as those recommended by other city parents. I've tried to go beyond the places you probably already know about to include good ethnic restaurants and other places off the beaten path.

Before you go out, consider your child's ability to sit still and eat in a somewhat mannerly fashion. And if she's having a tired or cranky day, forget it. Some days it's just better to stay home and order in.

north

❋ *Arya Bhavan*
2508 W. Devon
773-274-5800
In the heart of Chicago's Indian neighborhood, Arya Bhavan serves vegetarian North and South Indian cuisine, making it a good choice if some members of the family prefer spicy Indian food (Southern) and others don't (Northern). Arya Bhavan wins points for its friendly and laid-back service, fresh and inexpensive food, and a buffet said by some to be the best of its kind in the city.

❋ *Boxcar Café*
723 W. Wrightwood
773-325-9560
www.boxcarcafe.net
Kids love this cute café where toy trains deliver your order to your table. The Caboose Menu for kids features really cheap hot dogs, cheeseburgers, and sandwiches. Other offerings

include soups, salads, paninis, smoothies and milkshakes, ice cream, and coffee beverages.

❋ Calliope Café

2826 N. Lincoln Ave.

773-528-8055

On those cranky days when you just can't deal with cooking, a visit to the riotously colorful Calliope Café just might cheer everyone up. The very reasonably priced menu changes often and features an array of fresh-made soups, salads, and sandwiches, many with decidedly upscale or unusual ingredients, such as grilled salmon or dandelion greens. The luscious desserts will keep the kids happy.

❋ Costello Sandwich & Sides

2015 W. Roscoe St.

773-929-2323

This neighborhood sandwich shop is very veg-friendly and in warm weather is an especially nice place to visit for its outdoor patio and sidewalk café.

❋ Czerwone Jabluszko (Red Apple Restaurant)

3121 N. Milwaukee Ave., 773-588-5781

6474 N. Milwaukee Ave., 773-763-3407

Buffets tend to be good options with kids, and this is one of the most impressive in the city. The three dozen or so dishes comprise mainly Polish fare and include kid-pleasers like potato pancakes, cheese blintzes, pierogi, carrot-raisin salad, Jell-o, and apple fritters. Prices are cheap, and kids' meals are discounted according to their age.

❋ Ethiopian Diamond

6120 N. Broadway

773-338-6100

My friend Judy loves to take her kids here because the staff is "super-friendly"—they offer children free juice, and they don't mind restless kids running around the spacious restaurant. Ethiopian food can be a fun experience for kids because you're actually supposed to eat with your fingers, scooping up various stews—meats, lentils, vegetables—with the spongy, pancake-like bread called injera. The prices are reasonable, the paintings tracing Ethiopia's history create a nice atmosphere, and some foodies swear it's the best Ethiopian food in the city.

❋ Goose Island Brewpub

1800 N. Clybourn Ave.

312-915-0071

A brewpub may not seem like the place to take the kids, but according to Chicago magazine, Goose Island is the best restaurant in the city for a family lunch. It wins points for the free box of crayons given to every kid and a children's menu with favorites like macaroni and cheese and chicken fingers. Meanwhile, grown-ups can enjoy a variety of burgers and sandwiches along with more than a dozen house brews.

❋ Gulliver's

2727 W. Howard St.

773-338-2166

There are, of course, hundreds of pizza places in the city, but Gulliver's has been famous for serving a delicious, garlicky pie since the mid-

1960s, and on weekend nights you'll find a microcosm of Chicago lining up to eat at this Rogers Park joint. The decor is a lot more interesting than other family-friendly pizza places too, with stained glass, antiques, statues, and collectibles filling the three dining rooms. Definitely worth a trip.

❊ Heartland Café

7000 N. Glenwood

773-465-8005

Activist and owner Michael James has been keeping the spirit of the '60s alive at the Heartland Café since its founding in 1976. The food at this neighborhood hangout is hearty and wholesome, with many, many vegetarian dishes, but also meat dishes like Tamari-Maple Chicken, a buffalo-meat burger, and Panfried Catfish. We love to take Clare here for a hearty weekend breakfast, but I'll be honest: My dad wasn't crazy about the place, given that it's a bit worn about the edges, and definitely draws a funky, urban clientele (lots of piercings).

❊ O'Famé

750 W. Webster Ave.

773-929-5111

If you're in the mood for some adult food and a nice glass of wine but don't have a baby-sitter, take the kids along to O'Famé. Known for its delicious pizza, this Lincoln Park eatery also features a large menu of Italian pastas and entrees, as well as an excellent wine selection. The decor is pleasant, with candlelit tables and exposed-brick walls, and the staff is very friendly toward children.

❊ R.J. Grunts

2056 N. Lincoln Park West

773-929-5363

The restaurant that launched Rich Melman's Lettuce Entertain You empire, R.J. Grunts features music and a decor reminiscent of the '60s and '70s: lots of plants, stucco walls, and wooden booths. The menu is a kid-pleaser, with 13 kinds of burgers, lots of chicken, nachos, sandwiches, and giant shakes and malts. R.J. Grunts was one of the first restaurants in town to have a salad bar of any note, and it's still distinctive, with more than 50 items to choose from.

❊ Sunshine Café

5449 N. Clark St.

773-334-6214

This way-cheap, homey Japanese restaurant is one of my friend Patti's favorite places to take her kids. You'll find all kinds of noodle dishes—generally a hit, even with picky eaters—as well as meat and seafood entrees. The decor is nothing special, but the staff is very friendly and accommodating to families.

downtown

To me, what makes Chicago great is its distinctive neighborhoods, and when we eat out, I find that the most interesting places are off the beaten path, generally in an area known for a particular ethnicity. But I'd be remiss if I didn't include downtown restaurants that cater to families. Just know that during the summer and on many weekends these places tend to be mobbed with out-of-towners. That doesn't mean they're not worth a visit—Ed Debevic's can be especially fun with kids, thanks to the '50s-style diner menu and sassy waitstaff—but you might want to go at an off time to avoid the crowds.

❈ Dick's Last Resort

North Pier, 435 E. Illinois
312-836-7870
A wacky, boisterous place where you can order things like chicken and ribs by the bucket—literally.

❈ Ed Debevic's

640 N. Wells St.
312-664-1707
1950s-style diner with purposely smart-mouthed waiters.

❈ foodlife

Water Tower Place
835 N. Michigan Ave.
312-335-3663
An unusual, upscale food court notable for an emphasis on healthful menu options.

❈ Hard Rock Café

63 W. Ontario
312-943-2252
Good old American fare and a mind-boggling array of rock memorabilia.

❈ Johnny Rockets

901 N. Rush St.
312-337-3900
Also locations at Northbrook Court and Old Orchard Shopping Center
1950s-style diner.

❈ Rainforest Café

605 N. Clark St.
312-787-1501
Also locations at Woodfield Shopping Center and Gurnee Mills
Jungle plants, waterfalls, a starry sky, simulated thunderstorms, saltwater aquariums, and more provide so much entertainment the extensive menu is almost secondary.

west

❈ Amarind's Thai Restaurant

6822 W. North Ave.
773-889-9999
Owned by a former chef at the upscale Arun's, Amarind's features truly outstanding and elegantly prepared Thai food at surprisingly cheap prices: Most entrees are less than $10. You can get all the Thai standards here (pad thai, curries, nourishing soups), but the attention to preparation and presentation set it apart from other Thai restaurants. The chive dumplings with dipping sauce are one of my favorites and a good bet for kids, too, at least those who will eat something with a bit of green in it.

❈ The Flat Top Grill

1000 W. Washington Blvd.
312-829-4800
Also:
319 W. North Ave.; 312-787-7676
3200 N. Southport Ave.; 773-665-8100
Also locations in Evanston and Oak Park
You can order off the menu if you want, but the main draw at Flat Top Grill is the do-it-yourself

stir-fry bar. You visit a buffet with more than 70 ingredients (meats, seafood, tofu, vegetables, rice and noodles, special sauces), load up your bowl with whatever you like, then hand it off to be prepared to order, whether as a stir-fry or a soup. This is great option for picky kids who like to choose their own food. Even better is that there's no charge for children four and under.

Flo

1434 W. Chicago Ave.

312-243-0477

This charming, cozy neighborhood spot makes a terrific breakfast and draws quite the crowd, so it's best to get there early—not a problem if your toddler's been up since the crack of dawn. The offerings emphasize fresh ingredients, and many dishes have a Southwestern flair. Lunches are good, too, and feature creative soups, sandwiches, and salads. Flo is not open for dinner.

Irazu

1865 N. Milwaukee Ave.

773-252-5687

One of the few restaurants in the city serving real Costa Rican food, family-owned Irazu is off the beaten path and draws a crowd that ranges from hipsters in black to older Latino couples. This is a no-frills place where you order at the counter, but customers rave about the food, especially the burritos. Portions are big and inexpensive, and the menu is vegetarian friendly. While grown-ups try more adventurous fare, kids can enjoy hamburgers, the addictive plantain chips, and more than a dozen varieties of the milkshakes for which Irazu is famous. Be forewarned: The restaurant is small and often crowded, so you may have to experiment to find a time when you won't end up waiting.

Margie's Candies

1960 N. Western Ave.

773-384-1035

Sure, you could take the kids here for a burger, but the real reason to go to Margie's is for the legendary ice cream sundaes, as well as hand-dipped chocolate candies. Established in 1921, Margie's is still an old-fashioned ice cream parlor where you can get enormous hand-dipped ice cream drinks and sundaes that come with a pitcher of sauce on the side. If you're with a large group, try what's billed as the world's largest sundae, made with a half-gallon of ice cream. Who needs dinner?

Silver Cloud Bar & Grill

1700 N. Damen Ave.

773-489-6212

When you're in the mood for comfort food, check out Bucktown's Silver Cloud, where the menu includes childhood favorites like meatloaf, pot roast, and chicken potpie. Selected by Chicago Tribune readers as one of the top five outdoor dining spots in the city, Silver Cloud also wins points for its charming decor, fast service, and clean bathrooms. And kids love that the dessert options include some of their favorites: s'mores, root-beer floats, and sundaes with Hershey's syrup.

Sweet Maple Café

1339 W. Taylor St.

312-243-8908

This homey neighborhood restaurant, near the University of Illinois campus, serves home-cooked breakfasts and lunches like your grandma would make. In addition to generous portions of pancakes and waffles, egg dishes, hash, and meats, you can get Southern favorites like grits and biscuits and gravy. This is a great place to take the family but it gets packed on the weekends. Go early if you don't want to wait.

Wishbone

1001 W. Washington Blvd.; 312-850-2663

3300 N. Lincoln Ave.; 773-549-2663

Nationally known for its "Southern reconstruction cooking," Wishbone specializes in comfort food made with fresh ingredients in plentiful portions. The weekend brunch is especially popular and features dishes like Crawfish Cakes, Andouille Hash, Shrimp and Grits, and—my favorite—Corn Cakes, served with a sweet red pepper sauce. Kids love the pancake-and-egg dishes, and the yummy corn muffins that come with everything. All the menus (breakfast, lunch, dinner) are very vegetarian-friendly, which isn't always the case with most Southern joints. Wishbone gets packed on the weekend, so be prepared to wait. Dinner at the Lincoln Avenue location may be an easier option, and you'll be surrounded by other families from Lakeview and Roscoe Village.

south

BJ's Market

8734 S. Stony Island Ave.

773-374-4700

One reviewer says that eating at BJ's is like having Thanksgiving dinner. The emphasis is on comfort foods in the soul genre, like mustard-blackened catfish, red beans and rice, and peach cobbler. The atmosphere is pleasant and family-friendly, the prices are reasonable, and service is fast.

Manny's Coffee Shop & Deli

1141 S. Jefferson St.

312-939-2855

As a child during the '70s, my husband spent many a Saturday hanging out at Manny's with his family, and it's still a classic Chicago place to take the kids. Mingle with cops, firefighters, and aldermen while you enjoy Manny's legendary corned beef, potato pancakes, chicken noodle soup, and other Jewish deli food. The crowd is noisy, the portions are huge, and even the pickiest eater will find something to enjoy here.

Mellow Yellow Restaurant

1508 E. 53rd St.

773-667-2000

This Hyde Park restaurant is a kid-friendly place to visit before or after a trip to the Museum of Science and Industry. The menu features award-winning chili, crepes, soups, sandwiches, burgers, and salads. The big dish here is rotisserie chicken, a flavorful, juicy portion big enough to share with the kids so everyone still has room for a milkshake or a slice of one of the cakes or pies spinning in the dessert case.

Soul Vegetarian East

205 E. 75th St.

773-224-0104

I love this family-friendly place where you can get delicious soul food made entirely without meat—a real rarity. Many dishes are based on seitan (also known as wheat gluten) and include burgers, BBQ, and chili, as well as greens, sweet potatoes, cornbread, and other traditionally southern dishes. I once had vegan macaroni and cheese here that I couldn't believe was made without any dairy products; it was creamy and delicious. Be warned that service can be rather lax—don't go when you're in a hurry to get in and out.

Top Notch Beefburgers

2116 W. 95th St.

773-445-7218

An institution in the Beverly neighborhood for 40 years, this is a beloved place that many displaced South Siders make a point of visiting whenever they're in the area. The ultra-juicy burgers are made from round steak ground fresh each day, and many sources say they're best in the city. Kids like the free crayons and dinosaur placemats, as well as the shakes and fries.

other

Leona's

Six North/West Side locations

Three South Side locations

Eight suburban locations

No matter where you live, there's a Leona's near you. Leona's claim to fame is its pizza, but the burgers, chicken, and sandwiches are good too. Warm bread with pizza sauce and a coloring book and crayons keep the kids busy while they wait for their food, and some locations have rooms where kids can play or even watch a movie after dinner.

Potbelly Sandwich Works

Twenty-nine locations across Chicago

I remember discovering Potbelly when I was new to Chicago in the '80s. Back then the only location was on Lincoln Avenue, and I loved the place for its toasty sandwiches and cozy, antique-filled charm. Those elements are still integral to Potbelly's appeal, but now you'll also hear live local musicians at the 15 locations all over the North Side (and one in Midway Airport), and 14 more throughout the suburbs. Potbelly sandwiches are made to order and include meatball, roast beef, and pizza subs, as well as Big Jack's PB&J. The milkshakes are huge and come with a little butter cookie ring on the straw, while the desserts are made from scratch.

upscale restaurants

Some days you just can't face looking at even one more grilled cheese or frozen pizza on your dinner table. You need to get out and eat some real grown-up food, something exquisitely prepared and full of sophisticated flavors, but with all the baby-sitters booked, what are you supposed to do? Give the kids a bath, put them in their dressiest clothes (no Power Rangers shirts allowed), and pack the whole family off to one of the upscale restaurants I've listed here.

❄ Bistro Campagne

4518 N. Lincoln Ave.

773-271-6100

Though it doesn't have a kids' menu, Bistro Campagne makes the list for two reasons: its proximity to the Old Town School of Folk Music, site of myriad family concerts and classes, and its nearly exclusive use of organic ingredients. Children's bodies are far less able to handle pesticides than adults', and it's good to know there's a place to get upscale country French food that's good for you, too. The offerings are on the pricey side ($20 to $30 for an entree), but the waitstaff is welcoming and the child-friendly fare includes steak frites, pork chops, and roast chicken. You and your mate, meanwhile, can enjoy some more sophisticated French fare and a glass of wine, and everyone goes home satisfied.

❄ Brasserie Jo

59 W. Hubbard St.

312-595-0800

An upscale Lettuce Entertain You restaurant, Brasserie Jo gives children special attention that makes a meal there enjoyable for everyone. The special kids' menu is pasted on the back of an Etch a Sketch, so once your child has made her selection, she has plenty of entertainment at hand. Children's dinner items run about $7 and include tomato and cheese tart, pasta, and salmon, and for dessert there's a pint-sized portion of chocolate mousse. Visit the first Thursday night of the month for "Les Chapeaux of Brasserie Jo," when anyone who dines in a hat wins the reward of a free dessert. Photos of customers and their hats appear on the wall opposite the private dining room.

❄ The Dining Room at the Ritz-Carlton

160 E. Pearson St.

312-573-5223

If you want to take your family out to enjoy some of the city's most exquisitely prepared food in an opulent setting, the Sunday brunch buffet at the Ritz-Carlton can't be beat. The selection is unbelievably lavish and includes prime rib, seafood, omelet and waffle stations, various egg dishes, and much, much more. The service is, of course, superb, as you would expect when you're paying $57 per adult. Kids four to twelve, however, eat for just $15 each, and children under three are free—quite a bargain for such an expensive eatery.

❄ The Oak Terrace at the Drake Hotel

140 E. Walton Place

312-787-2200

Like the Ritz-Carlton, the Oak Terrace restaurant's Sunday brunch is huge and delicious, with more than three dozen hot and cold items, plus an omelet station and huge dessert selection. However, the view from the venerable Drake is stunning, with the wide-open vista of Lake Michigan as the backdrop. We were a bit nervous about taking Clare to such a nice brunch for her cousin's birthday, but the place was full of youngsters and we breathed a sigh of relief. Moreover, it was fun seeing kids decked out in their Sunday best instead of the usual jeans and character T-shirts. Clare feasted on pancakes, fruit, and scrambled eggs, then made two trips to the dessert table to pick out her own petite fours. Brunch is $39.50 for adults, $19 for children six to twelve, and free for kids five and under.

✳ *Vong's Thai Kitchen (VTK)*

6 W. Hubbard St.
312-644-8664

This incarnation of the more formal, even intimidating Vong has a much warmer and more casual atmosphere—and cheaper prices: Adult entrees are between $14 and $20, and kids can eat for under $10. Children are greeted with a little bowl of warm rice, a nice way to tide over a grumpy kid waiting for his dinner. The VTKids menu includes crispy chicken strips and grilled chicken with rice noodles. In warmer weather, the outdoor patio is a nice place to eat with the family.

✳ *South Water Kitchen*

225 N. Wabash Ave.
312-236-9300

At this dining room in the Hotel Monaco your child can find not just good food but food that does good, too: Half the proceeds from kids' menu items goes to the Chicago Coalition for the Homeless. The menu here is all-American, to the point that even the wine list has only domestic offerings. Food is of the comfort variety: pork tenderloin, roasted chicken, pot roast. To entertain children while waiting for their order, the host passes out crayons and a chef's hat to decorate. Kids' menu items include burgers, chicken, and pizza, as well as ice cream.

the big firsts

A baby is to celebrate! First you mark the new arrival with a printed birth announcement, something special, of course, but where do you find exactly the right thing? In the ensuing months, as you watch your baby grow, there will be many joyful and singular moments to celebrate—"the big firsts." For each of these milestones, Chicago can provide an expert who will help you make the most of these once-in-a-lifetime occasions. This chapter lists the best stationers for buying ready-made or personalized birth announcements, the most fun and unusual party places, the absolute best bakeries for ordering that first—and second, and third—birthday cake, the most skillful and entertaining hair cutters, the most reliable shoe stores, and the most artful photographers for that important first portrait.

You will be amazed at how fast your baby grows. Just when you are wondering when your baby will ever have enough hair to warrant a real haircut, it will be time to consider another important first: preschool. This is a rite of passage in Chicago, or anywhere, and I conclude with a few suggestions on how to start exploring the options.

birth announcements

Even in this day of e-mail and Web sites, printed birth announcements are still a very popular way to get out the word about the new addition to your family.

There are several options available. You can purchase ready-made cards at a stationery or party store and fill in your new baby's name, weight, size, and birth date.

Or you can order through an online source, such as K & T Announcements.com (www.kandtan-nouncements.com; 800-964-4002). The price for 100 announcements and plain envelopes is $99; envelopes printed with the return address are an additional $24. Another alternative—and an economical one, too—is to buy plain cards and print announcements from your computer at home. If you have a digital camera, you can even print a snapshot of your little bundle of joy on the card.

It's a good idea to choose your announcements a month or so in advance of your due date. If you are ordering from a store or catalog, plan on at least two weeks for printing; some stores require even more time. Get your envelopes early, and address them in advance. Then, after the baby is born, call the shop with all the details, such as height, weight, sex, and date and time of birth.

Chicago stationers have everything you could possibly want, and many will ship your selection directly to you. Below, I list the best. I've included prices where the selections of custom-order announcements are pretty straightforward; if you want to have your announcements custom designed as well, the options vary widely, and you'll need to consult with an individual store to come up with a price. Keep in mind these are also great sources for special birthday party invitations for the years to come.

❖ *All She Wrote*
825 W. Armitage Ave.
773-529-0100
This bright, cheery neighborhood store carries all kinds of paper goods for both adults and children and will do custom-engraved baby announcements chosen from a huge selection of design books.

Alphabétique

701 W. Armitage Ave.

312-751-2920

If creating a truly beautiful, one-of-a-kind announcement appeals to you, check out Alphabétique. The store's staff will help you create the announcement of your dreams from among the hundreds of gorgeous handmade papers and dozens of ink colors and typefaces. Alphabétique specializes in letterpress printing, the old art of inking and pressing metal type into each piece of paper, leaving subtle indentations.

Calligraphy Concepts

708-442-9663

www.calligraphyconcepts.com

Nearly 15 years, ago Monica McInerney left an unrewarding job to go into business as a calligrapher. After some time spent pounding the pavement, she's used her talent to build a business whose clients include the Mayor's Office of Special Events, Lettuce Entertain You Enterprises, and Saloman Smith Barney. Monica's calligraphy is really lovely; she offers three different writing styles and different ink colors to choose from. She also can copy any sample you might have. Prices are $2.50 and up per announcement.

Crane & Co.

Water Tower Place

835 N. Michigan Ave.

312-397-1936

(also at Oakbrook Center)

Crane & Co. sells a decent variety of preprinted announcements you fill in yourself, or you can order custom printed ones from about a

half-dozen choices. Prices range from $137 to $243 for 50 announcements.

Greer

2117 N. Clifton Ave.

773-529-3509

At this fine stationers you can custom order your announcements from a wide selection of traditional-looking styles on beautiful papers.

I've Been to a Marvelous Party

2121 N. Clybourn Ave.

773-404-9400

This fun store is mainly a party store, with everything from invites to decorations, but they also do custom-order baby announcements from designs in their many idea books.

Jane Weber, Ink!

900 N. Michigan Ave.

312-642-0747

This Magnificent Mile mainstay specializes in custom-order announcements, invitations, and fine stationery. They also carry a nice selection of writing and gift items.

Mite Invitations

180 W. Washington

312-236-3278

Mite has a big selection of announcements you can have custom printed. An unusual feature of the store is that it offers a variety of printing processes, most of them done on the premises: offset (flat printing, generally quickest and least expensive), thermography (raised letters but cheaper than engraving), engraving, and letterpress (old-fashioned and elegant, makes an impression in the paper).

❖ Original Expressions

845 W. Armitage Ave.

773-975-2010

This cute storefront has loads of ready-made announcements to choose from, in styles that range from traditional to whimsical.

❖ Paper Boy

1351 W. Belmont Ave.

773-388-8811

Attached to an art gallery, this colorful paper and gift store has a very creative feel to it. You can find fun ready-made announcements, or look through the store's idea books to choose unique custom-designed ones.

❖ Paper Source

232 W. Chicago Ave.; 312-337-0798

919 W. Armitage Ave.; 773-525-7300

2100 Central St. (Evanston); 847-733-8830

1109 Lake St. (Oak Park); 708-445-7700

I love the Paper Source. They have a mind-boggling selection of stunningly beautiful papers, many of them handmade. If you're of a creative bent, you can browse the many, many display samples of announcements, invitations, and cards for ideas to make your own announcements; Paper Source has what is probably the city's biggest selection of rubber stamps, which can be fun to incorporate in your design. Or you can consult with the store's designers to come up with a unique design that will be custom printed for you.

❖ Paper Trail

5309 N. Clark St.

773-275-2191

This hip little store carries a wide array of invitations, cards, gifts, and novelties, as well as invitations by Crane, Mara-mi, and Mudlark Papers. Paper Trail also will do custom-order birth announcements. You pick what you like from their selection of idea books and they'll order them for you.

❖ Papyrus

Water Tower Place

835 N. Michigan Ave.

312-266-9945

Papyrus carries lots of preprinted announcements. Or you can order custom printed ones from a selection of about two dozen choices that range from cute to sophisticated. Depending on the announcement, prices range from about $50 to $290 per 100.

❖ Tiffany & Company

730 N. Michigan Ave.

312-944-7500

Tiffany & Co. has a large stationery department offering both the Tiffany brand and some Crane lines. The Tiffany cards are simple, elegant, engraved, and costly. The starting price for 100 announcements is between $300 and $400.

birthday parties

Many parents love extravagant birthday parties, especially their child's first one. When your baby hits the magic age of one, the birthday party is mostly for Mom, Dad, grandparents, and friends. A cake and a few balloons will make most one-year-olds very happy, and you'll get great photos of your baby mushing up his icing. If you're interested in hiring a party planner or entertainment—clowns, magicians, balloon artists—the classifieds at the back of Chicago Parent magazine are chock-full of options.

I like the idea of having the first birthday at home, but this may not be possible if you have a big family, many friends, and a small apartment. Happily, Chicago is full of places that organize parties for a one-year-old. Keep this list handy for future reference—two- through six-year-olds can have even more fun at a party place.

Keep in mind that many of these places host parties only on the weekend. Most require that you bring your own food and cake, though they often have a list of suggested caterers in the neighborhood. Prices are noted, but they tend to change over time. Call ahead. Many of the below listings are great for older birthdays, too.

Another option for warmer weather is a party in one of Chicago's many parks, where the cost is minimal and the options are limited only by your imagination. For parties of more than 50 people, you need a permit from the Chicago Park District Permits Division; you can download a permit application from the Web site at www.chicagoparkdistrict.com. Park parties should be planned with a rain date or a back-up plan in case of inclement weather. That aside, plan for lots of outdoor games, such as circle time, hot potato, and freeze dance (bring batteries for your portable radio), or have a friend or professional play guitar. Any entertainers you would hire indoors can be hired outdoors as well. You can even have pizza delivered! You gotta love this town.

Five Great Places to Have a Two-Year-Old's Party

1. Your home, if you have room, or a common space in your apartment building.
2. A nearby park. Hang streamers and balloons in the tree branches to create a secret-garden atmosphere.
3. Corner Playroom.
4. Chicago Children's Museum.
5. Sing 'n' Dance.

✳ Bubbles Academy

1504 N. Fremont
312-944-7677
www.bubblesacademy.com

For birthday parties, Bubbles offers different staff-led activities depending on the children's age. For a one- or two-year-old, the program is Musical Motion, which involves singing, puppetry, and play with musical instruments, a parachute, and bubbles. An hour-and-a-half party for up to fifteen children costs $485 if you are currently registered in a Bubbles class, or $685 if you are not; an additional half-hour is $65. Bubbles does not provide food or cake, but you can bring in your own.

❋ Chicago Children's Museum

700 E. Grand Ave. at Navy Pier
312-464-7737 (for birthday party inquiries)
www.chichildrensmuseum.org/index.cfm

The Children's Museum offers a variety of party packages, all of which include two hours' use of the brightly decorated Birthday Party Parlor (which has tables and a sink, refrigerator, and freezer) plus all-day admission to the rest of the museum. You can add on a variety of extras, including an art activity led by museum staff, face painting ($75), and a food package (pizza, salad, drinks, and cake, for $250). Prices range from $195 for members for the basic package ($225 for nonmembers), up to $370 ($400 for nonmembers) for art activities.

❋ Corner Playroom

2121 N. Clybourn Ave.
773-388-2121
www.cornerplayroom.com

For $285 you get two hours' exclusive use of the playroom and party room, an assistant to help with set up and supervision, paper goods, and ice. You supply food, drinks, and cake. Parties are held only on Friday afternoons and evenings, Saturdays and Sundays.

❋ Dorby Magoo

2744 N. Lincoln Ave.
773-935-2663

Kids love parties in this shop designed to look like a house, with toys spilling from the living room, den, library, kitchen, even a bathroom. The owner declined to quote me prices because they vary so much depending on the package selected. One thing kids will want you to include, though, is a trip to the bedroom, where they can choose a predetermined number of goodie bag toys from more than 300 inexpensive choices like play jewelry and fake bugs. Take note: Dorby Magoo takes only cash and checks—no credit cards.

❋ Emerald City Theatre Company

2936 N. Southport Ave.
773-529-2690
www.emeraldcitytheatre.com

If you're planning a party for just your child and other one-year-olds, you may want to wait till they're older for an Emerald City party. But if your group is mixed ages, you might want to consider a visit to this children's theater company; it's a pretty good deal. For $11.50 per person, plus a $90 party fee, you get a two-hour event that includes personalized invitations to mail out, setup and cleanup, decorations, a performance of the company's current production, a visit with a character from the play that includes photos and autographs, a quarter sheet cake, and juice. For additional fees, you can have pizza and a bigger cake.

❋ Gymboree Play and Music

3158 N. Lincoln Ave.
773-296-4550
www.playandmusic.com/b2c/customer/home.jsp

For $385 (plus a $25 membership fee if you haven't previously taken a class there), you get an assistant who will help with the set up, cleanup, and supervision and a teacher who leads up to 25 children in a 45-minute developmentally appropriate class. The fee also covers invitations, paper goods and silverware, party hats, blowers, balloons, a goodie bag, and thank-you notes, all with a Gymboree theme. You provide the food and cake, which the staff will roll out on a slide, a fun touch. Gymboree parties are held only on Sundays, for two hours.

✳ Hands On Children's Art Museum
1800 W. 103rd St.
773-233-9933
www.handsonart.org/index.php
Hands On offers two 90-minute birthday packages, the light and the deluxe. Both include a half-hour of open play, a half-hour of guided art activity with a staff member, then a half-hour to use the party room. This constitutes the light package, which is $13 per person with an eight-person minimum. In addition to the above, the deluxe package includes all paper goods, ice cream and juice, and goodie bags; it costs $17 per person, again with an eight-person minimum.

✳ Happy Child Studios
741 Main St. (Evanston)
847-733-9545
www.happychildstudios.com
Happy Child Studios gives you two options: You can hold the party there, or the party can come to you. For $170, a staff member will come to your home for a 45-minute performance. For one-year-olds, the best choice is probably a music class (songs, fingerplay, movement), but the staff is open to whatever theme or activity you have in mind. For $320

you can have a two-hour party at Happy Child; the fee covers the space rental, a party helper, a 45-minute performance, and a goodie bag on whatever theme you like. You can bring in your own food and cake.

✳ The Little Gym of Chicago
3216 N. Lincoln Ave.
773-525-5750
www.tlgchicagoil.com
This is a great place to turn a bunch of one-year-olds loose. For $325 for nonmembers ($300 for members), you get the Little Gym for an hour and a half for 16 kids. A staff member will lead the children in age-appropriate activities, as well as allow free play with the gym's toys and equipment. The fee also includes invitations that the staff will address and mail for you, setup and cleanup, decorations, paper goods and utensils, balloons, juice, and a T-shirt for the birthday kid. You bring your own food and cake.

✳ My Gym Chicago
1880 W. Fullerton Ave.
773-645-9600
For $350 you get two hours at My Gym, including a wide variety of teacher-led activities. You supply the food and paper goods.

✳ Old Town School of Folk Music
4544 N. Lincoln Ave.
773-728-6000
www.oldtownschool.org
For $160, you can book a Wiggleworms teacher to come to your party for a 45-minute performance. Other performers from the

school are available as well; because availability and prices vary, call the school's referral coordinator for more information.

Partners in Play

In United Lutheran Church, 409 Greenfield St. (Oak Park)

708-386-2788

Partners in Play offers parties for children ages two to five. For $125, you get an hour and a half to use the program's gym space, and a teacher will lead the children in age-appropriate activities. You bring your own food and paper goods.

Sing 'n' Dance

2632 N. Halsted St.

773-528-7464

www.singndance.com

Sing 'n' Dance offers an hour-and-a-half birthday package that includes exclusive use of the play space and a half-hour developmentally appropriate class of music and movement. You supply the food and decorations. The cost is $400.

Ukrainian Village Children's Center

918 N. Damen

773-342-7415

http://uvcc.home.mindspring.com/

This cozy art center will work with you to choose an age-appropriate art activity that the staff will help children make at the party. Cost is $10 per child, plus the cost of the art project; you supply food, drinks, and cake for the hour-and-a-half event.

Windy City Field House

2367 W. Logan Blvd.

773-486-7300

www.windycityfieldhouse.com

Windy City offers a variety of birthday packages, all of which include organized and supervised games, sports of your choice, setup, and cleanup. You can add on face painting, balloon artists, inflatable games, additional staff organization and help, and catering. Prices vary widely depending on the package you create, so call for further information.

birthday cakes

Everybody has a local bakery that makes perfectly fine, even fabulous birthday cakes. Explore your neighborhood, and be sure to ask other moms where they get cakes. Heck, you can get a cake from Jewel complete with your baby's name and ubiquitous frosting flowers; the cake people there can even use a special decorating machine to reproduce any photograph you give them. (I did that for my parents' birthdays with a picture of six-month-old Clare, and they loved it.)

But for your child's first birthday, you may want to go all out. I've listed some makers of outstanding birthday cakes, and clued you in on which ones will incorporate themes such as Superman, ballerinas, or Peter Rabbit. Don't panic, though. You can always run out and pick up an Entenmann's cake—they can be quite tasty when they're fresh, and for $3.99, who's complaining?

Ben & Jerry's

26 W. Randolph St.; 312-252-2900
700 E. Grand Ave. (Navy Pier); 312-595-5496
338 W. Armitage Ave.; 773-281-5152
1634 Orrington Ave. (Evanston); 847-869-2640
Have your cake and ice cream all in one with an ice cream cake from Ben & Jerry's. You choose any two ice creams, which are separated by layers of crumbled brownies, then the whole thing is frosted with whipped cream and decorations. I could spend an hour contemplating the combinations (Coconut Almond Fudge Chip with Coffee, Dulce Delicious with New York Super Fudge Chunk, Cherry Garcia with Brownie Batter . . .). A sheet cake to serve 25 costs about $45.

Bittersweet

1114 W. Belmont
773-929-1100
If an occasion calls for cake, my sister-in-law Sara will be there with a fabulous creation from Bittersweet. This European-style bakery is one of the most popular wedding cake makers in the city. For birthdays, you can choose white, yellow, chocolate, carrot, almond, or banana cake, with a luscious variety of fillings that include brulée custard, lemon curd, fresh fruit, and milk chocolate mousse. A basic filled cake to serve 25 starts at about $50. Bittersweet also offers elaborately hand-decorated butter cookies that make lovely party favors. They generally have several shapes on hand—including birthday cakes—but with a couple of weeks' notice, they'll decorate any shape you want, though you may have to provide the cookie cutter if it's really unusual. Cookies range from $1.50 to $4.50 apiece, depending on the intricacy of the design.

House of Fine Chocolates

3109 N. Broadway
773-525-5700
Known for its spectacularly artistic wedding cakes, House of Fine Chocolates also will create a fabulous cake for your child's birthday. These are elegant, European-style cakes, and they come in a huge variety: yellow, white, chocolate, carrot, or almond cake, with fillings that include dark chocolate mousse, fudge and fresh bananas with English walnuts, and key lime mousse. A cake to serve 25 people starts at $38.50—much less than I expected for these works of art.

JR Dessert Bakery

2841 W. Howard St.
773-465-6733
This nationally known cheesecake bakery offers an untraditional alternative with its birthday cheesecakes, decorated and iced with buttercream or whipped cream. You can choose classic plain cheesecake or go with varieties that include chocolate chip, marble, raspberry, strawberry, and lemon. A decorated cheesecake to serve 25 is about $54.

Original Ferrara Inc.

2210 W. Taylor St.
312-666-2200
An old-time bakery in the Italian Taylor Street neighborhood, Ferrara's specialty is the canno-

li cake, a sensational layered creation filled with strawberries, Italian custard, and cannoli cream, all frosted with whipped cream. (For a child's birthday, you may want to request that the bakery not soak each layer in rum, however.) You also can choose other cakes and fillings if you prefer; tres leches, for instance, is a rich, milk-soaked cake you won't find just anywhere. A cannoli cake to serve 25 is $48. For an extra $6, you can choose from a variety of kid's characters to decorate the top.

❈ Roeser's Bakery

3216 W. North Ave.

773-489-6900

The oldest family-run bakery in Chicago, Roeser's is an old-fashioned kind of bakery considered by many to be the place for special-occasion cakes. Roeser's will do a cake with any of the typical kids' characters—Big Bird, Thomas, any Disney creatures—as well as just about any theme you might dream up; they once even did a cake shaped like a mushroom cloud topped with Albert Einstein's visage. A decorated, filled cake to serve 25 runs about $50.

❈ Swedish Bakery

5348 N. Clark St.

773-561-8919

This neighborhood pastry shop has been around for 75 years, making incredible European tortes, as well as breads, cookies, pies, and traditional Swedish baked goods. Cakes and tortes are made with yellow or chocolate cake and a huge variety of frostings and fillings, including strawberries, cherry chocolate whipped cream, and lemon coconut buttercream. For birthdays you can choose from the bakery's standard selection of cakes (Chocolate Suicide Torte anyone?) and have it personalized with decorations and writing. My friend Lisa had a Swedish Bakery torte for her daughter Emma's first birthday; the salutation was written on a ribbon of marzipan, and the cake was lovely and delicious. Cakes to serve 20 people start at around $35.

❈ Sweet Thang

1921 W. North Ave.

773-772-4166

Wicker Park's Sweet Thang is the brainchild of Bernard Runo, who previously worked as a pastry chef at the Ritz-Carlton, the Fairmont Hotel, and the Hotel Intercontinental. Sweet Thang specializes in traditional French pastry and creates beautiful cakes and tortes with an unusual variety of fillings that include mint chocolate, peanut butter, and passion fruit, among other, more standard offerings. Sweet Thang will decorate a cake with the typical children's characters, or you can go for the more unusual with a cake shaped like a train, a castle, a gift-wrapped package—whatever you can think of. A basic decorated cake to serve 25 people starts at around $37.

❈ Weber's Bakery

7055 W. Archer Ave.

773-586-1234

Located in the vicinity of Midway Airport, Weber's Bakery makes delicious, kid-friendly birthday cakes with just about any character you can name: Bear in the Big Blue House, Thomas the Tank Engine, Elmo, Barbie, Bob the Builder, Barney, Teletubbies, and on and on. They'll even make it while you wait (though they prefer at least a day's notice). In addition to the standard chocolate and yellow cake, you can get banana cake, an appealing change of taste for toddlers. A decorated, filled cake to serve 25 people costs about $43.

❋ Whole Foods Market

30 W. Huron; 312-932-9600

1000 W. North Ave.; 312-587-0648

3300 N. Ashland Ave.; 773-244-4200

If your child has food allergies, Whole Foods is a good bet for a vegan cake, which means it's free of eggs and dairy products. You can pick up a ready-made cake at the store's bakery or special order a decorated cake. The latter can run anywhere from $62 to $80 for a cake to serve 25, depending on the type of cake you choose.

haircuts

Most Chicago moms take their babies to their own hair salon, or attempt to give that first trim themselves. But you might want to try one of the few shops that specialize in children's haircutting. Little kids are notoriously bad at sitting still, and these places offer fun distractions like Barney or Sesame Street videos to watch, and toy cars for your child to sit in.

❋ Bear with Me Hair for Kids

72 E. Oak St., 2nd floor

312-664-6170

Bear with Me actually will cut the hair of any-

one in the family, but they have accoutrements that appeal especially to kids: a car-shaped cutting chair, videos, and toys. It's not as cheap as other places—$30 for a child's cut—but this is Oak Street after all.

❋ KidSnips

Deerfield: 655 Deerfield Road; 847-374-8000

Arlington Heights: Northpoint Center; 847-797-9690

Wilmette: Edens Plaza; 847-853-0099

Wheaton: Town Square; 630-653-3300

Vernon Hills: Westfield Hawthorn; 847-247-1110

Oakbrook: Oakbrook Center; 630-571-1500

KidSnips is not in the city, but I mention it because there are so few kids' salons around, and if you're able to find a way out to the suburbs, this one really has a lot to offer: a very clean environment, car-shaped chairs, videos, and Nintendo, plus a balloon and toy from the Treasure Chest afterward. For your child's very first haircut, you get a Polaroid and a lock of hair mounted on a special certificate. The salons also have a variety of toys and novelty items you can purchase. Cuts for children 12 and under are $15 to $17. KidSnips does adult hair, too, so it's a good chance for you to get a cut yourself while the kids are entertained.

❋ Snippets Mini Cuts

2154 N. Clybourn Ave.

773-755-1000

Moms have great things to say about Snippets, where the stylists get children in and out quickly—key with restless toddlers—and the haircuts are good, too. The styling chairs come in fun shapes (a taxi, a VW Beetle, a lion), cartoons play on the TV, and toys and Nintendo are available to play with. A children's cut is $20.

shoes

Buying your child's first walking shoes is an exciting and important task. Because your one- or two-year-old can't tell you whether the shoes are comfortable, watch carefully as she is being fitted. If it seems difficult to get the shoes on and off, they are probably too small. Shoes should generally last at least two months: if they seem small three weeks after you bought them, go back and have them checked.

The salesperson at the shoe store should measure your child's foot while he is standing with toes uncurled. Ask about the width of your child's foot and don't buy a shoe that narrows greatly at the toes. Also, look for a soft, flexible sole. A soft sole is necessary for the first year. After that, when your child is really walking and running, you can buy any shoe your heart desires, except slip-on penny loafers. Your youngster won't develop the gripping action that a slip-on shoe requires until he is four or five.

❋ Alamo Shoes

5319 N. Clark St.

773-784-8936

My friends in Andersonville and Rogers Park have bought many, many pairs of children's shoes at Alamo, an old-fashioned kind of shoe store that carries high-quality brands like Stride Rite, Elefanten, and Teva.

❋ Carrara Children's Shoes

2506-1/2 N. Clark St.

773-529-9955

Fine Italian footwear isn't just for grown-ups. Carrara specializes in imported Italian shoes, though it also has familiar brands of athletic shoes as well. The staff is helpful and has a good cache of toys to keep kids entertained.

❋ Little Soles

2121 N. Clybourn Ave.

773-525-7727

The staff here is very knowledgeable and keeps toys on hand for the kids. Little Soles carries brands that include Stride Rite, Elefanten, Jumping-Jacks and more.

❋ Piggy Toes

2205 N. Halsted St.

773-281-5583

Co-owned by a former shoe buyer for Nordstrom and her interior designer mother, Piggy Toes is the place to go for hip kids' shoes—and they even have a decent selection for moms, too. Specializing in sturdy European-made shoes, this fun boutique carries such brands as Moschino, Oilily, and Rocket Dog.

photographs

Since Clare was born, my mom has developed a first-name relationship with the photo guy at her supermarket—and she lives three hundred miles from us! You can just imagine how many hundreds of baby photos we have ourselves. If you're like us and this is your first child, you'll probably always have a camera at hand to record such things as haircuts and parties. But with the second and third child, you might find it easy to overlook either photographing or videotaping their big firsts. To make sure you never miss a special moment, keep a disposable camera in your stroller.

It won't take long for your drawers to become stuffed with photos taken of your adorable baby by you and your relatives. But there's a reason you've left them in the drawer. When you want a picture to put in that beautiful silver frame you got as a baby gift, it's time to go to a professional.

If your budget is limited, you can actually get very nice photos at places like Sears, JCPenney, and Picture People (located in various suburban malls). My friend Anne has gotten some lovely portraits at Sears that I thought she had taken at a photo studio. When her daughter Penelope was a toddler, for instance, Anne took her to Sears in a sweet, floppy hat and diaper and posed her with her big brother, wearing jeans and no shirt, against a plain earth-toned background. The results were beautiful. And every year we take Clare, who has a February 9 birthday, to Picture People for a portrait with Valentine props. Her one-year photo in a red diaper and gold-trimmed angel wings is one of my all-time favorites.

If you have a bigger budget, though, you can hire a fine-art photographer, who will work in your home, the park, or her studio, and can include parents or grandparents in the shots, as well as props such as stuffed animals, antique toys, costumes, and more. If you don't know a photographer, here are some of the best children's portrait artists in Chicago. Ask to see their portfolios, and if you don't see the kind of work you want, ask your friends for some recommendations.

Marc Harris Photography
1875 N. Milwaukee Ave.
773-342-1960
www.marcharris-photo.com
Marc Harris takes portraits mainly at his Bucktown studio, though he is willing to go on location if you prefer. His work is primarily black and white, though he does do color photography as well. Marc charges $275 per session, which lasts about an hour; $75 of the fee is applied toward your print order.

Joi de Vivre Family Photography
773-848-3013
www.joidevivre.com
Joi Rosenbaum takes wonderful black-and-white portraits that capture children in their many moods: joyful, silly, grumpy, loving, thoughtful. Rosenbaum's photos have a spontaneous, natural feel, largely because she prefers to get out of the studio and take pictures where kids most comfortable, whether that's their home, the beach, or a park. She also takes lovely photos of pregnant women and families—even pets are welcome. Rosenbaum includes a free consultation to plan the photo session. A session lasts anywhere from one to three hours and costs $225, which includes $70 toward your photo order.

Barb Levant
773-395-2002
www.barblevantphoto.com
A professional photographer for more than 25 years, Bucktown-based Levant is one of the city's top children's portrait artists and has

done work for many of Chicago's most famous families. She's full of energy, and her love of kids really shows in her work. Barb is particularly known for her hand-colored and sepia-tone work. A full, one-hour session costs $175 plus film costs (usually five rolls, at $175). Prints are extra.

❋ Jennifer Mau Photography
773-549-5579

www.jennifermau.com

Jennifer takes both black-and-white and color pictures. In addition to portraits, she also will photograph happenings, like a birthday party or family reunions; a series of these photos feels like documentary work that captures not just the event but the spontaneous, emotion-filled moments. My neighbors Margaret and Bart hired Jennifer to photograph their son, Simon, when he was a toddler and ended up with some really lovely black-and-white portraits.

❋ Menarchy-Pace
656 W. Hubbard

312-666-7400

www.menarchypace.com

A team for the past decade, photographer Marybeth Menarchy and costume designer Leslie Pace create ravishingly beautiful children's portraits unlike anyone else in the city. Pace has a huge cache of costumes and props to use for portraits, and the pair puts a tremendous amount of effort into choosing the backdrop, which might be their studio, the lakefront, or a snowy field. After a shoot,

Menarchy painstakingly manipulates the photo images with a computer, and the end results are portraits that are lushly imaginative and uniquely beautiful. A studio session starts at $600. Prints are extra.

❋ Modern Madonnas
312-543-2265

www.modernmadonnas.com

Marcia Dabrowski specializes in artful, black-and-white studio portraits of pregnant women, as well as photos of children and families. She's based in Naperville but is willing to travel just about anywhere—even California—for a shoot.

❋ Jill Norton Photography
312-403-1222

www.jillnorton.com

Jill says children are her favorite subject to shoot, and it shows in her work. Her black-and-white portraits of children are unposed and full of feeling; she's taken some especially sweet sibling photos. Jill will create custom cards and invitations from the pictures she shoots, at prices that are relatively reasonable for what you get: $1.50 to $3.00 per card, plus a set-up fee. She also offers framing. A photo session costs $360, with prints extra; travel to a location more than ten miles from Evanston adds travel fees of $30 per hour of travel time.

❋ Kirk Shepherd Photography
9841 S. Hoyne Ave.

773-238-8608

www.ksphoto.net

In my humble opinion, color portraits often can

have a stiff, unnatural feel to them. But Kirk Shepherd takes really lovely color children's photos, thanks to his practice of using only natural light instead of hot lights or flashes—in fact, he doesn't even have a studio. Kirk will take pictures just about anywhere you like, including indoors, as long as there is a source of natural light, be it a window or a skylight. Because Kirk shoots digitally, he can also provide black-and-white prints. A session with one subject costs $200, with additional subjects generally adding $100 each; for three children, for instance, he charges $400, which covers individual shots of each child as well as group shots.

❊ *Audrey Woulard Photography*

312-661-9019

www.alwphotography.com

The mother of four children, Audrey Woulard knows how to bring out kids' personalities for black-and-white photos that are natural and unposed. She prefers to shoot outside the studio, whether that means in your home or an outdoor location, for photos that are emotional and full of natural light. Woulard charges $250 for a session, which lasts about one to three hours. Photos are extra.

a word on preschools

My husband and I began checking out preschools the winter Clare turned three, and I was shocked to learn we had just about missed the boat. Many pre-

school applications for the next year are due in January—or sooner—and I had virtually no time to do the kind of thorough research I had applied to everything from finding my midwife to potty-training. I highly recommend you begin your preschool research between your child's first and second birthday, to be sure you have adequate time to get information and to meet deadlines.

As you begin to check out preschools you will probably be subject to intermittent panic attacks. You'll hear rumors that this or that school is "hot" this year. You'll be baffled by the complexity of the admissions process. You'll feel as though you're trying to get an 18-year-old into Harvard, not a two-year-old into a sweet little place where she'll play and eat crackers and juice. Try to relax. Things will work out.

Here are some basic facts to keep in mind as you and your child march on toward preschool:

❊ Many children begin preschool at age three or three and one-half years old; others begin as early as two years. Schools decide on cutoff ages for admission and often change these arbitrarily—a one-year-old born before March 15 can apply for admission for the following September; the next year, perhaps, a child born before March 31 can apply. Schools hold tight to their birth date policies, and there are few exceptions.

❊ There are many excellent preschools in Chicago. Get a copy of the Northside Parents Network's School Information Booklet, which provides the lowdown on 96 preschools and elementary schools ($5 for network members or

$15 for nonmembers; see page 66 for contact information).

✳ As you begin your search, look for a school in your neighborhood if possible. Try to keep your travel distance to about 10 blocks. The preschool day is only two or three hours, and you'll waste valuable chore or—if you're lucky—alone time if it takes you long to get back and forth.

✳ Talk to friends about their experiences with preschools. Make arrangements to visit the schools you're interested in. Tours typically take place from October through January. Some schools will not schedule a tour until they receive a completed application; others supply applications only after you have toured the school.

✳ Apply promptly. Schools have been known to stop sending applications by the second week of September, when they have already received enough applicants to fill their classes three times over. Apply to four or five schools. If you have a first choice, indicate it in a letter to the director of admissions of that particular school. It also helps greatly if you know families that attend the school you're most interested in. If possible, have them write or call for you.

Your child will almost surely find a place in a preschool you like, and you will almost surely wonder a year from now what all the fuss was about.

Chapter Nine

maternity clothes

Whatever clothing your lifestyle demands, you can find it in Chicago's maternity stores. From hip city-mama clothes at Belly Dance, rental evening gowns from As You Wait, and office wear at Mimi Maternity, these stores have everything you need to stay comfortable and look great.

If you're not much of a shopper, or if you're sticking to a budget, the Belly Basics Pregnancy Survival Kit can be a staple of your wardrobe from day one of your pregnancy. The kit includes boot-cut leggings, a skirt, a long-sleeved tunic, and a baby doll dress, all of which are made of black cotton and lycra. You can mix and match the pieces or wear them with non-maternity clothes.

This chapter describes the Chicago maternity stores—their focus, style, quality of merchandise, and price range. Most of these stores hold their biggest sales in January and July.

shopping tips

Before you shop, here's some tried-and-true advice from experienced moms.

❈ Hold off on buying maternity clothes for as long as you can. Remember, nine months is a long time, and you'll need new and different things as you grow bigger.

❈ In the first and second trimester, shop in regular clothing stores for larger sizes and skirts, shorts, and pants with elastic waists. The Gap, The Limited, and Victoria's Secret often offer inexpensive, machine-washable items with elastic waists. Buy one or two sizes larger than you usually do. You'll wear these items again post-

partum, when you can't bear to wear maternity clothes a day longer but still can't fit into your old clothes.

❈ Don't buy shoes in your first trimester; your feet will probably expand. In fact, even when your pregnancy is over, you may find your feet remain a half-size or even a full size larger.

❈ Buy fabrics you are used to and comfortable with. If you never wear polyester or rayon, there's no need to start now. Stick to cotton or other natural fabrics that breathe, such as heavy-weight cotton blend suits you can wear when you go to a business meeting or out to dinner.

❈ Buy new bras, pantyhose, and maternity underwear. You may go up as many as three cup sizes during your pregnancy, and bras with good support are essential. (Can you imagine going from an A to a D? It'll happen.) Maternity pantyhose by Hue and underwear by Japanese Weekend are two favorites.

❈ For the last two months, invest in a maternity support belt, sold at every maternity store. The belt is a large, thick band of elastic that closes with Velcro under your belly to help hold it up. You will be able to walk more comfortably and for longer periods of time.

❈ A pretty vest is an easy way to dress up an oxford shirt and a skirt or pair of leggings.

❈ Look in your husband's closet. A man's oxford shirt over a long elasticized skirt or leggings provides comfort and a clean, crisp look. You might even buy some men's sweaters and shirts to wear, then pass them on to your spouse when you're finished with them.

❋ Don't be afraid to wear fitted clothes. As more and more fashion models become pregnant, it's become the trend to wear form-fitting tops and dresses! Feel sexy and be pregnant at the same time. Liz Lange Maternity specializes in that sophisticated pregnancy look.

the stores

❋ *A Pea in the Pod*

46 E. Oak St.; 312-944-3080

Oak Brook Center (Oak Brook); 630-575-0211

www.apeainthepod.com

Return policy: Exchange and store credit only. This is a top-of-the-line maternity store. It carries its own exclusive line and also commissions suits, dresses, and weekend wear by Carole Little, Joan Vass, David Dart, Shelli Segal, ABS, Lou Nardi, and Adrienne Vittadini. A Pea in the Pod is the only store to carry Lily Pulitzer's maternity line. Amenities abound— big bathrooms, extra-large dressing rooms with space to sit down, magazines for bored husbands. The salespeople are helpful and trained to fit you with maternity and nursing bras. Prices run in the $150 to $200 range for most designer pieces. You can find jeans and leggings for about $60 to $70.

❋ *Belly Basics*

www.bellybasics.com

Sure, there are plenty of places to shop online, but the Belly Basics line is so stylish and versatile that it's worth special note. Besides the aforementioned Pregnancy Survival Kit, you also will find everything from twin sets to swimwear— and a diaper bag in city-essential black.

❋ *Belly Dance Maternity*

1647 N. Damen Ave.

773-862-1133

www.bellydancematernity.com

Return policy: Within two weeks with receipt and original tags; sale items are final.

This hip boutique carries a variety of sexy, chic maternity wear, ranging from the lower priced Olian line (about $60 for tops and bottoms) to higher-end designers Cadeau, Earl, Japanese Weekend, Nom, and others (about $120 and up). Because its owner believes that "all pregnant women look fabulous," Belly Dance uses mainly friends and customers as models on its Web site. If you'd like to model for the store, send an e-mail to info@bellydancematernity.com.

❋ *Motherhood Maternity*

51 E. Randolph St.; 312-332-0022

7601 S. Cicero Ave.; 773-884-1805

Return policy: Store credit or exchange only, within 10 days of purchase.

This was my favorite place to shop for maternity clothes, because the clothing is stylish, the quality is good, and the prices are more reasonable than just about anywhere else. At Motherhood you can find the store's line of career clothes, jeans, pants, shorts, skirts, dresses from casual to special occasion, sweaters, swimwear, nursing apparel, sleepwear, and accessories. Hardly anything is over $50, and most items run between $20 and $40—even less if you hit a sale.

❊ Mimi Maternity

Water Tower Place, 835 N. Michigan Ave.;
312-335-1818
On Marshall Field's third floor, 111 N. State St.;
312-629-9151
Return policy: Store credit or exchange only, within 10 days.
From the same owners as A Pea in the Pod, Mimi Maternity offers clothing that is much more affordable while remaining stylish and well made. You'll find a fashionable assortment of career suits, daytime and evening dresses, and casual clothing by Mimi, Mother's Work, BCBG, Paris Blues, and other labels. Prices range from about $30 to $100. The Mimi's in Field's is quite a bit larger than the one in Water Tower Place, and often runs sales you won't find at the other store.

❊ Swell

1206 W. Webster
773-935-SHOP (Shop Girl)
www.swellmaternity.com
Return policy: Within 10 days for store credit.
This trendy boutique specializes in hip, sexy maternity wear, from designers that include Noppies, Meet Me in Miami, Japanese Weekend, Blue Cult, Michael Stars, and the new Kate Prange for Swell, designed by the store's owner. Pants start at around $69, tops at about $60.

Swell also carries evening clothes and outerwear, as well as accessories and some baby items.

❊ While You Wait and As They Grow

703 Washington St. (Evanston)
847-869-6222
Refund policy: Exchange or store credit on new items; all sales final on resale items.
Recognizing that pregnancy is short term (really, it is) and many women don't want to invest a lot of money in a temporary wardrobe, While You Wait sells not just new but also gently used clothing. You can find one- or two-year-old fashions from lines like Gap and Pea in the Pod for as much as half of the retail price. New clothing also is discounted 10 percent off retail. While You Wait carries career clothing, evening wear, casual tops and bottoms, sleep wear, and nursing bras and tops. Also, you can rent evening dresses that cost as much as $300 for two days for as little as $50. As They Grow is the children's store under the same owner, also selling new and used clothing.

Best Alternatives to Maternity Stores

• Your husband's shirts and sweaters.
• A friend's maternity clothes.
• Target. The Liz Lange for Target line is really stylish—and really inexpensive.
• Jumpers and dresses with no waist; at reasonable prices in Victoria's Secret catalogs.
• The Pregnancy Survival Kit from Belly Basics.
• Rental clothes from While You Wait for special occasions.
• Secondhand stores.

baby furniture
and accessories

Walk into any baby furniture store and you'll face a sea of cribs, changing tables, and strollers. A year from now you'll be an expert on all of these items—but for new moms, some advice is in order. This chapter tells you what you need and why you need it.

While cost and style will influence your choice of your baby's new stroller, crib, or changing table, city mothers-to-be must also consider space. Is your apartment a roomy two-bedroom plus dining room, or is it basically a large studio? Portability will also be a consideration. It's very hard to maneuver a super-deluxe stroller in and out of a bus or taxi.

Don't run out and buy everything at once. You'll need the crib and stroller immediately, but wait until after the baby is born for the rest. You may receive useful gifts. Also, try to borrow some things, such as bouncy seats and swings. When you are ready to shop, read through the listings that follow. Baby "superstores" carry almost everything you will need; the information here will give you an idea of what you want before you go shopping.

Many items can be called in and ordered by phone or through the Internet. It saves time and anything that saves time helps—especially if this is your second or third child. If you need to order your furniture, do it at least 12 weeks before your due date. Finally, if you are a second-time parent, be aware that many car seats, pack-and-plays, and toys have been recalled in the past few years. Please call the Consumer Products Safety Commission (800-638-2772) or visit its Web site (www.cpsc.gov) to see if previously used products are still okay before you use them.

Ten Tips for Furnishing a Baby's Room

1. Good overhead lighting is key for convenience and safety.
2. A humidifier can be important in overheated Chicago apartments.
3. Have as many dressers, drawers, or shelves as possible—you'll need them.
4. Design the closet in the baby's room to allow for more toy than clothing space; baby clothes are tiny.
5. Baby proof the room (see page 159).
6. Have all diaper supplies within arm's reach of your changing table.
7. A glider or rocker can save the day (or night).
8. Curtains or shades help baby sleep.
9. If possible, leave a play space somewhere in the room.
10. Keep it simple—a busy or overdecorated room gets old quickly.

bassinets

A bassinet is a lovely basket for a newborn to sleep in. It is usually suitable for about three months. It can be handy if you want your baby to sleep in your bedroom, or if a full-size crib seems too big for that tiny infant. There are a lot of styles, from bassinets with wheels, to those that rock, to those that lift off the stand, and some come with full bedding ensembles, including linens, coverlets, and fitted sheets. Prices generally range from about $75 to $130, though you can pay up to $700 for a full, top of the line bassinet set. The Kids Line bassinet is a good one; it features carry straps on the detachable basket for portability, and full bedding. The unit collapses for easy storage or travel and the bassinet linens (available in a variety of colors and patterns) are removable for washing.

Here are some popular brands of bassinets:
- ❊ Badger
- ❊ Kids Line
- ❊ Lee Hy
- ❊ Century
- ❊ Graco

cribs

The many choices of styles, colors, and finishes in cribs can be overwhelming. You can find cribs in sleigh-bed styles and distressed wood finishes, in traditional styles or sleek, modern designs, but in almost all cases, the choices you're making are purely aesthetic. Finding a safe crib is easy; look for the seal of the Juvenile Products Manufacturers Association (JPMA), which develops standards and certifies many baby products, including cribs, strollers/carriages, highchairs, and playpens. JPMA safety specifications require that the space between crib bars is no more than two-and-three-eighths inches apart, the crib mattress fits snugly, and the crib has firmly locking dropsides and childproof lock-release mechanisms.

This is one area in which you should not use a hand-me-down or resale purchase unless you are absolutely certain the crib meets current JPMA standards; you can find them at www.jpma.org.

Here are the questions to ask when you shop for a crib:

- ❊ Do both sides, or just one drop? One drop-side provides more stability and is easier to operate while holding a baby in the other arm.

- ❊ Can you raise or lower the crib's sides with one hand while holding the baby, or do you need both hands? Some American cribs have kick-stands under the side rails, making them easier to raise and lower. More and more American companies (and most European companies) use an easy, leg-operated side-track mechanism.

- ❊ Is the crib stable when you shake it? A loose crib frame, or the sound of metal knocking against metal might indicate faulty construction or assembly.

- ❊ Does the crib include stabilizer bars, which are metal rods fastened to the endboards and located underneath the crib? These bars provide additional stabilization and protection for baby.

- ❊ Do the wheels have locks to prevent the crib from "walking"?

- ❊ Can the crib be converted into a youth bed (i.e., is one side completely removable)? This may or may not be important to you; I specifically purchased a crib that converted, but by the time Clare was big enough for a bed, I wanted one I could also lie on, for reading and snuggling together, so we went straight to a twin.

The crib you bring home should have a mattress that fits snugly—a gap of no more than one-and-one-half inches between the mattress and the crib's sides and ends. Bumpers should be securely tied on with at least six ties or snaps. Personally, I'm not a fan of bumpers. I worried about suffocation and took them out; I figured Clare wouldn't be moving fast enough that she'd actually bang her head on the crib. Keep the crib clear of any items—mobiles, clothing, and toys—that have strings longer than seven inches. Don't set up the crib near any potential hazards in the room, such as a heater, window, or cords from blinds.

Below are some better-known crib manufacturers. Most of these lines are well known and established in the baby market, while others, like Mibb and Million Dollar Baby, are only a few years old. Some lines, like Legacy and Renaissance, are newer, exclusive divisions of established lines (Child Craft and Simmons, respectively). The choice comes down to what you like and what you can afford. Shop around: Prices range from $200 for a very nice Kinderkraft to more than $700 for a Bellini. Ask whether the store delivers and what they charge, and confirm they will assemble the crib in your home. They should.

❊ Bassett

❊ Bellini

❊ Bonavita

❊ Child Craft

❊ Cosco

❊ Delta

❊ Legacy

❊ Mibb

❊ Million Dollar Baby

❊ Morigeau

❊ Pali

❊ Ragazzi

❊ Renaissance

❊ Simmons

changing tables

Today's most popular changing tables are dressers with changing kits on top, built to grow with your child. The top of the dresser becomes a changing area when you place the changing kit, fitted with a pad, on top of the dresser. Remove the kit once you're beyond the diaper stage, and you have a standard chest of drawers that's great for a bigger kid's room. De Arthur, Morigeau, Bellini, Child Craft, and several new, upscale companies carry this type of table, which typically cost upwards of $500.

Conventional changing tables have a little pad with a small guardrail that goes all the way around the top (picture a rectangle) so your baby can't roll off. There are shelves underneath for storing diapers and wipes. However, you should never leave a baby unattended, no matter how secure your baby might seem.

Popular brands for these tables include Simmons and Child Craft. Most crib manufacturers also carry coordinating changing tables as part of nursery suites that also include chests and cribs. You can find changing tables for as low as $70, up to about $150.

gliders

A glider or rocking chair is optional, but if you have the space and the money, you may find having one helpful when you're feeding your baby or trying to get him to sleep. Dutalier gliders are practical for Chicago apartments and retail for about $500. You can find lower-priced versions, such as those from Shermag, with less padding for about $200. I recommend spending the extra money for the gliding ottoman too; this was our only baby furniture indulgence and totally worth it in terms of comfort. Clare is four and still loves me to rock her in "the blue chair." The popular sleigh glider is very compact. They come in your choice of white or wood finishes, with different fabric patterns for the cushions. But beware: Babies who get trained to fall asleep while being rocked or nursed will expect to be rocked or nursed whenever they wake in the middle of the night as they get older. I refused to believe this was true and did it anyway, then paid the price later. I wouldn't do it differently now—rocking Clare at bedtime was awfully sweet—but just know what to expect.

carriages/strollers

Newborns and toddlers alike spend many hours in the stroller going to the park, the supermarket, or window-shopping. Chicago is a walking town, and your stroller is the equivalent of a suburban minivan.

Whether you choose a carriage (a bassinet-like construction on wheels) or a stroller (easily collapsible) depends on your personal needs. While suburban mothers and fathers may be content with an inexpensive umbrella stroller that spends most of its time in the trunk of a car, city parents know a sturdy carriage is a must-have for babies and toddlers, especially since you'll use it to carry the groceries home, too.

Strollers sold today are safe (the JPMA sees to that), but not every type may be right for you. Consider what time of year your baby is due before you purchase your carriage or stroller. For winter babies, a carriage with a boot (an enclosed end) might be the best bet to keep your infant warm. For summer babies, look for a carriage with good ventilation and a sunshade. Also consider where you live. If your building has a doorman, you can usually get some help carrying a heavier stroller up the stairs and inside. If you're in a walk-up, look for one that's light and portable, and practice folding it to get it down to a quick routine; you're going to be wrestling that stroller in and out of buses and cabs for a good couple of years.

Other desirable features include a stroller seat that reclines (a must for newborn to three-month-olds), plenty of storage space underneath, brakes on all four wheels, and a handle that reverses to allow the baby to face you or to face out. The latest innovation is the popular stroller/car seat combination. This is an infant car seat that straps and snaps into a stroller base. New moms swear by this for taxi travel and city walking. Popular models include the Snap N' Go by Baby Trend, Century 4-in-1 Plus by Century, the Circus and Sterling LiteRiders by Graco, the Evenflo Trendsetter by Evenflo, and the Kolcraft Secura Travel System by Kolcraft.

For umbrella strollers, the English-made Maclarens have withstood the test of time for parents who reuse them with their second child. One mom I know of has had her Maclaren for five years now, without a single repair! They retail for $170 to $300, depending on the model. For a full carriage/stroller, it is generally agreed that the Peg Perego strollers are the best of the lot. These Italian-made strollers are so popular in some neighborhoods, the playgrounds look like Peg Perego parking lots. They are sturdy, attractive, stand folded upright for storage, and have a multitude of features that make life easy for mom and baby (reversible handle, large removable storage basket, full boot, and large canopy). Depending on the model, a Peg Perego ranges from about $200 to $350.

Jogging strollers are also very popular with parents who exercise with their babies. Their cost is between $100 and $400, depending on wheel size—the bigger the wheels, the more smoothly they roll. For parents of twins or two small children, side-by-side or tandem strollers might be good options. Side-by-sides are great for twins or children close to the same weight, while tandem strollers are great for kids of different sizes—with larger kids in front, and smaller in back.

When preparing to buy, tell the store clerk how you plan to use the carriage, and ask for a recommendation. Take the carriage for a "test drive" in the store to see whether it feels comfortable for you and your mate; check the height of the handles or bar, and make sure neither of you has to hunch over to reach it comfortably.

Here is a list of popular brands:

❋ Aprica

❋ Baby Trend

❋ Century

❋ Chicco

❋ Combi

❋ Emmaljunga

❋ Evenflo

❋ Graco

❋ Inglesina

❋ Kolcraft

❋ Maclaren

❋ Peg Perego

car seats

Even if you don't have a car, you must have a car seat. The hospital will not release your newborn unless you have one, and while you could borrow a seat from a friend, purchasing your own will be a practical investment.

By law, babies must always ride in a car seat whenever in an automobile. (In fact, recent Illinois law dictates that all children under age eight be in a car seat or booster seat.) City taxis should come equipped with rear seat belts to attach over the car seat, so double check before you get into a cab. That said, it's very difficult to carry both a car seat and a stroller around with you. Hence, the new stroller/car seat combo, with the removable infant car seats that strap and snap into a base, is a great alternative. Prices range from $100 to $180.

The more ungainly convertible seats can be used from birth through the toddler years and have a reclining mechanism so that they face rearward for infants and forward for toddlers and young children. With more features and an advanced five-point tethering system, the Britax Roundabout (about $200) is by far the most popular model on the market. Other top sellers include Century and Evenflo. As of September 2002, all forward facing car seats have come equipped with tether straps for extra protection. They've been doing this in Europe for years.

Three designs of restraining straps or harnesses are available in car seats: the five-point harness, the T-shield, and the bar shield. Most experts agree that the five-point harness is the safest, but all three are sound options. The five-point harness is also the most time-consuming to put on and off, which can be annoying to impatient toddlers. All of this will make sense once you see them in the stores.

Though convertible seats can be used from birth, experts advise you to buy an infant carrier car seat for babies from birth up to twenty pounds (these range in price from about $70 go $170), and the convertible car seat when the child weighs more than twenty pounds. Infant car seats are smaller, recline better, often come with a sunshade, and are more heavily padded than the convertible. They're portable and can easily be carried in and out of the car without disturbing a sleeping baby. Remember that these seats must be rear-facing in your vehicle; toddler seats are forward-facing.

Booster seats and high-back boosters are designed for kids over 40 pounds—too big for convertible seats, but still too small for regular seatbelts. They have a raised, rigid base that allows children to use adult belts. Prices range from about $80 to $250.

baby swings

A swing might be your lifesaver during your baby's first few months—or maybe not. This is something your child either loves or hates. If you can, borrow one from a friend or relative before making the investment. However, keep in mind that swings have been a frequent recall item and check it out at www.cpsc.gov first. Do not use any swing that has only a waist belt (with no strap between the legs) and a hinged or removable tray as a restraint; babies have been injured or strangled when they slide down in the seat and fall to the ground or become trapped by the belt and tray.

The Graco Swyngomatic is a widely available swing. There are two models on the market—with and without the overhead bar. The benefit of the Graco Advantage is that without the bar, you can't bump your baby's head on it. Fisher Price and Regalo also make baby swings. A baby swing runs about $50 to $90.

bouncy seats

The bouncy seat is another potential lifesaver; it was the only way I got to shower for a while. It's portable; you can move it from the living room to the kitchen to the bathroom so you can always see your baby and he can always see you. Plus, the newest bouncy seats are more plush than ever, and have a vibrating feature that can lull a fussy baby right to sleep. The bouncy seat is great for feeding your baby when he's starting to eat solid food but is still too small for a highchair. Combi's "Activity Rocker" is popular; it's well made, it vibrates—and it's fancier than other brands. The European style of rocker-bouncers is very popular as well, such as the one from Chicco. Bouncy seats are about $20 to $40, or more with more bells and whistles. Here's a list of good bouncy seats:

❊ Chicco

❊ Combi

❊ Evenflo

❊ Kids II

❊ Summer

highchairs

When you are buying a highchair, it is advisable to:

❊ Buy a chair with a wide base to limit the chances of the chair tipping over.

❊ Find a chair with an easy, one-hand tray release mechanism, which makes it easier to take your baby in and out.

❊ Look for a wrap-around tray—easier to eat from and keep clean.

❊ Find a chair with a detachable seat cushion. These chairs become dirty easily and you will want it to last more than a year.

Most highchair accidents occur (usually with children under one year) when a child has not been strapped in properly and tumbles out. Don't rely on the chair's tray to keep your baby enclosed; use the safety belt—be sure it has a strap both around the waist and between the legs—and never leave your baby unattended.

Before buying a highchair, decide if you want wood or metal and vinyl. Wooden highchairs are beautiful, but they don't collapse—so they are not ideal for those with limited apartment space. Also they require the use of both hands to take the tray off. Some models require you to flip the tray over the baby's head. If you're not careful, this can be a dangerous maneuver.

Right now, the most popular and functional highchairs are metal and vinyl. They have one-handed tray release mechanisms, reclining and height features. They have easy to clean seats, and comfy cushioning.

By far, the most popular highchair on the market is the Peg Perego Prima Pappa—with seven height adjustments and four recline positions, a thickly padded seat, a wrap-around tray, and a wide wheeled base, this highchair is ideal. This is also the most expensive model, at around $170. Highchair prices start at $90 for a Million Dollar Baby.

First Years' Reclining Three Stage Feeding Seat is a great alternative to a highchair because like a booster seat, it straps onto a regular chair. This seat has three recline positions for each stage of early childhood: newborn, infant, and toddler. To adjust, you simply press two buttons and slide the seat. This product is ideal for traveling, as well as smaller apartments where space is limited. It retails for approximately $30.

Finally, I must repeat: Never leave your baby unattended in a highchair, even for a few seconds!

Here are some of the best and most popular brands:

❉ Peg Perego

❉ Chicco

❉ First Years

❉ Rochelle

❉ Million Dollar Baby

booster seats/hook-on seats

Although you may want to buy a portable hook-on chair to use when you take your baby or toddler to a restaurant or other place where no highchair is available, Consumer Reports does not recommend using hook-on seats at all; the hazards are just too serious.

Booster seats are safer and more practical than hook-ons. They can be used for children up to preschool age, and the Safety 1st (about $30), can be easily folded. Put this on a chair in your kitchen and you may be able to live without an expensive highchair! Other popular brands include Cosco, First Years, and Kids II, with prices ranging between $12 and $25.

playpens/portable cribs

Playpens—now known as "playards"—are a great place to park your baby when you need five minutes to yourself to shower, answer the door, talk on the phone, or make dinner. Some babies might amuse themselves in the playpen for up to thirty minutes at a time, but not all children like them; Clare wouldn't stay ten minutes without screaming her head off. Playpens are also big and difficult to store and transport, so you might want to go for the portable crib instead. It can function as a playpen, but it's smaller and can easily be put away. Portable cribs have a thin mattress and sheets, so they can be used as a crib when you're traveling. Many of the playpens and cribs are fundamentally the same, but each brand offers different additional features. Beware when inheriting a hand-me-down portable crib; many have been recalled. When shopping for a playpen, be sure to compare and contrast different brands to find the best features for your specific needs. Prices range between $75 for the Graco Pack 'N' Play, to $175 for Arm's Reach Concepts' dual playpen/bassinet. Popular brands include:

❉ Arms Reach Concepts

❉ Century

❉ Fisher Price

❉ Graco Pack 'N' Play

❉ Regalo

bathtubs/bath seats

At first, bathe your tiny baby in the kitchen or bathroom sink. When he's a little bigger and you'd prefer to use the bathtub, you may want to buy a special baby tub that fits into the big tub. Most baby tubs are similar; they come either with or without a sponge insert. The sponge tends to get a mildew odor, is hard to wring out, and takes days to dry—so I'd skip it. The Cuddletub by Graco ($25) is a great bathtub that is carried by many stores. It has an adjustable foam cushion with mesh underneath for newborns to rest on. It can be removed once your baby can sit up on his own. The best-selling Evenflo Two-Year tub is the sturdiest of tubs and can be used for a child up to two years old. It has an insert for infants up to three months old, which can be easily removed as the child grows.

When your baby is old enough to sit up on his own, he's ready for a bath seat. The Safety 1st bath seat is a ring that attaches to your bathtub with suction cups. It is roomy enough to hold a two-year-old. Once she can sit up on her own, your baby will also enjoy the inflatable Kel-Gar Snug-Tub. It looks like a mini pool and is lots of fun for older babies (over six months).

baby carriers

You see these pouch-like, soft cloth carriers strapped onto the fronts of mothers and fathers everywhere. They're often called "snuglis" for the company that invented them. While the actual Snuglis are attractive and functional, Baby Bjorn has surpassed them in quality and price.

This is another item that you may use for only a short time if you have a big baby; I had a tenth-per-centile baby and used mine for seven or eight months. Bigger babies quickly become too heavy to carry strapped onto your shoulders though. Try to borrow one from a friend and test it with your baby before purchasing to see if you're comfortable with it. Baby carriers are popular with second or third time moms who might have a stroller to push or other hands to hold.

Prices range from about $25 for a Snugli, to $79 for the best-selling Baby Bjorn. Nojo makes a popular Baby Sling (about $40), which allows you to hold your baby horizontally as well as vertically, allowing baby to sleep more comfortably. This product is wonderful for breastfeeding because you simply pull the fabric up over baby's head and you are guarded from exposure.

backpacks

Women who use backpacks swear by them for comfort and convenience; I used mine constantly, especially because I had a child who complained every time I put her down to vacuum or cook dinner. Your baby is ready for a backpack once she can sit up on her own. Borrow one from a friend, and try it out with your baby on board before you decide to purchase your own.

The most popular brand is the Kelty backpack, which is strong and durable. Kelty is well known for its outdoor equipment and this product is just as heavy-duty. It costs slightly more than the other brands (about $100), but will last forever.

Evenflo, Gerry, and Tough Travelers also make dependable backpacks, starting at about $70.

baby monitors

Here's how to be in one room and hear your baby crying in another. These gadgets give you lots of options. Some monitors are battery-operated and can be carried throughout the apartment. It is difficult to say which brand is the most functional because of varying frequencies in different areas. The most secure method in buying the right monitor is to ask other parents in your neighborhood or building which monitors work best for them. Many Chicago apartment buildings pick up "noise" from other apartments. You may hear another baby crying and think it's your own. Here are some of the most recent and popular additions to the monitor category:

❋ 900 Megahertz (MHz) monitors: For about $50, these offer greater range and clarity than earlier models, and they are offered by several companies including First Years Crisp 'N' Clear, and Safety 1st's Sensitive Sound or Grow with Me.

❋ Monitors with two receivers: These are great and functional for larger living spaces because you can leave monitors in separate rooms. Graco makes a popular model (about $50).

❋ Rechargeable Monitors: Available from The First Years, these work much like your portable or cellular phone, except it is a direct line to your little darling.

Safety 1st makes Angel Care, which is a sound and movement monitor created to guard against SIDS. It is an ultra-sensitive sensor pad that is placed under the baby's mattress. If the pad does not sense motion, including heartbeat and breath for twenty seconds an alarm sounds to alert you. It costs about $100. Beware: This can drive you crazy and keep you up at night, even when your baby is asleep. Still, if you have a tummy sleeper, it may be worth the investment.

Safety 1st has also created a Child View Monitor which has 2.4 Gigahertz (GHz) for clarity and additional privacy. It has a camera for sound and image as well as a little television monitor for $150.

You may have to try a few different monitors out before you settle on one—sometimes you pick up your neighbors' conversations instead of the baby's cries.

diaper bags

Diaper bags come in two basic styles: over-the-shoulder, which zips or snaps closed, and the increasingly popular backpack. I had a backpack and would recommend it over a bag with a shoulder strap. A backpack leaves your hands and arms much freer, and it won't create muscular imbalance and tension, which you likely have enough of from nursing, favoring one side for carrying the baby, and doing everything one-handed.

You won't believe how much stuff you have to carry for your baby. Find a roomy bag with lot of pockets (for bottles, wipes, and the like) and a plastic lining. A changing pad is another great feature. The superstores have terrific selections. Babies Alley makes a popular Chanel look-alike, in quilted black with gold chain straps. Peg Perego has patterns that match their carriages. Pierre Deux's pretty (and functional) bag comes in a variety of colors, and Baby Mania offers a funky, fake fur bag for $129.95. Chic designers like Kenneth Cole, Donna Karan, and Kate

Spade have also gotten into the act with stylish, subdued bags (mostly in basic black, of course), available at Bellini and other upscale stores. Prices range from $20 for a Babies Alley diaper bag to $200 for a Pierre Deux. Baby Bjorn and Evenflo make popular knapsacks that don't even look like diaper bags.

the stores

Baby superstores are not necessarily large in size, but I consider them super because they provide one-stop shopping. Here you can buy all the furniture you need (crib, changing table, dresser), as well as sheets, towels, diapers, nipples, bottles, layettes or clothing for newborns, strollers/carriages, highchairs, playpens, baby carriers/knapsacks, and much, much more. You get the idea. I like them because they make your life easy. Most sell toys, too, but be aware that the selection is limited and the prices are often higher than at Toys "R" Us or other toy stores.

Some stores are ritzier than others, some more value oriented. The proximity of the store to your home should help you decide where to shop. Many expectant moms in Chicago visit too many stores in their quest for the perfect crib, sheets, and towels. You don't have to! Find a place that's convenient, and use it for all your needs. Patronize one store consistently, so the staff gets to know you and will go that extra mile when necessary. Also, buy in bulk. Many stores never "officially" discount, but may give you a better price if you are placing a large order. Don't be afraid to ask. And there's no harm in asking if they'll match a better price that you have seen somewhere else. Also check out the store's delivery policy. Policies vary widely.

superstores

❋ The Baby's Room

640 N. LaSalle St.; 312-642-1520

6133 N. Lincoln Ave.; 773-583-8112

www.mybabysroom.com

Return policy: Within 60 days, unused with receipt, for full refund.

When my friend Judy was pregnant with her first child, a year before I was pregnant with Clare, it seemed she and her husband were constantly off to The Baby's Room to get more baby stuff. Then when I was in the baby market myself, I understood why: The Baby's Room has about two dozen room displays with absolutely everything you might need for the nursery and getting around town: bassinets, cribs, changing tables, dressers, rockers, lamps, coordinated linens, strollers, car seats, highchairs, and more. The prices are reasonable—cribs range from as low as $300 up to $1,000—and the staff is helpful. Delivery is available for a flat fee of $130, which includes assembly.

❋ Toys "R" Us

10 S. State St.; 312-857-0667

3330 N. Western Ave.; 773-525-1690

87th Street and the Dan Ryan; 773-846-2600

6420 W. Fullerton Ave.; 773-637-1166

8900 Lafayette St.; 773-846-2600

www.toysrus.com

Return policy: Refund with receipt, otherwise store credit only.

Toys "R" Us is great. They sell furniture and accessories at some of the best prices in town. You'll find cribs for under $200, strollers, highchairs, playpens, bottles, bibs, and waterproof bed pads, as well as diapers and formula (available by the case). While Toys "R" Us favors the mass-market labels, you can find some of the better brands such as Peg Perego and Graco, plus Cosco, Evenflo, Kolcraft, Aprica, and Fisher-Price. Weekdays and evenings are your best bet for shopping; these stores are mobbed on the weekends. Delivery service is available; prices depend on the size of the items to be shipped.

specialty stores

❊ Bellini

2001 N. Halsted St.
312-943-6696
www.bellini.com
Return Policy: Store credit.
Customers who shop here rave about the top-of-the-line furniture and service at this Tiffany's of baby stores. The staff at this particular location (there's also one in Highland Park) is especially good at helping you design for a small city-sized space. The store is beautiful and carries a huge list of baby necessities. The staff will spend hours helping you select the perfect crib (this is the only place in town to find Bellini cribs, which start at $770), and coordinating furniture, bedding, and accessories. They custom-make bedding sets and have a library of fabrics you can choose from. Special knit items like sweaters and christening outfits are exquisite. Furniture delivery is a flat rate of $100 and includes assembly.

❊ Cradles of Distinction

2100 N. Southport Ave.
773-472-1001
www.cradlesofdistinction.com
Return policy: Within thirty days with receipt for store credit only; no returns on special orders.
Like Bellini, Cradles of Distinction caters to a high-end clientele, featuring gorgeous sets of cribs, dressers, armoires, and changing tables; some brands can even be custom painted, in designs like antique roses, paper dolls, stars and stripes, and nautical themed. Regular cribs run between $300 and $700; hand-painted ones are about $1,700. The store also carries beautiful linens, rugs, unique clothing, strollers, great gift toys (what little girl couldn't use a leopard purse?), baby accessories, and lovely painted child's furniture, including rockers ($300) and little tables and chairs ($720). The store's designers will work with you to coordinate furniture and accessories, to create a truly distinctive nursery.

❊ Elizabeth Marie

3612 N. Southport Ave.
773-525-4100
Return policy: Within 14 days with receipt only. The owner of Elizabeth Marie specializes in doing interior design for babies' and childrens' rooms and sells beautiful custom-made bed linens (about $300 for a set) and handmade baby items. Though there isn't enough space for furniture on the floor, she does represent the Maine Cottage and Relics lines, and also

chapter ten: baby furniture and accessories

will track down a special item you may want, for instance, an antique armoire. Hours are limited to Monday and Thursday through Saturday, from 10 a.m. to 3 p.m.; other times are by appointment only.

❋ The Land of Nod

900 W. North Ave.

312-475-9903

Land of Nod sells unbelievably cute furniture for nurseries, boys' and girls' rooms, and playrooms, as well as colorful linens, window treatments, rugs, and more. Part of a joint venture with Crate & Barrel, Land of Nod is of the same stylish, high quality. Cribs come in a range of prices, from $329 to $1,095. And it's a haul from the city, but if you can get out to Wheeling, you'll find Nods & Ends Outlet Store (1110B Larkin Drive; 847-459-9900), which has some really good deals.

❋ Pottery Barn Kids

2111 N. Clybourn Ave.

773-525-8349

Also at Oakbrook Center and Old Orchard Center

www.potterybarnkids.com

Like Pottery Barn for grownups, Pottery Barn Kids features stylish, solidly made furniture and accessories in colors and designs that will please both grownups and children as they grow. You'll find sets of cribs, dressers, changing tables, armoires, bookcases, and nightstands in natural wood or white-painted finishes; cribs are between $500 and $700 and convert to toddler beds, making them usable up to at least age three or four. Pottery Barn Kids also sells rockers and gliders, bedding and bath linens, rugs, window treatments, playroom furniture, organizer baskets, accessories, and toys. Linens and accessories change seasonally, while the furniture styles tend to remain the same for several seasons.

❋ The Right Start

2121 N. Clybourn Ave.

773-296-4420

www.therightstart.com

Return policy: 30 days with receipt for carseats and strollers; 60 days for everything else. Without receipt, store credit only.

Right Start doesn't sell cribs or furniture, but it does carry just about everything else you'll need in the way of baby equipment, including bassinets, strollers, car seats, highchairs, linens, bouncy seats, swings, diaper bags, and accessories. Right Start also sells a great co-sleeping product called the Snuggle Nest by Baby Delight ($52.95), a three-sided, fifteen-inch wide rigid foam sleeper that enables you to keep the baby in your bed without worrying about rolling over on her. Or you can find the Arm's Reach Mini Co-Sleeper Bassinet ($139.95), a rolling bassinet with storage in the bottom and a drop side that allows you to keep the baby right next to you without actually being in the same bed. This is a product I thought about buying, didn't because of the cost, then wished I had when Clare ended up in our bed for months, and I ended up with killer back pain from being in the middle.

baby proofing

Little did you know your apartment was a danger zone. Beware if you have—as do most of us—a glass or sharp-edged coffee table, electrical outlets, lamps, lamp cords, drawers, cleaning solutions and cosmetics under sinks/vanities, or anything sitting on a table.

Baby proofing your home is one of the most important tasks you'll undertake. Keep in mind that it doesn't all have to be done before the baby arrives, however. You'll find that when the baby begins to roll, you can start at the floor level, then work your way up the walls and furniture as your baby learns to crawl, pull up, and climb. My friends and I have found that the extent of our baby proofing also depends on the type of kids we have: Some children will scale the bookshelves the instant you look away, while others are content to sit on the floor and look at a book.

Here are several ways to get baby proofing help:

❋ Buy a book or video such as Mr. Baby Proofer, a thirty-minute video that shows parents how to create a safe environment for newborns.

❋ Ask for advice at any of the baby superstores. A salesperson will talk you through what you need in order to create a safe home.

❋ Consult a baby proofing expert. Local ones include A & H Childproofers (847-680-1924; the consultation in your home is free) and ABC Baby Proofing (312-243-7233).

❋ Check out the Safety Matters Web site (www.safetymatters.com). Founded by Highland Park couple Leslie and Larry Stone, professional baby proofers authors of the book The Safe & Sound Child, the site sells baby-proofing products and has a helpful page called "Ask Larry and Leslie."

Many people baby proof their own apartments. Here are some safety tips:

❋ Poisons or toxic materials (i.e., all cleaners) should not be stored under the sink; place them high up, out of your baby's reach.

❋ Attach all busy boxes, mirrors, or crib toys on the wall side of the crib, so that your baby cannot use the objects to climb out of the crib. Do not mount a wall hanging above the crib, where your child can pull it down and perhaps dislodge nails.

❋ Toilet lids should be locked closed.

❋ Keep all trash containers locked up and out of baby's way.

❋ Remove tall lamps or coatracks or block them with furniture, so that your baby can't pull them over.

❋ When cooking, all pot handles should be turned inward so your baby cannot reach them. Use back burners when possible.

❋ Separate plants and babies. Some plants are poisonous, and a young child may eat the leaves or pull the whole plant on top of himself.

❋ Hanging cords from answering machines, phones, lamps, and appliances should be out of your baby's reach.

❋ Do not take pills or medication in front of children; they mimic what they see.

❋ Remove all soaps, razors, and shampoos from around the edge of the bathtub.

❋ Do not use tacks or staples to secure electrical cords to walls; they can fall out or be pulled out and swallowed. Use tape.

❋ Discard plastic dry cleaner bags before entering the house. Babies can suffocate in them or pull off pieces and choke on them.

❋ Keep emergency phone numbers, including poison control center, near all telephones.

❋ To prevent carpeting from sliding, use a foam grid padding beneath it.

❋ Babies like to pull off the tips from doorstops. Place some glue inside the cap, then stick the cap back onto the doorstop.

❋ Remove magnets from your refrigerator door. If they fall to the floor and break, a child may pick up the pieces and swallow them. Invest in baby magnets or plastic non-breakable ones.

❋ If you have a fireplace, place a piece of carpet or foam on the whole base so your child won't bang into the brick.

❋ Get a bathtub spout cover to prevent your child from hitting his head against it.

❋ If you have a home gym, keep that room closed when you're not in it. Babies can get their fingers stuck in the spokes of exercise bikes, put their fingers in the gears, or pull weights onto themselves.

❋ Glass panels in coffee tables can break under the weight of a child. Replace with acrylic.

❋ Mobiles should be removed when a child is five to seven months old. A baby of that age can pull the mobile down or get injured if the little strings from the mobile become wrapped around his fingers.

❋ Cords for window blinds should be lifted high and out of reach. Babies can accidentally wrap them around themselves.

❋ Wash out cleaning fluid bottles before putting them in your recycling bin. Just a drop of cleaning fluid can cause serious injury to a baby.

❋ Never leave infants alone in the bathtub. Ignore telephone calls and doorbells. Babies can drown in just an inch of water. Never leave a tub or any buckets or pails with water standing in them.

❋ Check the underside of upholstered furniture for loose staples or sharp points.

baby and toddler clothing

If you've always thought baby clothing was the cutest thing in the world, you're going to love this chapter. Chicago stores have all the baby clothing you need, want, or have dreamt of. There is tons of adorable stuff to choose from, but don't bring all of it home at once. Babies grow very, very quickly, and the outfit that fit the last time you put it on may not even come close a few weeks later. I'll tell you about some of the best clothing shops in the city to help you save time, energy, and money.

If you're a first-time parent, you may find that only the "best"—meaning most expensive—will do for your little one. From dresses to pajamas, parents of first-borns often spare no expense. But with a second child, you'll probably opt for a different strategy: Buy on sale! Shop resale stores, Children's Place, and Old Navy. The quality is good, and the bargains can't be beat.

shopping tips

If your shower gifts include too many outfits in three- and six-month sizes, return most of them for a credit, or exchange them for twelve- or eighteen-month sizes. Don't dawdle, either. If you put it off, you'll find the stores won't take them back or they'll have been marked down. Also, wait until all the baby gifts are in—you may not need as much as you think.

❊ Pay attention to a store's return policy. Most of the independent shops are very strict when it comes to returns. Department stores tend to be the most lenient; goods can usually be brought back for cash or credit for up to one year.

❊ Ask about the sales. Small shops often have January and June/July special pricing events; some have quarterly sales. Department stores always seem to have sales. In some shops, you won't be able to use gift certificates on sale items.

❊ If you plan to shop with your little one in tow, use a baby carrier or small stroller. Some of these stores are small and crowded, and you may have to walk up a flight of stairs.

❊ Onesie outfits are practical. You can't have too many of these pullover, short sleeve T-shirts with bottom snaps to layer under winter clothes or to use as-is in hot weather. All the stores carry onesies, in a variety of price ranges. Buy the least expensive ones you can find, and always in 100-percent cotton.

❊ Think cotton. It's cozy, soft, and easily washable. Your pediatrician may tell you to wash your baby's clothes for the first year in the nondetergents Dreft or Ivory Snow, which do not irritate a baby's sensitive skin. However, my husband's skin is about as sensitive as it comes, so we used our usual—and much cheaper—Purex on Clare's clothes and she was fine.

❊ You'll find it convenient to have many sleeping outfits, but test several before buying a bunch to see which your baby prefers. Some babies are uncomfortable with their feet restricted in drawstring-bottom sleepers and do better in sleeper pajamas. Unfortunately, all sleepwear must be 100-percent polyester to be flame retardant.

❊ Don't buy any infant clothes with strings around or near the neck, which can be dangerous.

Most manufacturers have stopped making baby clothes with strings, but if you purchase clothes at resale shops, they may predate this safety precaution.

✳ Use clothing with snaps around the bottoms, for easy changing. Baby girls may look adorable in tights, but you'll be cursing them by the third diaper change.

✳ Give some thought to how and when you'll do laundry. Your baby will go through several outfits a day (and so, most likely, will you if you don't enjoy being covered with spit-up and baby poop). If you have a washer and dryer in your apartment, and it's easy to throw in a load at odd moments, a large layette may be unnecessary. If you use a machine in your building's basement or take clothing to a neighborhood laundromat, it may be more convenient and easier on your pocketbook to stock a relatively large supply of clothing. Either way, all clothing should be machine washable.

✳ Buy ahead whenever possible. I've made a practice of hitting stores at the end of the season to buy clothes a year ahead at incredible prices. (By the next year I've forgotten what I bought, so it's always fun to open the "clothes for Clare to grow into" box.) Winter coats are often on sale in January. Also, try to borrow expensive items, such as snowsuits.

✳ If you receive many gifts in small sizes, always exchange some for larger ones.

✳ Many stores have prepared an essential layette list for you—some of them incredibly long! Take such lists with a grain of salt, keeping in mind your own budget and storage space.

✳ Because hours change frequently, call ahead. Most stores are open seven days a week, from 10 or 11 a.m. until 6 p.m.

Here's a practical layette:

for baby

✳ 6 onesies

✳ 2 side-snap or side-tie shirts (until umbilical cord falls off)

✳ 6 stretchies or coveralls, which cover your baby from neck to feet, and have snaps (these in heavier material are good for sleeping)

✳ 4 sleep gowns or sleeper bags

✳ 2 caps

✳ 6 pairs of socks

✳ 1 snowsuit (for winter babies)

✳ 4 receiving blankets (to lay the baby down on and wrap her up in)

✳ 2 heavier blankets (one for stroller, one for crib), waffle-weave

❄ 3 hooded towel/washcloth sets

❄ 12 cloth diapers (for burping the baby)

❄ 4 bibs

❄ 1 outdoor hat (keeps winter babies warm, protects summer babies from sun)

❄ 1 pair cotton mittens (to prevent your baby from scratching her face)

❄ 1 pair outdoor mittens (for winter babies)

❄ baby nail clipper, digital thermometer and probe covers, nasal aspirator (a good one, not the flimsy one from the hospital), hairbrush/comb

❄ bath tub

for crib

❄ 2 quilted mattress pads

❄ 2 waterproof liners

❄ 3–4 fitted crib sheets

❄ 6 crib bibs (to protect sheets from baby spit-up)

❄ 1 bumper pad

the stores

From expensive designer boutiques to discount department stores, children's shops dot the retail landscape of Chicago. The prices at some of the European boutiques found on Oak Street or Michigan Avenue are mind-boggling; I wouldn't pay $100 for a child's T-shirt from France, but apparently someone does. Just a few blocks away, in the heart of the Loop, you can find reasonably priced clothing at stores like Children's Place and Old Navy. And boutiques all over the North Side offer unique, trendy clothes in a variety of price ranges.

the big chains

❄ *The Children's Place*
39 S. State St.
312-332-9111
www.childrensplace.com
Return policy: No sale is ever final.
This growing chain with shops in the city and suburbs is a real find, and could well be the next Gap. The store is clean, its return policy is flexible, and the clothing is comfortable, high quality, stylish, and more affordable than the Gap. The collections are basic and come in bright and traditional colors, with some fashion sense. You can find beautiful fall/winter corduroys in rich, royal colors—deep blue, ruby red, and emerald green—as well as bright, multicolored summer clothing and bathing suits. You can also find socks, hats, headbands, scrunchies, and adorable sunglasses.

❊ babyGap

Many locations throughout Chicago, including
The Gap Outlet, 2778 N. Milwaukee Ave., 773-
252-0594

www.gapkids.com

Return policy: Lenient

Who doesn't love the Gap? There are about a
dozen babyGap stores in town, usually within
grown-up Gap stores. Nothing outrageous
here. The Gap's baby clothing is often 100-per-
cent cotton, and in traditional colors and
styles. But the sales are great. Comfortable
play clothes hold up well after repeated wash-
ings. (Just be prepared to see other babies at
the playgroup wearing the exact same outfit.)

❊ Gymboree

Water Tower Place

835 N. Michigan Ave.

312-649-9074

www.gymboree.com

Return policy: Lenient

The large, roomy Gymboree stores specialize
in trendy play clothes and active wear for boys
and girls from infant to eight years. It's also
one of the few places where you can find preemie clothes. The moderately priced clothes
are 100-percent cotton and come in brightly
colored designs, with new collections arriving
every six to eight weeks.

❊ Old Navy Clothing Co.

35 N. State St.; 312-551-0522

7601 S. Cicero; 773-284-7710

4805 W. North Ave.; 773-862-1774

1730 W. Fullerton Ave.; 773-871-0601

www.oldnavy.com

Return policy: Refund with receipt within 30 days

The Old Navy Clothing Co. is owned by the
Gap and is a lower-priced alternative. These
warehouse-like stores are great to visit, even if
you don't need kiddie clothes. You'll find reasonably priced, 100 percent cotton items for
newborns to adults. There are adorable overalls for $10, infant dresses for $10 to $16, and
onesies in bright colors, in addition to sunglasses, socks, hats, bathing suits, and whatever else is currently fashionable. Be warned: Old
Navy can be mobbed on weekends.

❊ Talbot's Kids

Chicago Place

700 N. Michigan Ave.

312-943-0255

www.talbots.com

Return policy: Refund with receipt, otherwise
store credit only

This large store sells attractive clothes for boys
and girls from size 2 to 16. Their high-quality,
preppy style of clothing is worth a look. Classic
polo shirts and elastic waist khakis are perfect
for husky boys. They have excellent sales, with
prices often half the original. The clothes are
very well made and hold up well even over several years as hand-me-downs.

the independents

❊ Active Kids

838 W. Armitage Ave.

773-281-2002

www.activeendeavors.com

Return policy: 14 days with tags and receipt for full refund; 14 more days with tags and receipt for store credit or exchange

Previously more of a kids' sportswear store, Active Kids now focuses on trendy casual clothes, with jeans, shorts, tops, and sweaters from Paper Denim, Juicy Couture, Petit Bateau, and James Perse, among others. You'll also find a variety of casual, sturdy shoes, and a selection of baby gear, including strollers and backpacks.

All Our Children

2217 N. Halsted St.

773-327-1868

Return policy: Within 45 days, for exchange or store credit only

This roomy Lincoln Park store carries a wide range of high-quality kids' clothing for boys and girls, from infants through size 14. Among the brands you'll find are Jean Bourget, Petit Bateau, Lilly Pulitzer, Charlie Rocket, and Wes & Willy. All Our Children also carries some toys and accessories, and the staff is incredibly helpful. Girls love Princess Day, an event held every few months, when they can get a manicure, hair braiding, lemonade, cookies, a photo, and a goodie bag, all for $12. For boys (and girls if they wish), the store recently started bringing in a magician to teach magic tricks for $5 a half-hour session. Finally, photographer Barb Levant (see page 137) periodically does photo shoots in the store; a portrait session is $185.

Anne's Kids

4509 N. Clark St.

773-506-4917

Return policy: Exchange or store credit only

If you're looking for kids' dress-up clothes at relatively affordable prices, this is the place to go. The store itself isn't fancy; in fact, it doesn't even have dressing rooms. What you will find are loads of children's clothing in sizes infant through 18. Most of it is party wear for girls, but you also can find suits and tuxes for boys, and some casual clothes for both boys and girls. The merchandise is constantly changing, so if you don't find anything suitable, it pays to stop in again soon.

Bebe Elegante

3338 N. Ashland Ave.; 773-477-2323

3903 W. Fullerton Ave.; 773-772-1538

Return policy: Exchange or store credit only

Specializing in children's clothing for special occasions, Bebe Elegante carries flowergirl dresses, tuxedos, first communion dresses, and christening outfits. You'll also find a few casual items—knit sweater sets for girls, sweatpants and shirts for boys—among the designer items, dress-up shoes, and accessories.

Camelot

2216 N. Clybourn Ave.

773-472-7091

Return policy: Exchange or store credit only

Camelot sells a mix of dressy and more casual designer clothing for infants up to size 16 for girls and size 10 for boys. Dressy designers include Charabia, Petit Faune, and Monkey

Wear, while trendy offerings come from Chevignon, Cakewalk, and Oilily, among others.

❉ Foxmoor Kids

105 S. State St.

312-759-9401

Return policy: Within 14 days, with receipt, for full refund

Foxmoor Kids sells the basics for babies, boys, and girls at reasonable prices: dresses, sweaters, tops, pants, jeans, shorts, and school uniforms. Most of the clothing is fairly casual, for school and play, but you can also find some dressier items for special occasions.

❉ Jacadi Paris

Water Tower Place

835 N. Michigan Ave.

312-337-9600

Return policy: 7 days for exchange only. Sale items are final.

Started in Paris in the late '70s, Jacadi Paris now has more than 400 stores worldwide, all selling the kind of clothing worn by French schoolchildren—who clearly are as stylish as their parents. The Jacadi line features comfortable, durable play clothes that are both really beautiful and really functional. Collections include clothing, shoes, and accessories, all in complementary colors and styles made for mixing and matching. Sizes range from newborn to 12.

❉ Jordan Marie

The Shops at North Bridge

520 N. Michigan Ave.

312-670-2229

www.jordanmarie.com

Return policy: Three days for specialty items (christening gowns, party dresses), two weeks for other items

Jordan Marie sells beautiful, upscale clothing for infants through size 4T. For newborns you'll find adorable sets of tops and leggings with matching hats and booties, as well as lovely christening gowns. For girls you'll find party dresses, unique tunic-and-pants sets, and the kind of pretty play clothes you hate to see get dirty; nearly every outfit has a cute hat to match. For boys you can find playwear that's a bit more rugged but still awfully cute. The store also carries lots of newborn accessories (blankets, bibs, towels), plush toys, and gift baskets.

❉ LMNOP

2574 N. Lincoln Ave.

773-975-4055

Return policy: Within two weeks, exchange or store credit

This boutique with a minimalist feel carries more than 100 different brands of designer children's clothing, in sizes newborn through ten. Among the labels you'll find are Fifi and Fido, James Perse, Confetti, Judith Lacroix, Quincy, and Haute Stuff.

❉ Madison and Friends

940 N. Rush St.

312-642-6403

www.madisonandfriends.com

Return policy: Within 30 days, for exchange or store credit only

Inspired by the far hipper children's clothing

stores they saw in California, owners David and Wendi Shelist launched their boutique to cater to an upscale clientele searching for cool clothes for kids, in sizes preemie to 16. Besides jeans, pants, dresses, sweaters, and tops by makers that include Diesel, Juicy, and Sean Jean, you'll find leather coats, cute sports-themed items (for girls, too—like a pink baseball sweater), even a baby tuxedo. The store also stocks baby toys, strollers, car seats, baby blankets, and gift items. The new Denim Lounge in the basement carries denim wear for men, women, and kids.

✳ Milani Boutique

65 E. Oak St.

312-587-0570

Return policy: Within 10 days, for exchange or store credit only

This ultra-exclusive shop sells not just off-the-rack clothing but also kiddie couture: custom-made children's wear fit for royalty. Among the designers featured are Dolce & Gabbana, Junior, Young Versace, Moschino, and Betsey Johnson Girls, for infants through size 20.

✳ Mini Me

900 N. Michigan Ave.

312-988-4011

Return policy: Within 30 days, for exchange or store credit only

Mini Me is a pricey boutique that offers European designer wear mainly for girls (infant through size 10), though you will find boys' clothing up to size 3. The exclusive clothing includes tops, bottoms, and dresses from mak-

ers such as Cashmere Cause, Sonia Rykiel, and Verde Mela.

✳ Oilily

The Shops at North Bridge

520 N. Michigan Ave.

312-527-5747

www.oililyusa.com

Return policy: Within 14 days, with receipt, for full refund

This Netherlands-based company sells well-made, higher-priced casual clothing in bright colors and bold prints; the girls' clothing in particular frequently comes in a brash, funky mix of patterns. You'll find clothing for babies through size 12 that includes tops, bottoms, dresses, skirts, and some outerwear. Oilily also sells unique shoes and boots, in the same kinds of wild colors and patterns you'll find in the clothing. Moms who want to match their kids can stop at the Oilily store for women on the first floor.

✳ Psycho Baby

1630 N. Damen Ave.

773-772-2815

Return policy: 14 days for cash refund, up to 30 days for store credit. Sale items are final.

If your tastes include funky, retro, and fun, you'll love the clothes at this Bucktown boutique. Clothing comes in sizes newborn to 6, and includes such labels as Queen Christine, Wild Mango, and the adorably packaged Fortune Tees. Psycho Baby also carries books, toys, and shoes, and has a play area to keep the kids out of your hair while you shop.

The Red Balloon

2060 N. Damen Ave.

773-489-9800

www.theredballoon.com

Return policy: Exchange or store credit only

Begun as a children's furniture store, the Red Balloon has expanded to include clothing, toys, books, wall art, and more. Kids clothing comes in size newborn to 6T, and is an appealing mix of sturdy fabrics, bright colors, and fun patterns. The boutique itself is a great place to shop, with brightly colored, inviting displays and fun wall art. You'll also find the store's signature item: handmade, hand-painted toy chests.

United Colors of Benetton Kids

The Shops at North Bridge

520 N. Michigan Ave.

312-494-9161

Return policy: Within 14 days, with receipt, for full refund

Like its adult line, Benetton Kids clothing is casual, trendy, and colorful. Clothing runs from newborn to size 10 for girls, and to size 6 for boys. You'll find sweaters, sweatshirts, pullover tops, jeans, knit dresses, and outerwear, all of it well made.

resale shops

On the other end of the scale, here's where you'll find real bargains—the big names, many hardly worn, at prices way below those of the boutiques.

First Seconds Resale

4266 N. Milwaukee Ave.

773-777-2200

First Seconds sells used children's clothing, furniture, baby equipment, books, videos, and toys. The service is good, and so is the quality of merchandise. If you're looking for stuffed animals, this is the place to get them; the shelves are loaded with not just modern ones, but also vintage Pooh Bears and other classics you probably haven't seen since you were a kid.

My Sister's Closet

5413 W. Devon Ave.

773-774-5050

Right next door to the fabulous Cut Rate Toys discount store, My Sister's Closet is a charming little resale store for children's clothing, shoes, and accessories.

Once Upon a Child

5316 N. Milwaukee Ave.

773-594-1705

This national chain carries both new and gently used children's clothing, furniture, baby gear, books, and toys. If you're looking to sell stuff, Once a Upon a Child has the advantage of paying on the spot, rather than requiring consigners to go through a waiting period of several months as other stores do.

The Second Child

954 W. Armitage Ave.

773-883-0880

Here you'll find designer clothes at resale prices: Oilily, Jacadi, Baby Lulu, Cakewalk, and

Lilly Pulitzer, in kids' sizes infant through 14. The clothing is high quality—no stains or missing buttons—and of recent vintage. You'll also find maternity clothes, including casual wear, business suits, and dressy outfits, as well as toys, books, and videos. The Second Child also carries used furniture that is JPMA-approved and car seats that are no more than three years old.

Unique Thrift

North Side:
3748 N. Elston Ave.; 773-279-0850
4441 W. Diversey Ave.; 773-227-2282
4445 N. Sheridan Road; 773-275-8623

South Side:
3000 S. Halsted St.; 312-842-0942
3542 S. Archer Ave.; 773-247-2599
9341 S. Ashland Ave.; 773-239-3127
2329 S. Kedzie Ave.; 773-762-7510
5040 S. Kedzie Ave.; 773-434-4886

My sister-in-law Molly is a huge fan of Unique Thrift and has been shopping there since her kids, now 14 and 12, were little. Molly is an extremely discriminating consumer with great taste, and she raves about the quality and selection the Unique stores offer. You can find everything here: clothes, linens, bikes, toys, books, household goods, furniture, jewelry, and more. The volume and turnover of merchandise is big and fast, and the organization makes shopping here much easier than other thrift stores; clothing, for instance, is arranged by type and color (black pants, red shirts, etc.). Every Monday the already rock-bottom prices are fifty percent off; get there when the store opens at 8 a.m. for the best stuff.

Village Discount Outlet

All inquiries:
12914 S. Western Ave. (Blue Island)
708-388-4772
www.villagediscountoutlet.com

North Side:
4898 N. Clark St.
3301 W. Lawrence
4635 N. Elston Ave.
4027 N. Kedzie Ave.
2043 W. Roscoe
2855 N. Halsted St.
2032 N. Milwaukee Ave.

South Side:
7443 S. Racine
6419 S. Kedzie
2514 W. 47th St.
4020 W. 26th St.

My friend Patti, who has three children under age five, compares Village Discount to the Salvation Army—except that the prices are even cheaper. The most expensive clothing items she's purchased were $2; most are between 10 cents and 90 cents, and the quality is really good. You'll find clothing for adults and children, toys, and household goods. The organization of stores seems to vary; the one Patti shops at, on Clark Street, is a bit messy, while Molly, my sister-in-law, says the ones she shops at on the South Side are better. You won't find better deals anywhere, except maybe some garage sales.

Funkiest Kids' Clothes

LMNOP

Madison and Friends

Psycho Baby

malls

Consider the possibility of leaving town from time to time to do your children's clothes shopping. Mall shopping makes for a good outing, and the food courts will keep the kids happy. I've listed malls in the area that have several children's stores and are within an hour of the city. All driving directions are from Chicago.

Many of the mall stores have been described throughout this chapter. Most, if not all, of these malls have large department stores with wonderful children's departments. Make a day of it. Pop into LEGO or the Disney Store to start the day off right, and then feed the kids an early lunch at the food court. Then while they nap in the stroller, you can shop for yourself.

north

❋ *Northbrook Court*

2171 Northbrook Court

Northbrook

847-498-8161

www.northbrookcourt.com

Directions: Take I-90/94 (the Kennedy) west,

and remain on I-94 (the Edens) past the split. Take Illinois 41 north and exit at Lake Cook Road. Go west on Lake Cook; mall will be on the left.

Stores:

Galt Toys • GapKids/babyGap • Gymboree • Gymboree Play and Music • Kids CDs • LEGO • Oilily • Snippets Mini-Cuts • Stride Rite • Land of Nod

❋ *Old Orchard*

34 Old Orchard Center

Skokie

847-673-6800

www.westfield.com/us/centres/illinois/oldor-chard/

Directions: Take I-90/94 (the Kennedy) west, and remain on I-94 (the Edens) past the split. Exit at Old Orchard Road, and go east. The center is on the right-hand side less than a quarter-mile from the exit.

Stores:

Big Toy Express • Children's Place • Disney Store • GapKids/babyGap • Gymboree • KB Toy Express • Mimi Maternity • Motherhood • Picture People • Pottery Barn Kids • Talbot's Kids

❋ *Woodfield Shopping Center*

Golf Road at Route 53

Schaumburg

847-330-1537

www.shopwoodfield.com/

Directions: Take I-90 (the Kennedy) west to Illinois 53 south. Exit onto Golf Road and go west; mall is on the left.

Stores:

Build-a-Bear Workshop • Children's Place • Disney Store • GapKids • Gymboree • Jiminee's Doll Clothes • Journey's Kidz • KB Toys • LEGO • Mimi Maternity • Motherhood Maternity • Picture People • Rainforest Café • Stride Rite

west

❈ *Oakbrook Center*

100 Oakbrook Center

Oakbrook

630-573-0700

www.oakbrookcenter.com

Directions: Take I-290 west. Exit onto the East-West Tollway to Aurora (I-88).

Pay one toll (40 cents) and exit at Cermak Road/22nd Street. At the bottom of the exit ramp, continue across Cermak Road. You are now on Spring Road. Mall is on the left.

Stores:

A Pea in the Pod • Build-a-Bear Workshop • Children's Place • Club Libby Liu • Disney Store • GapKids/babyGap • Guess Kids • Gymboree • Hanna Andersson • KB Toys • KidSnips • Motherhood Maternity • Picture People • Pottery Barn Kids • Talbot's Kids

south

❈ *Chicago Ridge*

95th Street and Ridgeland Avenue

708-422-0897

www.chicagoridgemall.com

Directions: Take I-90/94 (the Dan Ryan) south and remain on I-94 when I-90 splits off. Exit at 95th Street and go west to Ridgeland. Or, take Cicero Avenue (or another western main artery, such as Western Avenue) south to 95th Street, then head west to Ridgeland.

Stores:

Children's Place • Disney Store • Finish Line • Game Stop • Gymboree • KB Toys • Motherhood Maternity • Picture People • Stride Rite

Best Places for Sale Items Under $10

The Children's Place

Old Navy

Target

toys,
toys,
toys

You're about to rediscover the magic of toys, because you're going to be playing with them more than you can imagine. Having a baby is a great excuse to act like a kid again, and Chicago's toy stores, from the Disney Store to the tiniest neighborhood specialty shop, will help you to remember what it was like when a toy store was the greatest place in the world. Of course, the world of toys has changed since you were a kid, so here are some tips to get you started on picking the right toys, including where to find them.

Play is, essentially, a child's version of work. Play is how children learn, and healthy, happy, imaginative play is crucial to a growing child's development. The more creative playtime a child has, the more likely it is that she or he will become a creative, well-rounded adult. Creative thinking is important whether you are a doctor, an accountant, an actor, or a painter. Be creative with your child, play with abandon . . . but remember: No toy can replace you, and you can only enhance the toy.

Toys must be safe, durable, and age-appropriate—no buttons, long strings, ribbons, or small parts for children under three years of age. If a toy or toy part can fit inside a cardboard toilet paper roll, it's too small.

If you're looking for a specific item, call ahead. Some stores will gift wrap and deliver nearby, so you might be able to shop over the phone. There are a few Web sites (see the Web Directory) that are excellent for ordering toys. Once you know what you want, check the Web for the best prices. Pay attention to return policies and store credits. Some stores, like Toys "R" Us and Building Blocks, have an "anything, anytime" return policy, which can be useful if your youngster receives three Barney dolls.

age-specific toys

Here are some toy suggestions for specific age groups, but remember, more does not equal better. Stick to one or two toys that your child enjoys for each stage:

1st month

At this age, babies are just beginning to focus on the face, and see high contrast images. So consider black-and-white toys for a newborn.

⁂ Stim-Mobile (Wimmer Ferguson)

⁂ Pattern-Play Cards (Wimmer Ferguson)

⁂ B&W crib bumper books

⁂ B&W Board Books

⁂ B&W Gymini (Tiny Love): Hang one item at a time! Don't overwhelm your little one. By hanging single items you learn what their favorites are.

⁂ Infant Mirror (Wimmer Ferguson)

⁂ Tracking Tube (Early Start): Great for the stroller

⁂ Lullaby Light Show (Tomy) or IRC Lullaby Dream Show (Tomy)

2nd month

Baby can now grasp a rattle, and will begin to lift her head and roll over. Continue with above toys and introduce:

❋ Pat Mat: We recommend a pat mat with brightly colored objects rather than pastels.

❋ Activity Blanket (Discover & Go Playmat, Wimmer Ferguson)

❋ Bumper Books (Whoozit, Lamaze): Hang as low as you can in the crib so the baby can focus on the graphics.

❋ Small Rattles (Ambi, Haba, Sassy, etc.): Place the rattle in the palm of the baby's hand and watch her grasp it.

❋ Foot & Wrist rattles (Manhattan Baby, Eden)

❋ Whoozit (B&W Side) (Manhattan Toy)

3rd month

As your baby begins to turn in the direction of voices or sounds, it is a great time to introduce musical toys.

❋ Rattles with bells (i.e., Geo Rattles from Imagiix)

❋ Wiggly Giggler Rattle (HandsOn Toys)

❋ Pull-down musical toys (Winnie the Pooh from Gund)

❋ Whoozit Musical (Manhattan Toy)

4th month

Now the baby is beginning to raise her chest, and is reaching and teething.

❋ Crib Activity Gym (Fisher-Price Busy Box, Kick & Play Piano)

❋ Soft multi-textured blocks

❋ Clack Rattle (Lamaze)

❋ Smiley Face Mirror (Sassy)

❋ Discovery Links (Lamaze)

❋ Teethers

❋ 123 Discovery Lane (Tiny Love)

❋ Activity Arch (Tiny Love)

❋ Happy Sounds Ball (Tomy)

5th month

Your baby can now hold her head steady, roll over, reach for objects, grasp a rattle, raise herself up on her arms, and sit. And put everything in her mouth, too. You no longer need black-and-white toys. Your baby should be able to focus on more detail. In addition to the above toys, introduce more manipulative toys, such as:

❋ Twin Rattle (Ambi)

❋ Stroller Fun (Early Years)

❋ Fisher-Price Soft Snap & Lock Beads

6th–7th month

Now your child can sit, bear her own weight when held up, and comprehend cause and effect. He may pass object from hand to hand or look for objects dropped onto the floor. To help with separation anxiety, play lots of hide-and-seek games using cups, puppets, boxes, and your hands. Your baby will begin to understand that if the toy always comes back so will you.

❉ Stacking Cups (Small World Toys, Sassy, Galt, etc.)

❉ Fascination Station (Sassy)

❉ Activity Spiral (Early Years)

❉ Bath toys: Squirts, sieve, cups, floating toys, bath books

❉ Sand toys: small shovel, sieve, and bucket

❉ Neobaby Pick 'n' Pull (Tomy)

❉ Cloth & Vinyl Books

8th–9th month

Now your baby can bear weight on her legs. She'll work to get a toy out of reach, look for a dropped object, pull herself up to standing position, play patty-cake, and nest.

❉ Babysongs video series

❉ Balls in a Bowl (Early Learning)

❉ Lift-the-Flap Books

❉ Chuckling Charlie

10th–11th month

Your baby's becoming aware of his environment, and is beginning to interact with toys as well as becoming more independent. He may be pulling himself up, cruising, and making a razzing sound.

❉ Baby's First Blocks (TC Timber)

❉ Bouncing Billy (Tomy)

❉ Mozart Magic Cube

❉ Tommy Toot (Ambi)

❉ Plastic kazoo

1 year

Your baby may be walking, responding to your voice, cruising, making razzing sounds, and trying to nest, stack, and sort. It may be time to introduce:

❉ Simple Peg Puzzles

❉ Pull Toys Battat's Spinning Bus, Troller, Ambi Max, World on Wheels (Bozart)

❉ Push Toys: Fisher-Price Corn Popper

❉ Activity Cube (Anatex)

✳ Pounding Bench (either plastic or wood) or Pound a Ball (many versions)

✳ First Dolls (Corolle Calin, bath babies, Raggedy Ann, etc.)

✳ Stacking Rings (Fisher-Price, Sassy, Lamaze, Brio, etc.)

✳ Pop-up Friends (many versions): Creature pops up when correct manipulation is done.

✳ Umbrella Stroller

✳ Sound Puzzle Box (Battat)

✳ Flashcards

18 months

Your baby is gaining more control of fine motor skills, and is beginning to follow your direction.

✳ Lock Box (Tag Toys)

✳ Pathfinder (Anatex)

✳ Shape Sorter (Gazoobo)

✳ Brio Builder Pounding Board

2 years

At two years of age, your child is beginning to build and create, and is interested in how things work. She's becoming verbal, reciting her ABCs and 1,2,3s.

✳ Picture Cube Puzzles (Selecta)

✳ Magic Sound Blocks (Small World Toys)

✳ See Inside Puzzles (Ravensburger)

✳ Tricycle

✳ Figure 8 wooden train set (TC Timber, Brio, Thomas)

✳ Tomy Bring-Along CD Player

✳ Object recognition puzzles

✳ Bop Bag

✳ Trucks of all sizes

✳ Beginning phonics toys like LeapFrog's Phonics Bus

✳ Play pretend toys

✳ Art Supplies

✳ I Spy Preschool Game

✳ Brio Builder level 1

3 years

Can you believe it? Your child's a preschooler! His construction and manipulative skills are increasing, and he's learning to play well with others. He is beginning to understand the concept of counting and reciting the ABCs. His fantasy world is expanding, and he's able to make associations.

※ Tangrams (Mr. Mighty Mind)

※ Marble Maze (Quercetti)

※ Pretend & Play Cash Register

※ Gearations (Tomy)

※ Flashlight (Playskool)

※ LeapFrog Think 'n' Go phonics

※ Bingo Bears

※ Floor Puzzles (approx. 12–25 pieces)

※ Games: Barnyard Boogie Woogie, Hi-Ho Cherri-o, Footloose, Kids on Stage, Colorforms Silly Faces, Maisy's ABC Game, Four First Games, Snail's Pace, Lotto

※ Sequencing games: Things I Can Do (Educa), Tell-a-Story (Ravensburger), Step-by-Step (Educa), Magnetic Letters & Numbers

※ Animal Ball Park (Tomy)

※ Art supplies

※ Lacing aids: lacing cards, beads, shoes

the stores

※ *American Girl Place*
111 E. Chicago Ave.
312-943-9400
www.americangirl.com
Return policy: Receipt required for cash refund; without receipt, exchange or store credit only
Walk down Chicago Avenue early on a Saturday morning, and you'll see young girls and their moms lined up around the block, waiting to stream through the doors for a day of shopping and bonding. One of only two American Girl stores in the country (the other is in New York), this place boggles the mind with room after room overflowing with dolls, matching outfits for dolls and owners, furniture, books, and accessories. You can eat in the café, visit the Doll Hair Salon, and (if you're over age 6) watch a Broadway-style show called "Circle of Friends: An American Girls Musical." Plan to spend the day—and bring a bag of money.

※ *Building Blocks Toy Store*
3306 N. Lincoln Ave.
773-525-6200
Return policy: Extremely lenient
If you think they don't make toys like they used to, pay a visit to Building Blocks. This small, mom-and-pop establishment emphasizes wooden and European-made toys that promote interactive play; you won't find battery-powered or aggression-promoting toys. Building Blocks carries developmental toys for infants, arts-and-crafts materials, board games, books,

puzzles, science kits, and more. The large stockpile of Thomas & Friends trains is especially noteworthy. The store encourages hands-on play with its merchandise, and the free gift-wrapping and local delivery are added bonuses.

Cut Rate Toys
5409 W. Devon Ave.
773-763-5740
My mother-in-law certainly understood my glee over my recent discovery of this great discount store; she shopped at Cut Rate's previous Rogers Park location every Friday after Thanksgiving throughout her three kids' entire childhood. Now under new ownership, Cut Rate Toys nevertheless continues its 50-year tradition of selling quality name-brand new toys—LEGO, playmobil, Melissa and Doug wooden toys, and much, much more—at as much as 30 percent off retail. This is off the beaten path, but most definitely worth the trip.

The Disney Store
717 N. Michigan Ave.
312-654-9208
www.disneystore.com
Return policy: Anytime with receipt for full refund
Here's where you'll find the pantheon of Disney characters adorning every item imaginable: action figures, Disney Princess dolls and accessories, stuffed animals, playsets, videos and DVDs, CD-ROMs, audio CDs, posters, clothing and sleepwear, costumes, home decor, and bath accessories. Each new Disney movie brings a fresh wave of merchandise.

Dorby Magoo & Company
2744 N. Lincoln Ave.
773-935-2663
Returns: With receipt
Parents rave about this toy store owned by sisters Joan and Anne Frankel, who grew up in the business back in Cleveland. The shop is designed to look like a house, with toys spilling from the living room, den, library, kitchen, even a bathroom. Selections include vintage toys you'll remember from your youth, educational toys, puzzles, books, games, etc. The highlight for many kids is picking out their own toys in the bedroom, with more than 300 inexpensive choices like play jewelry and fake bugs. Take note: Dorby Magoo takes only cash and checks—no credit cards.

Galt Toys
900 N. Michigan Ave.
312-440-9550
(also at Northbrook Court)
Return policy: Within 30 days, with receipt, for full refund
This 150-year-old English company has a reputation for well-made toys that encourage learning through play. Here you'll find loads of arts and crafts, including activity packs for young children; Playnests, fabric-covered inflatable play rings for babies to sit in and enjoy multisensory, hands-on activities; developmental toys for infants and toddlers; puzzles and games; and construction sets. The Galt Baby department features European clothing, strollers, and furniture for babies and young children.

The LEGO Store

The Shops at North Bridge
520 N. Michigan Ave.
312-494-0760
Return policy: Within 90 days, unopened and with receipt, for full refund
If you have a LEGO lover in your house, this place will seem like heaven on earth. Crammed with every LEGO product imaginable—basic bricks, Bionicles, Star Wars pieces, Clickits sets to make jewelry, trains and trucks, dinosaurs, hard-to-find LEGOs—this is also something of an art gallery for kids. The displays, all made from the tiny LEGOs, are really incredible, and have included a model of the Magnificent Mile, Darth Vader, the White House, and, of course, Santa Claus. Kids are encouraged to play at huge tables loaded down with LEGOs, and you'll see children who've never met team up like little ants and get busy building. You'll also find bins full of replacement parts, a necessity when that tiny but key LEGO piece goes missing, as it inevitably will.

Little Strummer

909 W. Armitage Ave.
773-751-3410
Return policy: Within 30 days, with receipt
Little Strummer is the Old Town School of Folk Music's store for kids and is stocked with a colorful array that includes not just kids' instruments but also art supplies, books, CDs, and Wiggleworms accessories. The store also rents many instruments, including kid-sized guitars, cellos, and violins.

Pumpkin Moon

1028 North Blvd. (Oak Park)
708-524-8144
Return policy: Within two weeks, for store credit or exchange
If you're looking for the toys you remember from childhood, take a trek to Pumpkin Moon. This small, whimsical store specializes in nostalgic toys as well as cookie jars, lunchboxes, T-shirts, old-fashioned candy, cards, and more. Some toys are reproductions while others are actual vintage items. You'll find Felix the Cat, Betty Boop, Curious George, and the Three Stooges, among others. Pumpkin Moon also has lots of inexpensive, funky little toys kids will have fun picking out for gift bags and favors. For those without a car, the shop is right on the Green Line.

Sanrio

The Shops at North Bridge
520 N. Michigan Ave.
312-644-9783
Return policy: Within 30 days, with receipt, for refund
Japanese toymaker Sanrio is home to all things Hello Kitty: clothing, backpacks, cosmetics, school supplies, stickers, stuffed animals, and on and on. You can even buy working Hello Kitty items for the home, like a coffeemaker, TV, toaster, or telephone. This is the way a four-year-old girl would do interior design if she had the chance.

Think Small by Rosebud

3209 N. Clark St.

773-477-1920

Return policy: Within 30 days, with receipt; no returns on special orders or wallpaper

More than just a dollhouse supply store, Think Small also is a place where you can go to build your own structure in the store's workshop. The shop features everything you need to make a dollhouse, including floor plans, building materials, furniture, wants to work on a project and get expert help from the staff. You don't have to have purchased your materials at the store; however, certain dollhouses are not allowed to be brought in, because, the owner says, "they just frustrate people." So call before lugging in your project.

Timeless Toys

4749 N. Lincoln Ave.

773-334-4445

Return policy: Within 30 days, for exchange or store credit

This well-organized and roomy store has a good mix of toys for different ages, and they provide a nice selection within each category, which isn't always the case with smaller independent stores. You'll find dollhouses, trains, blocks, developmental toys, books, art supplies, and more. The staff is friendly and laidback—they don't get stressed when your kid has a tantrum.

Toys & Treasures

5311 N. Clark St.

773-769-5311

Return policy: Store credit or exchange only

Even when it was in a tiny space at the back of the Landmark shops in Andersonville, Toys & Treasures always had an interesting and varied selection. Now in its own, bigger space in the neighborhood, the store has an even wider array of what are mainly educational toys for babies and preschoolers, though there are some items for older kids as well.

Toys Et Cetera

5211-A. S. Harper Ave.

773-324-6039

711 Main St. (Evanston)

847-475-7172

www.toysetcetera.com

Return policy: For cash refund, need receipt before December 31st of the year purchased. Without receipt, exchange or store credit only. Toys Et Cetera was founded in the '70s by a mom who was looking for better toys for her own children, ones that were well made and fostered creative play. The result is a store filled with classic wooden toys (trains, rocking horses, looms, blocks), infant and toddler developmental toys, art supplies, science-oriented kits and crafts, games, cloth toys, puppets and puppet theaters, books, and CDs.

Toys "R" Us

10 S. State St.; 312-857-0667

6420 Fullerton Ave,; 773-637-1166

3300 N. Western Ave.; 773-525-1690

8900 Lafayette St.; 773-846-2600

87th Street and the Dan Ryan; 773-846-2600

www.toysrus.com

Return Policy: Refund with a receipt, otherwise store credit only

Toys "R" Us discounts every well-known name-brand toy. It carries a lot of Fisher-Price, Safety 1st, Playskool, and Mattel; these are all the latest toys, and the prices and selections on books, videos, and Barbie dolls are usually the best in town.

❊ Uncle Fun

1338 W. Belmont
www.unclefunchicago.com
773-477-8223
Return policy: Store credit or exchange only
Make sure to allot plenty of time to visit Uncle Fun; you could spend days exploring the mother lode of stuff here. Uncle Fun specializes in the nostalgic, the wacky, and the collectible—and the prices are great. You'll find silly toys like Groucho glasses and Whoopie cushions, character-themed items from Felix the Cat to Power Puff Girls, vintage reproduction toys, and wooden drawers crammed with hundreds of inexpensive party-favor toys. Grown-ups enjoy this place as much as the kids do.

❊ Zany Brainy

2163 N. Clybourn Ave.
773-281-2371
Return Policy: Refund with a receipt, otherwise store credit only
This big, bright, colorful toy store has fair prices on all the most popular brands, and carries puzzles, games, a large selection of educational toys, and arts-and-crafts supplies.

costumes

At least once a year (more if you have a child who loves to dress up like a superhero), you will need to pick up a costume for your little one. You can easily find selections at your regular toyshops, clothing stores, department stores, party stores. The following specialty stores, however, are authorities when it comes to Halloween and costume parties.

❊ Chicago Costume Company

1120 W. Fullerton Ave.
773-528-1264
www.chicagocostume.com
Carries a huge range of costumes for babies and young children, as well as teens and adults, including animals, favorite movie and television characters, ghosts, gargoyles, action figures, pumpkins, clowns, princesses, construction workers, and more. Also carries wigs, makeup, and accessories.

❊ Fantasy Headquarters

4065 N. Milwaukee Ave.
773-777-0222
www.fantasycostumes.com
Offers an enormous array of costumes for the whole family, including babies and toddlers. You'll find animals, holiday-themed costumes, movie and TV characters, action figures, religious costumes, action figures, and Disney characters, as well as wigs, makeup, accessories—and costumes for your pet.

Chapter Thirteen

books,
videos,
audio tapes,
cds, catalogs,
and magazines

No doubt about it: city babies—and their moms—love city bookstores! Together they can listen to stories, pick out videos and CDs, and, best of all, discover the joys of children's books. This multimedia universe is one of the most exciting aspects of baby culture today. In every case, talented writers, artists, and musicians are creating lasting treasures for your children.

This section lists the best bookstores in Chicago and all they hold, from the classic must-haves, like Goodnight Moon or Where the Wild Things Are, to useful adult titles such as Practical Parenting Tips. I have recommended audio tapes and CDs (essential for those long car rides) and videos, not only to entertain the kids but to provide you with a few moments of peace. We have also listed some of the best parenting magazines, along with a selection of catalogs to assist you with at-home shopping.

Of course, the Web has totally changed and enriched the way we get our parenting information. Don't fail to read through the many great sites listed in the Web Directory at the end of the book.

best bookstores for children

❖ *Barbara's Bookstore*

On Marshall Field's lower level, 111 N. State St.; 312-781-3033
At Navy Pier, 700 E. Grand Ave.; 312-222-0890
201 E. Huron; 312-926-2665
1350 N. Wells; 312-642-5044
1100 Lake St. (Oak Park); 708-848-9140
Started in Old Town in 1963, Barbara's is the oldest and biggest independent bookseller in the city. Known for its emphasis on quality literature and its knowledgeable staff, Barbara's stores also have terrific kids' sections. Last year Barbara's opened a 2,400-square-foot location in the lower level of Marshall Field's State Street store, where events are held in conjunction with Field's Go Read program, an initiative to foster reading skills and passion in preschoolers to third-graders. The Barbara's at Field's holds many children's and family events, including performances on the Children's Stage and appearances by beloved children's characters.

❖ *Barnes & Noble Booksellers*

1130 N. State St.; 312-280-8155
1441 W. Webster Ave.; 773-871-3610
659 W. Diversey Parkway; 773-871-9004
Barnes & Noble has a huge selection, and its children's sections are comfortable, with plenty of room to sit and read with your child. The Webster Avenue location has one of the largest children's sections in the city and holds numerous events for kids and families, including daytime story hours; a monthly Pajamarama Storytime, when kids come in their jammies to hear bedtime stories; and a monthly event where children can hear stories read by a favorite costumed character, such as Cat in the Hat, Curious George, Angelina Ballerina, and Clifford.

❖ *Borders Books & Music*

830 N. Michigan Ave.; 312-573-0564
2210 W. 95th St.; 773-445-5471
Borders has a lovely children's department

with small tables to sit at as you peruse books. Like Barnes & Noble, Borders is a megastore with everything: A coffee bar, the latest magazines, and a newspaper rack make this store complete. The Michigan Avenue location hosts a weekly storytime (see page 80), and the 95th Street store holds its Pajama Party on Fridays at 7 p.m., when kids come dressed in the pajamas to hear bedtime stories.

❋ Children in Paradise

909 N. Rush St.
312-951-5437
Back in the 1980s, when I was toiling in the lower ranks of book publishing, my fellow editorial assistant Jodi Block told me how she longed to own a children's bookstore. In 1994, she realized her dream when she opened the gorgeous Children in Paradise, the only children's bookstore within city limits. With roughly 10,000 titles in stock, Children in Paradise has just about every kids' book you can think of, from board books for babies to novels for teens. The store is painted beautifully; in the back, for instance, a vine-covered castle surrounds a domed area decorated with a nighttime sky featuring a book-shaped constellation of stars. This is a wonderful place to while away a morning or afternoon with your child.

❋ Magic Tree

141 N. Oak Park Ave. (Oak Park)
708-848-0770
This delightfully cozy children's bookstore has been around for twenty years and is especially noteworthy for its multicultural books, music, and accessories, including a Spanish-language section. Magic Tree has several book clubs for young people, and it hosts a wide variety of children's events and author appearances; its spectacular release party for the fifth Harry Potter book was featured by news outlets all over the country.

❋ 57th Street Books

1301 E. 57th St.
773-684-1300
Part of Seminary Co-op, one of the best academic booksellers in the world, 57th Street Books is a general interest bookstore with a great children's section. Each autumn the store holds its annual 57th Street Children's Book Fair, where the street is blocked off so area bookstores showcase new and used children's books; the fair also features readings, music, dancing, puppet shows, face painting, and other kid-friendly events.

❋ Women & Children First

5233 N. Clark St.
773-769-9299
Founded in a small storefront in 1979, Women & Children First has expanded over the years and is now located in Andersonville, a North Side neighborhood known for its diversity and large lesbian population. The children's section is smaller than other stores listed here, but it is well stocked, and the staff is very knowledgeable and helpful. Independent bookstores are a vanishing breed, and this is one worthy of support.

choosing a book for your child

There are so many benefits to reading with your child: it will familiarize him with speaking patterns, increase his vocabulary, develop his attention span, introduce him to new concepts, and most importantly, help him learn to enjoy reading. Books provide influences that will be key in forming his personality. As a Chicago parent, you have an abundance of resources available to help you find the newest in children's literature and give you an opportunity to rediscover old classics. Sometimes all of this information can be overwhelming, but there are a few pointers I can give you to make the process of choosing a book for you and your child to share as smooth as possible.

❈ Don't be afraid to ask for help from the children's department at your favorite bookstore or from the children's librarian at your local Chicago Public Library branch. That's what they're there for and they will be happy to help you!

❈ Especially for very small children, pick books that are durable—gnawing on the corners is popular with babies—and with pages that little fingers will be able to turn; cloth books and board books are good bets. Bright, simple illustrations are always great.

❈ For slightly older children, follow your child's interests. If he likes sports or history, choose books with simple story lines in these areas. Children especially enjoy books about kids their own age in different historical periods, such as the American Girl series.

❈ Books should be challenging and stimulating—they should give children a chance to ask questions, think about possible solutions, use their imagination, and have fun.

❈ Read your child the books that you read as a child. It will be more enjoyable for both of you if you like what you are reading too.

❈ Most importantly, let your child be active in choosing the books she wants to read. She might feel ready to start exploring simple chapter books (like Winnie the Pooh, Pippi Longstocking, or the Ramona series from Beverly Cleary) when she is about five or six years old and first learning how to read. Take turns reading aloud; you'll probably have to do most of the reading at first. Your child will grow into the book and enjoy the challenge.

❈ Many suppliers and carriers of children's books maintain web sites. You can go to these to find new releases, locate places to borrow or purchase a specific book, and even order a book.

❈ Barnes & Noble publishes a great book for choosing reading material for your child: The Barnes & Noble Guide to Children's Books. It can be purchased in the Children's Section of any Barnes & Noble store.

making the most of reading with your child

When reading aloud with your child, set aside a certain time each day and make it part of her daily routine. Snuggle up together and make it a time that you share. Let her be active in the reading process, encourage her to point out and describe pictures, suggest possible endings and ask questions. Older babies can participate by pointing and helping to turn the pages. Use silly voices for the characters—it will make storytelling more enjoyable for all involved. Introduce your child to the reading process early on, and tell short, simple stories to your newborn. A parent's voice evokes special responses from a child and it is never too early to take advantage of this. Also, don't be afraid to read just one or two words per page and skip the rest. This is how a one- or two-year-old reads. Toddlers like to jump around a lot, and the constant stimulation is good for them. Turn those pages quickly!

best books for young children

There are so many great books out there for children of all ages. For newborn babies to children ages five or six, there are three main categories to use as guidelines. Baby books (from infant to 2 years) are simple and repetitive with lots of pictures. These books are bright and colorful, and connected to the baby's surroundings in some way. They should be sturdy and rounded at the corners for safety. The most popular forms of these books are plastic bath books (great in the tub), cloth books (perfect for the crib), board books, and touch and feel books.

Once your child is around two, you can introduce her to preschool books. These books are con-cept-based and should be helpful in developing a sense of humor. They also begin to teach children about social interaction and the difference between right and wrong. They should be easy, fun, and colorfully illustrated. Preschool books are especially popular in pop-up form.

Finally, picture books should have slightly more complex story lines and illustrations. They often address a key life issue: siblings, sharing, potty training, starting school, and so on. These come in hard cover and paperback and some have plush figures as well. Classic books have been kept in a separate category—they're great for all ages. We've also included some special needs books that explain issues like divorce or adoption to young children.

It is important to remember that reading levels are just recommended ages and that what may be right for one three-year-old may be too advanced or too simple for another. Your child will let you know when she is ready to move on by showing interest in more difficult concepts and reading material. The age ranges given for the following books are generally appropriate for most children in that age group. Use your judgment and enjoy.

baby books

Board Books:

❊ *Little Spot Board Books by Eric Hill*
   (Spot's First Words, Spot at Home,
   Spot in the Garden, Spot's Toy Box)
   These books tell simple stories that are easy for small children to follow. Spot helps children learn to associate words and images.

Sesame Street Board Books
(Elmo's Guessing Game, Ernie and Bert Can . . . Can You?, Ernie Follows His Nose, Hide and Seek With Big Bird)
Sesame Street has been entertaining and educating children for years, and these books help even the youngest children learn useful concepts.

Neil Ricklen Board Books
(Daddy and Me, Mommy and Me, Baby's Clothes, Baby's Colors, etc.)
These books use one word per picture to describe familiar situations. They are adorable and use real baby photographs rather than illustrations.

Sandra Boynton Board Books
(Snoozers, A to Z, Moo, BAA, La La La!, Doggies, etc.)
Kids love the rhyming sentences with cute cartoon pictures. Even at four, Clare still likes me to read Doggies.

Anne Geddes Board Books
(Garden Friends, Colors, Dress-ups, Faces)
There's nothing babies love more than looking at other babies, and photographer Anne Geddes shows them in a whole new light. There are baby mushrooms, baby flowers, and many baby animals.

Helen Oxenbury Board Books
(Working, Dressing, Friends)
These great books teach little ones about the basics with simple illustrations and single words.

I Spy Board Books
(Little Animals, Little Wheels, Little Letter, etc.)
At first your baby will enjoy simply listening to the rhymes; as she gets older, she'll learn to match the objects incorporated in the rhymes to objects in the photo collage on the opposite page.

My First Word Board Book
by Angela Wilkes
Brightly colored photos with labels help children learn the words for everyday objects.

Thomas and the Freight Train
This is an early introduction to the beloved little train.

Touch and Feel Board Books
(Wild Animals, Home, Fire Engine)
These wonderful books combine reading with tactile exploration. In Wild Animals, for instance, the lion has a furry patch to stroke, the lizard has rough, bumpy skin to rub, and the tree frog has sticky fingers to touch.

Cloth Books:

Thomas the Tank Engine Says Good Night
This cute book is perfect for the crib.

Cloth Books by Eric Hill
(Animals, Clothes, Home)
These charming books by the creator of Spot are perfect for little ones.

Bath Books:

* *Bath Books by Eric Hill*
  (Spot Goes Splash, Spot's Friends, Spot's Toys)
  Make a splash with Spot, the adorable puppy!

* *Bath Books by Beatrix Potter*
  (Benjamin Bunny, Jemima Puddle-Duck, Mr. Jeremy Fisher, Mrs. Tiggy-Winkle, Peter Rabbit)
  Looking at these classic characters will make baths more enjoyable for your little one.

* *Babar's Bath Book*
  This elephant makes a great friend in the tub.

* *Sesame Street Bath Books*
  (Elmo Wants a Bath, Ernie's Bath Book)
  No one knows bath time like the experts, Ernie and his rubber ducky.

A Great Reading Tip

Carry a board book or two in your diaper bag, and you'll always have entertainment for your baby:
* On the bus
* In line at the grocery
* At the pediatrician's office

preschool books

* *Ten Little Ladybugs*
  by Melanie Gerth
  Beautiful illustrations, fun rhymes, and a surprise ending make this a charming counting book.

* *I Am a Bunny*
  by Ole Risom
  Children discover the seasons as they travel with Nicholas the bunny from spring to winter.

* *The Runaway Bunny*
  by Margaret Wise Brown
  The sweet and moving story of a little bunny who can't escape his mother's love.

* *Sheep in a Jeep* and the other *Sheep* books
  by Nancy E. Shaw
  Clare and I love the wacky rhymes that describe the high-spirited misadventures of Shaw's wooly-heads.

* *If You Give a Mouse a Cookie*
  by Laura Joffe Numeroff
  Kids love the story, and parents can relate to how a little creature's simple request leads to a whole series of demands—and messes.

* *Brown Bear, Brown Bear, What Do You See?*
  by Bill Martin, Jr.
  Illustrations by Eric Carle (The Very Hungry Caterpillar) and repetitive rhymes help kids learn animals and colors.

* *Chicka Chicka Boom Boom*
  by Bill Martin, Jr., and John Archambault
  The letters of the alphabet have an adventure in this book with text that mimics the rhythms of jazz music—lots of fun to read aloud.

* *The Napping House*
  by Audrey Wood

Chaos ensues as one creature after another piles into bed for a nap in this whimsically illustrated book.

❋ *Cat Heaven*
by Cynthia Rylant
Lovely rhymes and folk-art illustrations grace this book about what happens to cats when they die. We read it a lot after our cat Henry died when Clare was one.

❋ *Everyone Poops*
by Taro Gomi
This book uses simple illustrations and explanations, showing kids that going to the bathroom is perfectly natural. (You will love this book, too.)

❋ *Going to the Potty*
by Fred Rogers
Mr. Rogers patiently and supportively explains potty training to parents and children.

classics

❋ *Beatrix Potter books*
(*The Complete Tales, The Tale of Benjamin Bunny, The Tale of Peter Rabbit, The Tale of Squirrel Nutkin, The Tale of Tom Kitten, The Tale of Two Bad Mice*)
For generations, children have enjoyed the cute, trouble-making little animals in Beatrix Potter's stories.

❋ *Curious George by H.A. Rey*
(*The Adventures of Curious George,*

Curious George Gets a Medal, Curious George Learns the Alphabet, Curious George Rides a Bike, Curious George Takes a Job, Curious George Flies a Kite, Curious George Goes to the Hospital)
Curious George loves life in the city with the man in a yellow hat, but his curiosity for new things can get him into trouble.

❋ *Dr. Seuss Books*
(*One Fish, Two Fish, Red Fish, Blue Fish, etc.*)
These are silly, rhyming stories with amusing drawings and creative characters with the power to bring you back to your own childhood as well.

❋ *The Giving Tree*
by Shel Silverstein
(*Giraffe and a Half, The Missing Piece, The Missing Piece Meets the Big O*)
This is the story of the lifelong friendship between a little boy and a very generous tree.

❋ *Goodnight Moon**
by Margaret Wise Brown
Everyone loves this timeless, charming picture book about a little rabbit who says goodnight to everything, including the moon outside his window. Beware of giving it as a gift though—I received five copies before Clare was born.

❋ *Harold and the Purple Crayon*
by Crockett Johnson
(*Harold's ABC, Harold's Purple Crayon*)
Join Harold as he draws his way through adventures.

* *The Little Engine That Could**
by Watty Piper
This inspiring tale about the brave little engine has been popular for more than seventy years for good reason.

* *Madeline*
by Ludwig Bemelmans
(Madeline and the Bad Hat, Madeline and the Gypsies, Madeline in London, Madeline's Rescue, Mad About Madeline)
Follow Madeline and her friends on their adventures in Paris.

* *Make Way for Ducklings*
by Robert McCloskey
(Blueberries for Sal, One Morning in Maine, Time of Wonder)
This classic book tells the tale of Mrs. Mallard and her eight ducklings crossing a busy Boston street.

* *Pat the Bunny, Pat the Cat, Pat the Puppy*
by Dorothy Kunhardt
Your child will love touching the soft bunny and Daddy's scratchy face.

* *The Very Hungry Caterpillar**
by Eric Carle
(The Grouchy Ladybug, The Very Busy Spider, The Very Lonely Firefly)
This is a beautiful, interactive picture book about a caterpillar, who eats and eats until eventually, turning into a butterfly.

* *Where the Wild Things Are*
by Maurice Sendak

(Alligators All Around: An Alphabet, Chicken Soup with Rice: A Book of Months, One Was Johnny: A Counting Book, Pierre: A Cautionary Tale in Five Chapters and a Prologue, In the Night Kitchen)
When Max gets sent to his room without dinner, he sails off to the land of the Wild Things, where he can misbehave as much as he wants. But is this as great as it sounds? Also, check out Chicken Soup with Rice. This is a great way to learn the months of the year.

other great reading recommendations

* *Bus Stops*
by Gomi

* *Eating the Alphabet: Fruits and Vegetables from A to Z*
by Lois Ehlert

* *Goodnight, Gorilla*
by Peggy Rathmann

* *Jamberry*
by Bruce Degan

* *Jesse Bear, Jesse Bear, What You Will Wear*
by Nancy White Carlstrom

* *Lady with the Alligator Purse*
by Nadine Bernard Westcott

* *Peek-A-Boo*
by Jan Olmerod

* *Silly Sally*
  by Audrey Wood

* *Snowy Day*
  by Ezra Jack Keats

* *10, 9, 8*
  by Molly Bang

* *Time for Bed*
  by Mem Fox (illustrated by Jane Dyer)

special needs books

* *Adoption Is for Always*
  by Linda Walvoord Girard

* *At Daddy's on Saturdays*
  by Linda Walvoord Girard

* *Dinosaurs Divorce:*
  A Guide for Changing Families
  by Laurence Krasny Brown

* *Let's Talk About It: Divorce*
  by Fred Rogers

* *Lifetimes: The Beautiful Way to*
  Explain Death to Children
  by Bryan Mellonie

* *Over the Moon: An Adoption Tale*
  by Karen Katz

* *Tell Me Again About the Night I Was Born*
  by Jamie Lee Curtis

* *We Adopted You, Benjamin Koo*
  by Linda Walvoord Girard

* *What's Heaven?*
  by Maria Shriver

* *When a Pet Dies*
  by Fred Rogers

* *When Dinosaurs Die:*
  A Guide to Understanding Death
  by Laurence Krasny Brown

best books for parents

As a new mother, you'll want to stock your shelves with books by experts such as Penelope Leach, Dr. Spock, and T. Barry Brazelton. A word of advice though: Trust your instincts. As a new parent, it's easy to get caught up in trying to follow these authors' advice to the letter; I certainly did. But most of us don't have textbook kids, and textbook advice doesn't always work in a given situation. Use these books as a starting point, but pay attention to your gut feeling, and to the needs of your own child and family.

Having said that, here are a few more titles to consider. You can pick these books up at any of the major bookstores or order them online. Also, don't forget to take advantage of your local library.

general

* *The Baby Book: Everything You Need to*
  Know About Your Baby from Birth to Age 2
  by William Sears, M.D., and Martha Sears, R.N.

* *Games Babies Play**
  by Julie Hagstrom and Joan Morrill

* *Mother's Almanac**
  by Marguerite Kelly and Elia S. Parsons

* *The Parent's Guide to Baby and Child Medical Care*
  by Terril H. Hart, M.D.

* *The Pediatrician's Best Baby Planner for the First Year of Life*
  by Daniel W. Dubner, M.D. and D. Gregory Felch, M.D.

* *Practical Parenting for the 21st Century*
  by Julie Ross*

* *Practical Parenting Tips*
  by Vicki Lansky

* *Solve Your Children's Sleep Problems**
  by Richard Ferber
  This book is not for everyone, but it's definitely worth a close look.

* *25 Things Every New Mother Should Know**
  by Martha Sears, R.N. and William Sears, M.D.

* *What to Expect the First Year**
  by Arlene Eisenberg, Heidi E. Murkoff, and Sandee E. Hathaway
  A month-by-month guide to your baby's first year.

* *Your Amazing Newborn*
  by M. Klaus and J. Kennell

* *Your Baby's First Three Years*
  by Dr. Paula Kelly

breastfeeding

* *Breastfeeding: The Nursing Mother's Problem Solver*
  by Claire Martin, Nancy Funnemark Krebs, ed.

* *The Breastfeeding Book: Everything You Need to Know About Nursing Your Child From Birth to Weaning*
  by Martha Sears, R.N.

* *The Complete Book of Breastfeeding*
  by Marvin S. Eiger, M.D. and Sally Wendklos Olds

* *Successful Breastfeeding*
  by Nancy Dana and Anne Price

* *The Womanly Art of Breastfeeding**
  by La Leche League

toddlers

* *The Girlfriends' Guide to Toddlers*
  by Vicki Iovine
  The Vicki Iovine books are hilarious! Written for mothers by a mother who has seen it all with her four children.

* *Kids Book to Welcome a New Baby*
  by Barbara J. Collman

* *How to Take Great Trips with Your Kids*
  by Sanford and Joan Portnoy

❖ *The Smart Parents' Guide to Kids T.V.*
by Milton Chen, Ph.D.

special interests

❖ *In Praise of Single Parents*
by Shoshana Alexander

❖ *The Single Mother's Book: A Practical
Guide to Managing Your Children, Career,
Home, Finances, and Everything Else*
by Joan Anderson

❖ *Twins from Conception to Five Years*
by Averil Clegg and Anne Woolett

videos

Almost all the superstores and many toy stores
carry both children's entertainment and grown-up
videos, covering a range of topics concerning new
parents—breastfeeding, child development, and
baby proofing. Also, don't forget your local library,
Tower Records, Coconuts, and Blockbuster Video,
all of which sell and/or rent children's and parenting videos.

Keep in mind that according to the American
Academy of Pediatrics, too much television can neg-
atively affect young children's brain development.
AAP suggests that children under age two not watch
any TV at all, and children over two should be limited to no more than one or two hours per day.

best videos for children

During your child's first two or three years, he is
going to fall madly in love with Barney, Big Bird,
Ernie, Winnie-the-Pooh, or some character that has-
n't even been invented yet. You'll be renting or buying any number of videos featuring these lovable
creatures, even if, like me, you once swore no child
of yours would ever watch a purple dinosaur sing.

Here's a listing of videos based on popular television series (the titles give you an idea of what
each is about). All the tapes listed here offer either
fun or instruction:

❖ *Barney*
(Best for 9 months and up)
Children love sharing adventures with Barney
and Baby Bop. Your child will love the sing-a-
long songs, even if they drive you crazy.
Barney's Alphabet Zoo
Barney's Birthday*
Let's Pretend with Barney*
Riding in Barney's Car
Barney and Mother Goose*
And more . . .

❖ *Disney's Spot Series*
(Best for newborns to 9 months)
The Spot video series is just as charming as
Eric Hill's books.
Spot Goes to the Farm
Spot Goes to School*
Spot Goes to a Party
Where's Spot?*
Sweet Dreams Spot

❋ Disney Classics

(Best for age 2 or 3 and up)

Everybody loves the Disney classics, even Mom and Dad. The animation is enjoyable for all ages and the tales are timeless.

A Bug's Life

Aladdin

A Goofy Movie

Cinderella

The Fox and the Hound

The Great Mouse Detective

The Lion King

Mulan

Pocahontas

Snow White and the Seven Dwarfs

Toy Story

One-Hundred-and-One Dalmatians

The Aristocats

And more . . .

❋ Disney's Winnie-the-Pooh Series

(Best for 18 months and up)

Follow Winnie, Piglet, Tigger, and the others as they make their way from adventure to adventure. These videos are great because, aside from being fun, they teach valuable lessons.

Pooh Party

Pooh Learning

Cowboy Pooh

Sharing and Caring

Making Friends*

Winnie-the-Pooh and the Blustery Day

Winnie-the-Pooh and a Day for Eeyore

Winnie-the-Pooh and Tigger Too*

Winnie-the-Pooh and the Honey Tree

❋ Richard Scarry

(Best for toddlers ages 2 to 4)

Join the little worm Lowly and his friends in their animated adventures.

Richard Scarry's Learning Songs

Best Sing-along Mother Goose Video Ever!

Best Busy People Video Ever!

Best Counting Video Ever!

Best ABC Video Ever!

Best Silly Stories and Songs Ever!

Best Birthday Party Ever!

❋ Sesame Street

(Best for 12 months and up)

Sesame Street videos are as educational as the television show. Elmo, Bert, Ernie, Big Bird, and other beloved characters will help teach your little one how to sing, spell, and say their ABCs.

My Sesame Street Home Video

Play-Along

Sesame Street Sing Along

Big Bird Sings

The Best of Bert and Ernie

Do the Alphabet

The Best of Elmo

Sing, Hoot & Howl with the Sesame Street Animals

Sesame Street's 25th Birthday Celebration

❋ Miscellaneous

(18 months and up)

Here are some additional favorites:

Baby Songs

Shari Lewis' "Don't Wake Your Mom!"

Wee Sing Grandpa's Magical Toys

videos for parents

Videos are an easy, convenient way to pick up parenting tips and gain some know-how. They will save you precious time by allowing you to stay at home with your little one. The Lifetime cable channel also offers some interesting parenting programming. Check your local listings.

baby's early growth, care, and development

❋ **Baby's First Months "What Do We Do Now?"**
Developed by 12 pediatricians, this video leads parents from birth through their baby's first few months. New parents are instructed on the daily care of a newborn.

❋ **The First Two Years—A Comprehensive Guide To Enhancing Your Child's Physical and Mental Development**
This award-winning video observes babies involved in everyday activities. The developmental periods are divided by age: one day to three months, three to six months, six to 12 months, and 12 to 24 months. Other topics include breastfeeding, early child care, infant nutrition, physical growth, and mobility/motor skills.

❋ **Dr. Jane Morton's Guide to Successful Breastfeeding**
Using a case study and graphics, this video shows the critical steps to comfortable, effective breastfeeding, including how to avoid common problems.

❋ **Touchpoints: The Definitive Video Series on Parenting, Volume 1: Pregnancy, Birth, and the First Weeks of Life***
This practical guide to child development defines touchpoints as periods preceding rapid growth in learning, which are significant to future development. Points covered include pregnancy, delivery, preparation for birth, and the first weeks of your baby's life to three months.

❋ **What Every Baby Knows— A Guide To Pregnancy**
An instructive video with sensible information concerning the development of children from birth to three months. This tape also explores a father's emotional involvement during pregnancy, gives a detailed profile of one couple's delivery, and looks at typical issues that arise in the early months after birth.

❋ **Your Baby—A Video Guide To Care and Understanding with Penelope Leach**
A comprehensive and practical guide to newborn baby care and development, this video demonstrates techniques of everyday care in a variety of situations.

exercise/well-being

❋ **Jane Fonda's Pregnancy, Birth, and Recovery**
This exercise program demonstrates pregnancy and recovery workouts, baby massage, and infant care, and skills to physically prepare for birth.

❋ **Kathy Smith's Pregnancy Workout***

Both mothers-to-be and three different child-birth experts instruct mothers on how to maintain their energy and strength. Divided into prenatal and postnatal sections, the ninety-minute tape covers exercise for the new mothers up to six weeks after giving birth.

safety videos

❋ **Barney Safety**

Barney and friends instruct little ones on safety with cars, traffic, and in the home.

❋ **Choosing Quality Child Care**

This video answers questions such as how to recognize quality child care, how to make sure a child is safe, and what to ask during an interview.

❋ **CPR To Save Your Child or Baby***

This award-winning video carefully explains the step-by-step procedures of CPR, including instructions on the Heimlich maneuver and choking rescue. If you haven't had a chance to take a CPR-instruction class, this is the next best thing.

❋ **Fire Safety for Kids with Beasel the Easel**

This video, endorsed by educators and fire-fighters, teaches basic fire safety to children ages two and up. Children will enjoy the cast of characters and an original soundtrack.

❋ **Infant and Toddler Emergency First Aid (Volume 1: Accidents, Volume 2: Illnesses)**

These videos are endorsed by the American Academy of Pediatrics. The tapes explain emer-gency medical services including the proper procedures and actions to take when giving CPR or dealing with choking or poisoning.

❋ **Mr. Baby Proofer**

A tape designed to teach parents how to make their home a baby-safe environment, this hands-on guide also describes key safety products.

audio casettes and cds for children

Just because you have a baby doesn't mean you have to spend the next few years listening to terrible, sappy music. There's some great music being written for children these days; don't be amazed when you find yourself humming the tunes to yourself (even in the company of other adults). In fact, you can find a lot of the adult music you like re-recorded for children. Much of the music recommended here is in Baby's Best by Susan Silver, or the Music for Little People catalog (800-409-2757). Also, don't hesitate to listen to your own music in the car.

❋ *Ralph's World*

Ralph's World
At the Bottom of the Sea
Happy Lemons
Peggy's Pie Parlor

Chicago musician Ralph Covert spent years playing in the local band the Bad Examples and teaching music at the Old Town School of Folk Music before he rocketed to national fame with the release of Ralph's World in 2001. His tunes are catchy and original—and designed to be loved by parents too, even if you've heard them 500 times.

❊ They Might Be Giants

No!

My husband and I have been fans of TMBG for years, and now kids can enjoy the band's wacky, imaginative lyrics in songs aimed just at them.

❊ Jerry Garcia and David Grisman

Not for Kids Only

The late, great Grateful Dead frontman and legendary mandolin player David Grisman teamed up to create a wonderful album of folk-inspired tunes that will appeal even to adults without children.

❊ John Lithgow

Singin' in the Bathtub

Farkle & Friends

More than just a fantastic actor, John Lithgow is also the creator of some of the best kids' music ever. Backed by a big band and exuding more energy than a lot of toddlers I know, Lithgow writes and sings whimsical, eminently listenable tunes for kids of all ages.

❊ Trout Fishing in America

It's a Puzzle

Big Trouble

Family Music Party

Mine!

And more…

These guys remember what it was like to be kids; their music captures childhood experiences in way that's funny and smart and easy to listen to.

❊ Raffi

Baby Beluga

Bananaphone*

Grocery Corner Store and Others

Singable Songs for the Very Young

Raffi's a classic, and for good reason—kids love his songs.

❊ Other Suggestions

The Beatles for Kids

A Child's Gift of Lullabies, by Someday Baby

G'Night Wolfgang, by Ric Louchard

Hap Palmer's Follow Along Songs*

Hush-A-Bye Dreamsongs

Lullabies of Broadway, by Mimi Bessette

The Lullaby and Goodnight Sleep Kit

Lullaby Berceuse, by XYZ

Peter, Paul, and Mommy, by Peter, Paul, and Mary*

Shakin' It, by Parachute Express

Sleep, Baby Sleep, by Nicolette Larson*

Sugar Beats* (Rebecca and Benjamin love all of the Sugar Beats' music.)

children's catalogs

Shopping by catalog can be the world's greatest convenience; there are loads of them, all filled with great things for babies and children, and all of these great things can be delivered right to your doorstep. Most of these catalogs also have Web sites, which make shopping online easier than ever. Here are a few of our favorites offering one-of-a-kind accessories, toys, and practical imported clothing not available in stores.

Mia Bambini

360 Merrimack St.
Lawrence, MA 01843
For orders: 888-588-4900
www.miabambini.com
Cotton and dress-up clothing for infants, toddlers, and older children.

Cambridge Educational

P.O. Box 2153, Dept. PA7
Charleston, WV 25328
800-468-4227
www.cambridgeeducational.com
Extensive selection of videos on parenting, discipline, and health-and-safety issues.

Chinaberry Book Service*

2780 Via Orange Way, Suite B
Spring Valley, CA 91978
800-776-2242
www.chinaberry.com
Chinaberry has wonderful books for children, with incredibly detailed descriptions.

Constructive Playthings*

13201 Arrington Road
Grandview, MO 64030
800-832-0572
www.ustoy.com
An array of colorful, entertaining toys for young boys and girls, with a section called "First Playthings" that's especially good for newborns to one-year-olds.

The Walt Disney Catalog of Children's Clothing

800-328-0612
www.disneystore.com
All of the merchandise, including characters from your child's favorite Disney characters and movies.

Ecobaby Organics, Inc.

332 Coogan Way
El Cajon, CA 92020
888-ECOBABY
www.ecobaby.com
This catalog has more than organic baby accessories—they also have non-toxic furniture, and a selection of breast pumps. They augment the Natural Baby Catalog very nicely.

Hanna Andersson*

1010 NW Flanders Street
Portland, OR 97209
800-222-0544
www.hannaandersson.com
Hanna Andersson carries moderately priced, superior quality cotton play clothes for young children, including swimwear and hats, plus some matching outfits for parents. And these clothes last forever!

L.L. Bean Inc.

Freeport, ME 04033-0001
800-441-5713
www.llbean.com
Casual clothes for rugged kids. L.L. Bean is one of the few companies to offer clothing for larger body types.

Lilly's Kids

Lillian Vernon Corp.
Virginia Beach, VA 23479-0002
800-285-5555
www.lillianvernon.com
From Lillian Vernon, a catalog with well-priced toys, games, and costumes.

The Natural Baby Catalog

7835 Freedom Avenue
North Canton, OH 44720
800-922-7397
www.kidsstuff.com
The Natural Baby Catalog carries natural, eco-logical, and health-minded products, including cloth diaper covers, bedroom furniture, many beautifully crafted wooden toys, and books.

One Step Ahead*

75 Albrecht Drive
Lake Bluff, IL 60044
800-274-8440
www.onestepahead.com
One Step Ahead is good for baby products, including carriers/strollers, car seats, cribs, bottle holders, and some toys and clothing. Safety, travel, and mealtime helpers are also available.

Oshkosh B'Gosh

1112 Seventh Avenue, P.O. Box 2222
Monroe, WI 53566-8222
800-MY BGOSH (800-692-4674)
www.oshkoshbgosh.com
Oshkosh is simple, all-American kid's wear, including classic denim overalls and jeans for your toddler or young child, in both boys' and girls' sizes.

Patagonia Mail Order

P.O. Box 8900
Bozeman, MT 59715
800-336-9090
www.patagonia.com
Patagonia is known for its own brand of rugged everyday clothing and parkas, as well as its cozy fleece jackets.

Perfectly Safe*

7245 Whipple Avenue, NW
North Canton, OH 44720
800-837-KIDS (800-837-5437)
www.kidsstuff.com
Safety gates, bathtub spout covers, and other items to child-proof a home.

Play Fair Toys

P.O. Box 18210
Boulder, CO 80308
800-824-7255
www.playfairtoys.com
Games, blocks, nesting animals, videos, and many other play items that just may help your little one learn to play fair.

The Right Start Catalog*

Right Start Plaza
5334 Sterling Center Drive
Westlake, CA 91361-4627
800-LITTLE-1 (800-548-8531)
www.rightstart.com
Nursery accessories, safe plastic toys, diaper bags, car seats, jogging strollers, baby carriers, and more.

* *Rubens & Marble Inc.*

P.O. Box 14900
Chicago, IL 60614
773-348-6200
Rubens & Marble has basic white, 100-percent cotton clothing and bedding for infants. Excellent prices.

* *Toys to Grow On*

P.O. Box 17
Long Beach, CA 90801
800-542-8338
www.ttgo.com
Every kind of toy you can think of, for newborn to pre-teens.

magazines for parents

* *Chicago Parent*

141 S. Oak Park Ave.
Oak Park, IL 60302
708-386-5555
www.chicagoparent.com
There's always something to do with children in Chicago, and the award-winning Chicago Parent is the place to find out about it. In addition to terrific features and departments, the free monthly magazine also includes an extensive calendar section. Its advertisements are also a great way to find out about class and events for parents and kids.

national magazines

* *American Baby*

249 W. 17th Street bet. Seventh and Eighth Avenues
New York, NY 10011
212-462-3500
www.healthykids.com
A monthly magazine for expectant parents and parents of one-year-olds and under.

* *Baby Talk*

1325 Avenue of the Americas (on 53rd Street, bet. Sixth and Seventh Avenues)
New York, NY 10019
212-522-8989
A monthly magazine for expectant parents and parents of two-year-olds and under.

* *Child**

375 Lexington Ave.
New York, NY 10017
212-499-2000
www.child.com
A popular, authoritative magazine full of information for parents of newborns through teens.

* *Parents**

685 Third Avenue
New York, NY 10017
212-499-2000
www.parentsmagazine.com
A monthly magazine for expectant parents and parents of preteens and under.

❋ Practical Parenting Newsletter

8326A Minnetonka Boulevard
Deephaven, MN 55391
612-475-1505
A bimonthly newsletter for expectant parents and parents of grade school age children and under.

❋ Sesame Street Parents*

P.O. Box 52000
Boulder, CO 80322-2000
Provides information for parents about children age two through six, as well as a specially-sized little magazine for your children to read and color in, featuring favorite Sesame Street characters.

❋ Twins Magazine

5350 South Roslyn Street, Suite 400
Englewood, CO 80111
888-55-TWINS (888-558-9467)
www.twinsmagazine.com
The only bimonthly national magazine for parents of twins.

❋ Working Mother

135 W. 50th Street
New York, NY 10020
212-445-6100
www.workingwomannetwork.com
A monthly magazine for parents.

index